Teacher's Gu
ExpressWays
Second Edition

3

Steven J. Molinsky
Bill Bliss

Contributing Authors

Sarah Lynn
Jane Sloan

PRENTICE HALL REGENTS

A VIACOM COMPANY

Publisher: *Louisa B. Hellegers*
Production Editor and Compositor: *Kelly Tavares*
Interior Design: *Siren Design*
Manufacturing Manager: *Ray Keating*
Art Director: *Merle Krumper*

Cover Designer: *Tom Nery*
Cover Production: *Warren Fischbach*

The authors gratefully acknowledge the contribution of Tina Carver
in the development of the *ExpressWays* program.

© 1997 by Prentice Hall Regents
Prentice-Hall, Inc.
A Simon & Schuster Company
Upper Saddle River, New Jersey 07458

Printed in the United States of America

10   9   8   7   6   5   4

ISBN 0-13-385668-2

Prentice-Hall International (UK) Limited, *London*
Prentice-Hall of Australia Pty. Limited, *Sydney*
Prentice-Hall Canada Inc., *Toronto*
Prentice-Hall Hisponoamericana, S.A., *Mexico*
Prentice-Hall of India Private Limited, *New Delhi*
Prentice-Hall of Japan, Inc., *Tokyo*
Simon & Schuster Asia Pte. Ltd., *Singapore*
Editora Prentice-Hall do Brasil, Ltda., *Rio de Janeiro*

CONTENTS

To the Teacher   iv

Continuum of Language Learning Chart   vii

Language Proficiency Levels   viii

EXIT 1 • Meeting and Greeting People
Giving Information   2

EXIT 2 • Sharing News and Information   34

EXIT 3 • People and Places   60

EXIT 4 • Housing and Food   92

EXIT 5 • At Work   126

EXIT 6 • Health and Emergencies   160

EXIT 7 • Shopping   200

EXIT 8 • Recreation   236

Activity Workbook Answer Key   279

ExpressWays Picture Cards   295

Correlation Key   296

ExpressWays is a comprehensive 4-level course for learners of English. Its innovative spiraled curriculum integrates lifeskill topics, functions, and grammar in an imaginative highway theme that puts students *in the fast lane* for an exciting and motivating journey to English language proficiency.

The program consists of the following components:

- **Student Texts** — offering speaking, reading, writing, and listening comprehension practice that integrates grammar and functions in a topic-based curriculum.
- **Activity Workbooks** — offering reinforcement through grammar, reading, writing, and listening comprehension practice fully coordinated with the student texts. The activity workbooks also feature dynamic exercises in pronunciation, rhythm, stress, and intonation.
- *Navigator* **Companion Books** — visually exciting "magazine-style" texts, offering a complete lifeskill curriculum fully integrated with the *ExpressWays* student texts.
- **Teacher's Guides** — providing background notes and expansion activities for all lessons and step-by-step instructions for teachers.
- **Audio Program** — offering realistic presentations of conversations, listening comprehension exercises, and readings from the student texts and workbooks.
- **Picture Program** — featuring Picture Cards for vocabulary development, enrichment exercises, and role-playing activities.
- **Placement and Achievement Testing Program** — providing tools for the evaluation of student levels and progress.

The *ExpressWays* series is organized by a spiraled curriculum that is covered at different degrees of intensity and depth at each level. *ExpressWays 1* and *2* provide beginning-level students with the most important vocabulary, grammar, and functional expressions needed to communicate at a basic level in a full range of situations and contexts. *ExpressWays 3* and *4* cover the same full range of situations and contexts, but offer intermediate-level students expanded vocabulary, more complex grammar, and a wider choice of functional expressions.

The Dimensions of Communication: Function, Form, and Content

ExpressWays provides dynamic, communicative practice that involves students in lively interactions based on the content of real-life contexts and situations. Every lesson offers students simultaneous practice with one or more functions, the grammatical forms needed to express those functions competently, and the contexts and situations in which the functions and grammar are used. This "tri-dimensional" clustering of function, form, and content is the organizing principle behind each lesson and the cornerstone of the *ExpressWays* approach to functional syllabus design.

ExpressWays offers students broad exposure to uses of language in a variety of relevant contexts: in community, school, employment, home, and social settings. The series gives students practice using a variety of registers, from the formal language someone might use in a job interview, with a customer, or when speaking to an authority figure, to the informal language someone would use when talking with family members, co-workers, or friends.

A special feature of the course is the treatment of discourse strategies — initiating conversations and topics, hesitating, asking for clarification, and other conversation skills.

An Overview

Chapter-Opening Photos

Each chapter-opening page features two photographs of situations that depict key topics presented in the chapter. Students make predictions about who the people are and what they might be saying to each other. In this way, students have the opportunity to share what they already know and to relate the chapter's content to their own lives and experiences.

Guided Conversations

Guided conversations are the dialogs and exercises that are the central learning devices in *ExpressWays*. Each lesson begins with a model conversation that depicts a real-life situation and the vocabulary, grammar, and functions used in the communication exchange. In the exercises that follow, students create new conversations by placing new content into the framework of the model and by using any of the alternative functional expressions.

Original Student Conversations

Each lesson ends with an open-ended exercise that offers students the opportunity to create and present original conversations based on the theme of the lesson. Students contribute content based on their experiences, ideas, and imaginations.

Follow-Up Exercises and Activities

A variety of follow-up exercises and activities reinforce and build upon the topics, functions, and grammar presented in the guided conversation lessons.

- **Constructions Ahead!** exercises provide focused practice with grammar structures.
- **CrossTalk** activities provide opportunities for students to relate lesson content to their own lives.
- **InterActions** activities provide opportunities for role playing and cooperative learning.
- **Interview** activities encourage students to interview each other as well as people in the community.
- **Community Connections** activities provide task-based homework for students to get out into their communities to practice their language skills.
- **Cultural Intersections** activities offer rich opportunities for cross-cultural comparison.
- **Figure It Out!** activities offer opportunities for problem-solving.
- **Your Turn** activities provide opportunities for writing and discussion of issues presented in the chapter.
- **Listening Exercises** give students intensive listening practice that focuses on functional communication.
- **Reflections** activities provide frequent opportunities for self-assessment, critical thinking, and problem-solving.
- **Reading** passages in every chapter are designed to provide interesting and stimulating content for class discussion. These selections are also available on the accompanying audiotapes for additional listening comprehension practice.

InterChange

This end-of-chapter activity offers students the opportunity to create and present "guided role plays." Each activity consists of a model that students can practice and then use as a basis for their original presentations. Students should be encouraged to be inventive and to use new vocabulary in these presentations and should feel free to adapt and expand the model any way they wish.

Rest Stop

These "free role plays" appear after every few chapters, offering review and synthesis of the topics, functions, and grammar of the preceding chapters. Students are presented with eight scenes depicting conversations between people in various situations. The students determine who the people are and what they are talking about, and then improvise based on their perceptions of the scenes' characters, contexts, and situations. These improvisations promote students' absorption of the preceding chapters' functions and grammar into their repertoire of active language use.

Support and Reference Sections

End-of-Chapter Summaries include the following:
- **Looking Back** — a listing of key functional expressions in the chapter for review.
- **Construction Sign** — a listing of the key grammar structures presented in the chapter.
- **ExpressWays Checklist** — a self-assessment listing of key lifeskills presented in the chapter.

An **Appendix** provides charts of the grammar constructions presented in each chapter, along with a list of cardinal numbers, ordinal numbers, and irregular verbs.

An **Index** provides a convenient reference for locating topics and grammar in the text.

Suggested Teaching Strategies

We encourage you, in using *ExpressWays*, to develop approaches and strategies that are compatible with your own teaching style and with the needs and abilities of your students. While the program does not require any specific method or technique in order to be used effectively, you may find it helpful to review and try out some of the following suggestions. (Specific step-by-step instructions may be found in the *ExpressWays* Teacher's Guides.)

Chapter-Opening Photos

Have students talk about the people and the situations and, as a class or in pairs, predict what the characters might be saying to each other. Students in pairs or small groups may enjoy practicing role plays based on these scenes and then presenting them to the class.

Guided Conversations

1. SETTING THE SCENE: Have students look at the model illustration in the book. Set the scene: Who are the people? What is the situation?
2. LISTENING: With books closed, have students listen to the model conversation — presented by you, by a pair of students, or on the audiotape.
3. CLASS PRACTICE: With books still closed, model each line and have the whole class practice in unison.
4. READING: With books open, have students follow along as two students present the model.
5. PAIR PRACTICE: In pairs, have students practice the model conversation.
6. ALTERNATIVE EXPRESSIONS: Present to the class each sentence of the dialog containing a footnoted expression. Call on different students to present the same sentence, replacing the footnoted expression with its alternatives.
7. EXERCISE PRACTICE: (optional) Have pairs of students simultaneously practice all the exercises.
8. EXERCISE PRESENTATIONS: Call on pairs of students to present the exercises.

Original Student Conversations

In these activities, which follow the guided conversations at the end of each lesson, have students create and present original conversations based on the theme of the lesson. Encourage students to be inventive as they create their characters and situations. (You may ask students to prepare their original conversations as homework, then practice them the next day with another student and present them to the class. In this way, students can review the previous day's lesson without actually having to repeat the specific exercises already covered.)

CrossTalk

Have students first work in pairs and then share with the class what they talked about.

InterActions

Have pairs of students practice role-playing the activity and then present their role plays to the class.

InterView

Have students circulate around the room to conduct their interviews, or have students interview people outside the class. Students should then report to the class about their interviews.

Community Connections

Have students do the activity individually, in pairs, or in small groups and then report to the class.

Cultural Intersections

Have students do the activity as a class, in pairs, or in small groups.

Reflections

Have students discuss the questions in pairs or small groups and then share their ideas with the class.

Your Turn

This activity is designed for both writing practice and discussion. Have students discuss the activity as a class, in pairs, or in small groups. Then have students write their responses at home, share their written work with other students, and discuss in class. Students may enjoy keeping a journal of their written work. If time permits, you may want to write a response to each student's journal, sharing your own opinions and experiences as well as reacting to what the student has written. If you are keeping portfolios of students' work, these compositions serve as excellent examples of students' progress in learning English.

Reading

Have students discuss the topic of the reading beforehand, using the pre-reading questions suggested in the Teacher's Guide. Have students then read the passage silently, or have them listen to the passage and take notes as you read it or play the audiotape.

InterChange

Have students practice the model, using the same steps listed above for guided conversations. Then have pairs of students create and present original conversations, using the model dialog as a guide. Encourage students to be inventive and to use new vocabulary. (You may want to assign this exercise as homework, having students prepare their conversations, practice them the next day with another student, and then present them to the class.) Students should present their conversations without referring to the written text, but they should also not memorize them. Rather, they should feel free to adapt and expand them any way they wish.

Rest Stop

Have students talk about the people and the situations and then present role plays based on the scenes. Students may refer back to previous lessons as a resource, but they should not simply re-use specific conversations. (You may want to assign these exercises as written homework, having students prepare their conversations, practice them the next day with another student, and then present them to the class.)

We hope that *ExpressWays* offers you and your students a journey to English that is meaningful, effective, and entertaining. Have a nice trip!

Steven J. Molinsky
Bill Bliss

The Molinsky & Bliss Family of English as a Second Language Textbooks

A Continuum of Language Learning
– from Competencies to Content –
– from Literacy to Academic Proficiency –

Language Proficiency Level	CASAS Score	MELT Level	Competency-Based Core Text	Competency-Based Companion Text	General Language Development Text	Content-Based Text for Academic Skills & GED Prep	Picture Dictionary/ Vocabulary Development	English for Work / English for Citizenship
Literacy	165-180	I	Access		Access		Word by Word Basic WBW Basic Literacy Workbook	
Beginning–Low	181-190	II	Foundations	Navigator Basic	Foundations		Word by Word Basic WBW Basic Beginning Workbook	
Beginning–High	191-200	III	ExpressWays 1	Navigator 1	Side by Side 1	Classmates 1	Word by Word WBW Beginning Workbook	Day by Day / Voices of Freedom
Intermediate–Low	201-208	IV	ExpressWays 2	Navigator 2	Side by Side 2	Classmates 2	Word by Word WBW Intermediate Workbook	Day by Day / Voices of Freedom
Intermediate–High	209-215	V	ExpressWays 3	Navigator 3	Side by Side 3	Classmates 3		
Advanced–Low	216-224	VI	ExpressWays 4	Navigator 4	Side by Side 4	Classmates 4		
Advanced–High	225 +	VII	Communicator 1 / Communicator 2		Communicator 1 / Communicator 2	Social Studies / Math / Science / Health Classmates		

Language Proficiency Levels are based on the California ESL Model Standards for Adult Education Programs.
CASAS (Comprehensive Adult Student Assessment System)
MELT (Mainstream English Language Training Project, U.S. Department of Health and Human Services)
Students at the Advanced–Low level are ready for Pre-GED instruction.
Students at the Advanced–High level are ready for GED preparation classes.

Language Proficiency Levels

Language Proficiency Level	CASAS Score	MELT Level	General Language Ability	Vocational and Academic Preparedness	Comprehensibility
Literacy	165–180	I	Functions minimally, if at all, in English.	Can handle only very routine entry-level jobs that do not require oral communication, and in which all tasks can be easily demonstrated.	A native English speaker used to dealing with limited English speakers can rarely communicate with a person at this level except through gestures.
Beginning–Low	181–190	II	Functions in a very limited way in situations related to immediate needs.	Can handle only routine entry-level jobs that do not require oral communication, and in which all tasks can be easily demonstrated.	A native English speaker used to dealing with limited English speakers will have great difficulty communicating with a person at this level.
Beginning–High	191–200	III	Functions with some difficulty in situations related to immediate needs.	Can handle routine entry-level jobs that involve only the most basic oral communication, and in which all tasks can be demonstrated.	A native English speaker used to dealing with limited English speakers will have great difficulty communicating with a person at this level.
Intermediate–Low	201–208	IV	Can satisfy basic survival needs and a few very routine social demands.	Can handle entry-level jobs that involve some simple oral communication, but in which tasks can also be demonstrated.	A native English speaker used to dealing with limited English speakers will have difficulty communicating with a person at this level.
Intermediate–High	209–215	V	Can satisfy basic survival needs and some limited social demands.	Can handle jobs and job training that involve following simple oral and very basic written instructions but in which most tasks can also be demonstrated.	A native English speaker used to dealing with limited English speakers will have some difficulty communicating with a person at this level.

Language Proficiency Level	CASAS Score	MELT Level	General Language Ability	Vocational and Academic Preparedness	Comprehensibility
Advanced–Low	216-224	VI	Can satisfy most survival needs and limited social demands.	Can handle jobs and job training that involve following simple oral and written instructions and diagrams. Students at this level have sufficient language proficiency for Pre-GED and Basic Skills instruction.	A native English speaker not used to dealing with limited English speakers will be able to communicate with a person at this level on familiar topics, but with difficulty and some effort.
Advanced–High	225 +	VII	Can satisfy survival needs and routine work and social demands.	Can handle work that involves following oral and simple written instructions in familiar and some unfamiliar situations. Students at this level have sufficient language proficiency for GED preparation classes.	A native English speaker not used to dealing with limited English speakers can generally communicate with a person at this level on familiar topics.

Language Proficiency Levels are based on the California ESL Model Standards for Adult Education Programs.
CASAS (Comprehensive Adult Student Assessment System)
MELT (Mainstream English Language Training Project, U.S. Department of Health and Human Services)

Language Proficiency Levels and Basic English Skills Test (BEST) Scores

MELT Level	BEST	CASAS
I	0 - 2	< 165
II	3 - 7	165 - 185
III	8 - 21	186 - 190
IV	22 - 35	191 - 200
V	36 - 46	201 - 208
VI	47 - 53	209 - 216
VII	54 - 65	217 - 223
	> 66	224 - 231

MELT Levels are also referred to as Student Performance Levels (SPLs).
The Basic English Skills Test (BEST), developed by the Center for
Applied Linguistics, assesses language skills in lifeskill contexts.
Score correlations in this table indicate the relationship of the proficiency
levels to the BEST literacy section and the CASAS reading test.
(From the CASAS Technical Manual.)

EXIT 1

OVERVIEW
Student Text
Pages 1–18

Topics	Functions	Grammar

P. 2   Let Me Introduce Myself

Social Communication:
    Meeting People
Housing: Relations with
    Neighbors

Introductions
Greeting People
Asking for and Reporting
    Information

Question Formation
Tense Review
WH-Questions

P. 3   You're New Here, Aren't You?

Social Communication:
    Meeting People

Initiating Conversations
Introductions
Greeting People
Asking for and Reporting
    Information

Question Formation
Tense Review
WH-Questions

P. 8   Nice to Meet You

Social Communication:
    Meeting People
Personal Information:
    Family Members

Greeting People
Introductions

P. 10   Passport, Please!

Personal Information:
    Nationality
Travel: Customs and
    Immigration

Asking for and Reporting
    Information

Question Formation

Topics	Functions	Grammar

P. 12 I Have a Reservation

Travel:
   Accommodations —
   Checking In
Personal Information:
   Name

Asking for and Reporting
   Information
Correcting

Question Formation
Tense Review

P. 14 We Need Some Information

Personal Information:
   Address, Age, Date of
   Birth, Name,
   Occupation, Social
   Security Number,
   Telephone Number
Health: Checking In to a
   Hospital or Clinic

Asking for and Reporting
   Information

Question Formation
Tense Review

LOOKING AHEAD

Grammar This Exit

Simple Present Tense

Which apartment **do** you **live** in?
Where **are** you from?
I **have** a reservation.
I **don't** remember.

Present Continuous Tense

What **are** you **majoring** in?
You**'re staying** 3 nights.

Past Tense

When **did** you **move** in?
I **requested** a king-size bed.
We **had** the wrong information in our computer.
I **left** my membership card at home.

Future: Will

Somebody **will see** you in a few minutes.

Question Formation

Which apartment do you live in?
Where are you from?

Do you have medical insurance?

WH-Questions

Who is your supervisor?
What are you majoring in?
When did you move in?
Where are you from?
Why are you here?
Which apartment do you live in?
Whose English class are you in?
How are you enjoying your work?

Functions This Exit

Asking for and Reporting Information

Who *is your supervisor*?
What *floor do you live on*?
When *did you move in*?
Where *are you from*?
Why *are you here*?
Which *apartment do you live in*?
How *are you enjoying your work*?
How long *do you plan to stay*?
Whose *English class are you in*?

Where in _____ are you from?

How about you?
What about you?
And you?

We need some information.

What's your *last name*?
And your *first name*?

Could you spell that, please?
Could you please spell that?

Address?
  35 Winter Street in *Middletown.*
Telephone number?
  732-4495.
What's your date of birth?
  May 15th, 1975.
Occupation?
  Shoe salesman.
What's your Social Security number?
Do you have *medical insurance?*
Do you know your *I.D. number?*

Introductions

Introducing Oneself

Let me introduce myself.

My name is _____.
I'm _____.

Introducing Others

I'd like to introduce you to _____.
I'd like to introduce _____.
Let me introduce you to _____.
Let me introduce _____.
I'd like you to meet _____.
[*less formal*]
This is _____.

Correcting

Giving Correction

No, actually not.
Not really.

Greeting People

Hello.
[*less formal*]
Hi.
[*more formal*]
How do you do?

Nice to meet you.
It's nice to meet you.
Nice meeting you.
It's nice meeting you.

How are you?
[*less formal*]
How are you doing?
How are things?
  Fine (thanks).
  Good.
  All right.

Initiating Conversations

You're new here, aren't you?

PREVIEWING EXIT 1: CHAPTER-OPENING PHOTOS

Have students talk about the people and the situations and, as a class or in pairs, predict what the characters might be saying to each other. Students in pairs or small groups may enjoy practicing role plays based on these scenes and then presenting them to the class.

Text Page 2: Let Me Introduce Myself

FOCUS

TOPICS

Social Communication: Meeting People
Housing: Relations with Neighbors

GRAMMAR

1. **Question Formation**

   Which apartment do you live in?
   Where are you from?

2. **Tense Review**

   Where **are** you from?
   What floor **do** you **live** on?
   When **did** you **move** in?
   What **are** you **majoring** in?

3. **WH-Questions**

   Which apartment do you live in?
   Where are you from?
   What floor do you live on?
   When did you move in?
   Why are you here?

FUNCTIONS

1. **Introductions**

   Introducing Oneself
   Let me introduce myself.

   My name is _____.
   I'm _____.

2. **Greeting People**

   Hello.
   [*less formal*]
   Hi.

[*more formal*]
How do you do?

Nice to meet you.
It's nice to meet you.
Nice meeting you.
It's nice meeting you.

3. **Asking for and Reporting Information**

Which *apartment do you live in*?
Where *are you from*?
What *floor do you live on*?
When *did you move in*?
Why *are you here*?

VOCABULARY

Personal Information	**Housing**	**Countries**	**Education**
name	apartment floor neighbor	Greece Guatemala	Business Fine Arts major

COMMENTARY

1. In the United States, it is common to initiate a conversation by introducing oneself. People meeting for the first time may use just their first names if the situation is informal.

2. "How do you do?" is a formal greeting. "Hello" is both formal and informal. "Hi" is informal and is very common.

3. Appropriate questions to ask when people meet for the first time often involve what the two speakers have in common. For example, when the two people live in the same apartment building, one might ask, "Which apartment do you live in?"

4. In informal conversation, single words or short phrases are used in response to information questions. For example, "Which apartment do you live in?" "7A."

Culture Note

In the United States, it is common for people to shake hands during introductions in formal or official settings. It is less common to shake hands in more casual introductions.

GETTING READY

Review WH-questions.

a. Write the following on the board:

What	When	Where	Why	Which

b. Ask students questions, using the WH-words on the board. Point to the appropriate word as you ask the question. For example:

When does our English class meet?
Where is our classroom?
Why are you studying English?
Which book are we using in this class?

THE MODEL CONVERSATION

1. **Setting the Scene.** Have students look at the model illustration. Set the scene: "Linda and Helen live in the same apartment building. Today they're meeting for the first time."

2. **Listening to the Model.** With books closed, have students listen to the model conversation — presented by you, by a pair of students, or on the audiotape.

3. **Class Practice.** With books still closed, model each line and have the whole class repeat in unison.

4. **Reading.** With books open, have students follow along as two students present the model. Ask students if they have any questions and check understanding of vocabulary.

5. **Pair Practice.** In pairs, have students practice the model conversation.

6. **Alternative Expressions.** Present to the class each sentence of the dialog containing a footnoted expression. Call on different students to present the same sentence, but replacing the footnoted expression with its alternatives. (You can cue students to do this quickly by asking, "What's another way of saying that?" or "How else could he/she/you say that?")

THE EXERCISES

Examples

---

1. A. Hello. Let me introduce myself. I'm your neighbor. My name is George.
   B. Hello. I'm Miguel. Nice to meet you.
   A. Nice meeting you, too. Where are you from?
   B. Guatemala. How about you?
   A. Greece.

2. A. Hi. Let me introduce myself. I'm your neighbor. My name is Bill.
   B. How do you do? I'm Diane. It's nice to meet you.
   A. It's nice meeting you, too. What floor do you live on?
   B. The 2nd. How about you?
   A. The 4th.

Before doing each exercise, check students' understanding of the vocabulary and introduce any unfamiliar words or phrases. Have students use the footnoted expressions or any of their alternatives as they do the exercises.

Exercise Practice (optional). Have pairs of students simultaneously practice all the exercises.

Exercise Presentations. Call on pairs of students to present the exercises.

Language Note

Exercise 4: "What are you majoring in?" is a question one asks a college student. It means: "What field or course of study (such as Business or Fine Arts) are you specializing in?"

ORIGINAL STUDENT CONVERSATIONS

Have pairs of students create and present original conversations based on the model. (You may want students to prepare their original conversations as homework, then practice them the next day with another student and present them to the class.)

EXPANSION

1. Role Play: Introduce Yourself

a. Create a list of appropriate and inappropriate places or situations for introducing oneself. Write the list on the board. For example:

---

in a class at school
on the bus
standing in line at a restaurant
at a party
at work
at your child's school

---

b. For each place on the list, ask students: "Is it okay or not okay to introduce yourself here?" Encourage students to explain why they think it is appropriate or inappropriate.

c. In pairs, have students practice introducing themselves. Have each pair choose a place from the list on the board and role play introducing themselves in that situation.

d. Call on a few pairs of students to present their role plays to the class. Encourage students to say something to keep the conversation going after the introductions. For example:

Place: *At Your Child's School*

A. Isn't this a nice class?
B. Yes, it is.
A. Which child is yours?
B. Billy. He's the boy with the brown hair, over there.
A. Oh, I'm Sally's mother. She's the one wearing the red overalls. My name is Susan Brown.
B. Nice to meet you. I'm Richard Estevez.

2. Information Gap: Mystery Person

a. Give each student a card. Have the student write one fact about himself or herself that the classmates are not likely to know. For example, "I live on the tenth floor of an apartment building" or "I love Mexican food."

b. Collect the cards, mix them up, and give a cue card for a *mystery person* to each student in the class. Have students go around the room asking each other questions until they find their *mystery person*. At that point, each student should greet the person and introduce himself or herself.

3. Be an Observer!

a. Have students go into the community and observe people's introductions in public places, such as cafés or parks. Tell students to note the following:

   Do the people smile at each other?
   Do they shake hands?
   Do they look directly at each other?
   How close to each other do they stand?

b. Have students report their findings to the class.

4. Cultural Differences

a. Have students present introductions to the class in their own language. If possible, have students present introductions between men and men, women and women, and men and women.

b. Have the class observe the introductions. Tell students to note the following:

   Do the people smile at each other?
   Do they shake hands or bow?
   Do they look directly at each other?
   How close to each other do they stand?

c. Have the class discuss their observations.

5. Appropriate Questions Game

a. Divide the class into several teams.

b. Call out one of the following situations:

   two neighbors in an apartment building
   two students in a dormitory
   two classmates on the first day of class
   two people in a church or temple
   two parents at a school meeting

c. Have the students in each group work together to see how many appropriate questions they can imagine the two people asking in that situation. For example:

   [*two neighbors in an apartment building*]

   Which apartment do you live in?
   Where are you from?
   What floor do you live on?
   When did you move in?

d. The team with the most number of appropriate questions wins.

FOCUS

TOPIC

Social Communication: Meeting People

GRAMMAR

1. **Question Formation**

   Which department do you work in?
   Who is your supervisor?
   Whose English class are you in?
   How are you enjoying your work?

2. **Tense Review**

   Which department **do** you **work** in?
   What country **are** you from?
   When **did** you **start** working here?
   How **are** you **enjoying** your work?

3. **WH-Questions**

   Which department do you work in?
   Who is your supervisor?
   What country are you from?
   Whose English class are you in?
   When did you start working here?
   How are you enjoying your work?

FUNCTIONS

1. **Initiating Conversations**

   You're new here, aren't you?

2. **Introductions**

   Introducing Oneself

   My name is _____.
   I'm _____.

3. **Greeting People**

   Nice to meet you.
   It's nice to meet you.
   Nice meeting you.
   It's nice meeting you.

4. **Asking for and Reporting Information**

   Which *department do you work in*?
   Who *is your supervisor*?
   Whose *class are you in*?
   How *are you enjoying your work*?

VOCABULARY

Places on the Job	Countries	Education
Accounting department	Ethiopia	class
Personnel	Japan	English class
supervisor		

COMMENTARY

"Tell me" (line 5) is commonly used to introduce a question.

GETTING READY

Practice making information questions (WH-questions).

   a. Write the following sentences on the board:

> 1. Jackie works in the Personnel department.
> 2. Mr. Crane is Don's supervisor.
> 3. Enku is from Ethiopia.
> 4. Rose is in Mr. Frankel's English class.
> 5. Thelma started working here yesterday.

   b. Have students listen to each sentence and then make one or more information questions about each one. For example, for number 1:

> "Where does Jackie work?"
> "Which department does Jackie work in?"
> "Who works in the Personnel department?"

   c. Check students' understanding of the vocabulary. (Note that these sentences tell about the characters in the exercises for this lesson.)

THE MODEL CONVERSATION

1. **Setting the Scene.** Have students look at the model illustration. Set the scene: "Jackie Walden and Roger Bell work for the same company. Roger just started working there, and he is meeting Jackie for the first time."

2. **Listening to the Model.** With books closed, have students listen to the model conversation — presented by you, by a pair of students, or on the audiotape.

3. **Class Practice.** With books still closed, model each line and have the whole class repeat in unison.

4. **Reading.** With books open, have students follow along as two students present the model. Ask students if they have any questions and check understanding of vocabulary.

Culture Note

In this conversation, "department" refers to subdivisions within a company, such as the "Personnel" and "Accounting" departments.

5. **Pair Practice.** In pairs, have students practice the model conversation.

6. **Alternative Expressions.** Present to the class each sentence of the dialog containing a footnoted expression. Call on different students to present the same sentence, but replacing the footnoted expression with its alternatives. (You can cue students to do this quickly by asking, "What's another way of saying that?" or "How else could he/she/you say that?")

THE EXERCISES

Examples

> 1. A. You're new here, aren't you?
>   B. Yes, I am. My name is Don.
>   A. I'm Steve. Nice to meet you.
>   B. Nice meeting you, too.
>   A. Tell me, who is your supervisor?
>   B. Mr. Crane. How about you?
>   A. Mrs. Benson.

2. A. You're new here, aren't you?
   B. Yes, I am. My name is Enku.
   A. I'm Asako. It's nice to meet you.
   B. It's nice meeting you, too.
   A. Tell me, what country are you from?
   B. Ethiopia. What about you?
   A. Japan.

Before doing each exercise, check students' understanding of the vocabulary and introduce any new words or phrases. Have students use the footnoted expressions or any of their alternatives as they do the exercises.

Exercise Practice (optional). Have pairs of students simultaneously practice all the exercies.

Exercise Presentations. Call on pairs of students to present the exercises.

Language Notes

Exercises 1 and 3: "Mr." refers to both married and single men. "Mrs." indicates that a woman is married and has taken her husband's last name. For example, Mary Smith marries Joe West and becomes "Mrs. West." "Miss" is traditionally placed before a woman's name if she is unmarried. "Ms." is a relatively new term that refers to all women whether they are married or single.

Exercise 5: The expression "ups and downs" is used humorously for its double meaning in this context. The window washer moves from floor to floor ("up and down") as he does his job; and everyone experiences good times and bad times ("ups and downs") in their lives.

ORIGINAL STUDENT CONVERSATIONS

Have pairs of students create and present original conversations based on the model. (You may want students to prepare their original conversations as homework, then practice them the next day with another student and present them to the class.)

EXPANSION

1. Interviewing and Note-Taking

a. Divide the class into pairs, and have the students informally interview each other. Have students take notes on the information they learn about their partners. Sample interview questions and conversation starters are:

Where are you from?
Can you tell me a little about your city?
When did you start working/studying here?
How are you enjoying your work/classes?

Ask students to take notes on their partners' answers so that they can report back to the class. Explain that notes do not have to be complete sentences. Give some examples of notes, such as "from Senegal" or "is studying computers."

b. On another class day, have each student use the notes from the previous class to give a brief oral report. Or have students use their notes to write a short paragraph about the interview. Students can also use these reports to create a class newsletter.

2. Find Someone Who . . .

a. Collect some information about the students. Some examples might include their nationalities, occupations, travel experiences, and neighborhoods.

b. Put this information in the following form:

> Find someone who . . .
>
> 1. is from Ecuador. _____
> 2. lives on the West Side. _____
> 3. lived in Lebanon for three years. _____
> 4. is studying pharmacology. _____
> 5. is a secretary. _____

c. Have students circulate around the room asking each other questions to identify the above people.

d. The first student to identify all the people wins.

3. Tic Tac Question

This is a fun challenge for students after they have interviewed each other. It tests their knowledge of each other, as well as of question formation.

a. Draw a tic tac grid on the board, and fill it in with question words. For example:

What kind	Where	When
How	Who	Why
Does	Which	What

b. Divide the class into teams. Give each team a mark—X or O.

c. Have each team ask a question about a classmate that begins with one of the question words and then provide the answer to the question. If the question and answer are correct, the team puts its mark in that space. For example:

> X Team: What kind music does Maria like? Jazz.

X	Where	When
How	Who	Why
Does	Which	What

d. The first team to mark out three boxes in a straight line — vertically, horizontally, or diagonally — wins.

4. Famous People Party

a. Have students choose a living person whom they admire. Have them do a brief investigation into that person's life and find out some basic facts such as the person's home, family, occupation, hobbies, and attitudes.

b. Have the class role-play a party scene, in which students *become* the person they chose but not disclose their identity.

c. After 5 or 10 minutes of mingling, have people tell how many celebrities they were able to identify and what they learned about them.

What's the Word?

Have students do the activity individually, in pairs, or as a class. You may want to assign this exercise as homework.

1. Where	7. What
2. Who	8. Whose
3. What/Which	9. When
4. How	10. Who
5. When	11. How
6. Why	12. Where

Constructions Ahead!

Have students do the activity individually, in pairs, or as a class. You may want to assign this exercise as homework.

1. are	9. is
2. do	10. Are
3. am	11. Is
4. are	12. do
5. Does	13. are
6. is	14. does
7. Are	15. Do
8. Do	16. Am

Listen

Listen and choose the right answer.

1. Where's Michael?
2. Who are you?
3. When did you move in?
4. Where are you going?
5. How's Janet?
6. Which apartment do you live in?
7. What are you majoring in?
8. My name is Elsa.
9. How do you do?

Answers

1. b	4. b	7. b
2. a	5. b	8. b
3. b	6. a	9. a

More Questions!

Have students do the activity individually, in pairs, or as a class. You may want to assign this exercise as homework.

1. a	4. a	7. a
2. b	5. b	8. b
3. b	6. b	9. b

InterActions

Have pairs of students practice role-playing the activity and then present their role plays to the class.

Cultural Intersections

Have students do the activity in class, in pairs, or in small groups.

Figure It Out!

Have students practice their dialogs in pairs and then present them to the class. Have the rest of the class try to guess who the characters are and where the conversation is taking place.

Fill It In!

Have students do the activity individually, in pairs, or as a class. You may want to assign this exercise as homework.

1. Is
2. is
3. Are
4. am
5. is
6. Are
7. am
8. I'm
9. is
10. I'm
11. Does
12. does
13. are
14. Are
15. I'm

Matching Lines

Have students do the activity individually, in pairs, or as a class. You may want to assign this exercise as homework.

1. c
2. a
3. b
4. f
5. e
6. d
7. i
8. g
9. h

FOCUS

TOPICS

Social Communication: Meeting People
Personal Information: Family Members

FUNCTIONS

1. **Greeting People**

   How are you?
   [*less formal*]
   How are you doing?
   How are things?
       Fine, thanks.
       Good.
       All right.

2. **Introductions**

   Introducing Others

   I'd like to introduce you to _____.
   I'd like to introduce _____.
   Let me introduce you to _____.
   Let me introduce _____.
   I'd like you to meet _____.
   [*less formal*]
   This is _____.

VOCABULARY

Family Members

brother
daughter
father
husband
mother-in-law
wife

COMMENTARY

1. The greeting "How are you?" is used in both formal and informal situations. "How are you doing?" and "How are things?" are informal expressions.

2. "How are you?" "Fine. And you?" is a very common way of greeting people. In this context, "How are you?" is not really a request for information, but rather a way of extending a greeting. The response is usually an automatic "Fine."

3. "I'd" is a contraction of "I + would." *I'd like to* is a polite way of saying *I want to*.

16 EXIT ONE

THE MODEL CONVERSATION

1. **Setting the Scene.** Have students look at the model illustration. Set the scene: "Patty and her husband are at a health club. While they are there, they see a friend of her husband's."

2. **Listening to the Model.** With books closed, have students listen to the model conversation — presented by you, by a pair of students, or on the audiotape.

3. **Class Practice.** With books still closed, model each line and have the whole class repeat in unison.

4. **Reading.** With books open, have students follow along as two students present the model. Ask students if they have any questions and check understanding of vocabulary.

5. **Pair Practice.** In pairs, have students practice the model conversation.

6. **Alternative Expressions**. Present to the class each sentence of the dialog containing a footnoted expression. Call on different students to present the same sentence, but replacing the footnoted expression with its alternatives. (You can cue students to do this quickly by asking, "What's another way of saying that?" or "How else could he/she/you say that?")

Culture Note

These people are exercising at a health club or community recreation center. Many adults in the United States are interested in physical fitness, or staying in shape.

THE EXERCISES

Examples

1. A. Hi! How are you?
   B. Fine. And you?
   A. Fine, thanks. I'd like to introduce you to my husband, Philip.
   B. Nice to meet you.

2. A. Hi! How are you doing?
   B. Good. And you?
   A. All right, thanks. I'd like to introduce my brother, Carl.
   B. Nice to meet you.

Before doing each exercise, check students' understanding of the vocabulary and introduce any unfamiliar words or phrases. Have students use the footnoted expressions or any of their alternatives as they do the exercises.

Exercise Practice (optional). Have pairs of students simultaneously practice all the exercises.

Exercise Presentations. Call on pairs of students to present the exercises.

ORIGINAL STUDENT CONVERSATIONS

Have pairs of students create and present original conversations based on the model. (You may want students to prepare their original conversations as homework, then practice them the next day with another student and present them to the class.)

EXPANSION

1. Role Play: More Introductions

Have students role-play introducing a friend to someone and then developing a short conversation in a natural way. During most introductions, a bit of information is given that can be used as a springboard for continuing the conversation.

a. Divide the class into groups of 3 or 4 people. Have students take turns role-playing introducing each other to the group.

b. Read the following examples to show students how they can develop a short conversation by giving or asking for information about the person they are introducing.

> *(Jean is introducing Roger to Stan.)*
> A. Stan, I'd like you to meet Roger.
> B. Hi, Roger. Nice to meet you.
> C. Nice to meet you, too.
> A. Did you two see the baseball game on TV last night?
> C. No. I missed it. I had to work.
> B. I saw it. That was really a great game.

> *(Assad is introducing Kim to Bill.)*
> A. Bill, this is Kim. Kim is in my English class.
> B. Hi, Kim. How are you?
> C. Fine, thanks.
> B. What other languages do you speak, Kim?
> C. I speak Korean. How about you?
> B. I speak French and a little Spanish.

2. Class Discussion: What Is Appropriate?

a. Check your students' awareness of appropriate behavior in their own culture and in U.S. culture by answering the questions below. (There may not be one right answer to a question; what seems appropriate to one person may not be appropriate to another.) Have students explain the reasons for their answers.

b. Add your own questions to this list based on situations that relate to your students' lives.

(1) You're meeting the director of the school for the first time. Should you shake hands? How should you greet the director? For example, should you say, "Hi! How are you doing?"

(2) You're new at your job. Your supervisor is showing you around the company. She's introducing you to many different people. The supervisor is saying "Hi, Bill! I want you to meet _____ ." How do you greet your new co-workers? Should you shake hands with anyone?

(3) You're doing your laundry in the laundry room in the basement of your apartment building. A man is doing his laundry at the machine next to you. He asks you if you have change for a dollar bill for the machine. You have extra change so you give him some. Should you introduce yourself? If you do, how should you do it?

3. Expanding Vocabulary Game

a. Divide the class into teams.

b. Have each team list as many *family* words as they can think of. For example:

    daughter
    cousin
    father-in-law
    grandfather
    grandchild
    uncle
    aunt
    mother-in-law

c. After three minutes, the team with the longest list wins.

4. Class Discussion: Meeting People

As a class, in pairs, or in small groups, have students discuss the following:

How did you meet your five closest friends? (through friends, family, school, or hobby activities?)

Where are good places to meet people? Why?

How did your parents meet?
How do young couples meet these days?

Tell about a time you introduced yourself to a stranger.
    Where was it?
    What did you say to each other?

Fill It In!

Have students do the activity individually, in pairs, or as a class. You may want to assign this exercise as homework.

1. b
2. b
3. a
4. b
5. a
6. b

Meet My Family!

Have students do the activity individually, in pairs, or as a class. You may want to assign this exercise as homework.

1. wife
2. son
3. daughter
4. mother
5. father
6. brother
7. sister
8. husband
9. nephew
10. niece

Your Turn

Have students discuss the activity as a class, in pairs, or in small groups. Then have students write their responses at home, share their written work and photographs with other students, and discuss in class.

Students may enjoy keeping a journal of their written work. If time permits, you may want to write a response to each student's journal, sharing your own opinions and experiences as well as reacting to what the student has written. If you are keeping portfolios of students' work, these compositions serve as excellent examples of students' progress in learning English.

FOCUS

TOPICS

Personal Information: Nationality
Travel: Customs and Immigration

GRAMMAR

Question Formation

Where in Italy are you from?
How long do you plan to stay?

FUNCTIONS

Asking for and Reporting Information

How long *do you plan to stay*?

Where in *Italy* are you from?

VOCABULARY

Countries	Nationalities	People	Travel/ Accommodations
Brazil	Brazilian	Brazilians	
Italy	Italian	Italians	passport
Japan	Japanese	Japanese	passport control
Korea	Korean	Koreans	
Spain	Spanish	Spaniards	
Sweden	Swedish	Swedes	

COMMENTARY

1. In line 3, "Italian?" is a shortened form of the question "Are you Italian?" It is common for people performing routine interviews or asking routine questions to use shortened forms of questions.

2. In line 7, "sure" intensifies the meaning of the whole sentence.

3. When the clerk calls out "Next!" she is asking for the next person in line to come forward.

GETTING READY

1. Present and practice the vocabulary for countries and cities.

a. Write the list of countries and cities on the board. For example:

Brazil	Rio de Janeiro
Sweden	Stockholm
Italy	Florence
Japan	Tokyo
Spain	Barcelona

b. Have students use a world map or globe to locate the countries and cities.

c. Practice the names of the countries and cities by having students ask and answer questions about each one. For example:

A. Where is (Rio de Janeiro)?
B. It's in (Brazil).

A. Is (Stockholm) in (Canada)?
B. No. It's in (Sweden).

2. Present and practice the terms for nationalities and people living in each country.

a. Write on the board:

Country	Nationality	People
Brazil	Brazilian	Brazilians
Italy	Italian	Italians
Japan	Japanese	Japanese
Korea	Korean	Koreans
Spain	Spanish	Spaniards
Sweden	Swedish	Swedes

b. Model the following:

A. What's the country?
B. Brazil.
A. What's the nationality?
B. Brazilian.
A. Who lives there?
B. Brazilians.

c. Call on pairs of students to practice with all the countries on the board.

THE MODEL CONVERSATION

1. **Setting the Scene.** Have students look at the model illustration. Set the scene: "A visitor from Italy is entering the United States. He's showing his passport and answering questions."

2. **Listening to the Model.** With books closed, have students listen to the model conversation — presented by you, by a pair of students, or on the audiotape.

3. **Class Practice.** With books still closed, model each line and have the whole class repeat in unison.

4. **Reading.** With books open, have students follow along as two students present the model. Ask students if they have any questions and check understanding of vocabulary.

5. **Pair Practice.** In pairs, have students practice the model conversation.

THE EXERCISES

Examples

1. A. Passport, please!
   B. Here you are.
   A. Swedish?
   B. Yes.
   A. Where in Sweden are you from?
   B. Stockholm.
   A. There sure are a lot of people from Sweden visiting right now.
   B. I'm not surprised. Our school year just ended, and a lot of Swedes are on vacation.
   A. How long do you play to stay?
   B. About ten days.
   A. All right. Here's your passport. Welcome to Canada.
   B. Thank you.
   A. Next!

2. A. Passport, please!
   B. Here you are.
   A. Japanese?
   B. Yes.
   A. Where in Japan are you from?
   B. Tokyo.
   A. There sure are a lot of people from Japan visiting right now.
   B. I'm not surprised. Our school year just ended, and a lot of Japanese are on vacation.
   A. How long do you plan to stay?
   B. About ten days.
   A. Okay. Here's your passport. Welcome to Australia. ▾
   B. Thank you.
   A. Next!

Before doing each exercise, check students' understanding of the vocabulary and introduce any unfamiliar words or phrases.

Exercise Practice (optional). Have pairs of students simultaneously practice all the exercises.

Exercise Presentations. Call on pairs of students to present the exercises.

ORIGINAL STUDENT CONVERSATIONS

Have pairs of students create and present original conversations based on the model. (You may want students to prepare their original conversations as homework, then practice them the next day with another student and present them to the class.)

EXPANSION

1. Describing Locations

a. Choose expressions for describing locations, such as those shown below. Write them on the board, and check students' understanding of the words and expressions.

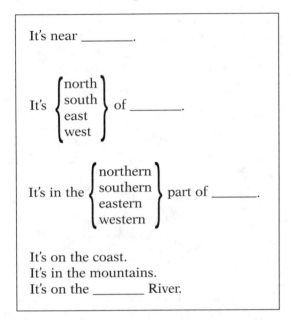

It's near _____.

It's $\begin{Bmatrix} \text{north} \\ \text{south} \\ \text{east} \\ \text{west} \end{Bmatrix}$ of _____.

It's in the $\begin{Bmatrix} \text{northern} \\ \text{southern} \\ \text{eastern} \\ \text{western} \end{Bmatrix}$ part of _____.

It's on the coast.
It's in the mountains.
It's on the _____ River.

b. Have each student choose a town or city and prepare to tell the class exactly where it is, using the expressions on the board. Encourage students to use a map to help explain and show locations. (If your students are from different countries or cities, they might like to talk about the places where they were born or grew up. In a class of students from the same city, they might instead talk about cities they want to visit or their favorite places.)

Variation: This can be done as a guessing game, in which the name of the city or town is a mystery. The class has to figure out what the city or town is, based on the student's description of its location.

2. Nations, Nationalities, and Languages

a. Divide the class into teams.

b. Call out a category such as the following:

North America
Latin America
South America
Western Europe
Eastern Europe
Africa
Mediterranean countries
The Middle East
Southeast Asia
The Far East
The Caribbean
Central Asia

c. Have the teams write down as many countries they can think of in the region, the languages spoken in those countries, and the name of the nationalities. For example: *Mediterranean countries*

Country	Language	Nationality
Italy	Italian	Italian
Libya	Arabic	Libyan
Greece	Greek	Greek
Spain	Spanish	Spanish
Morocco	Arabic and French	Moroccan

d. The team that comes up with the most correct and complete information wins the game.

3. It's on the Map!

a. Put a large world outline map on a bulletin board.

b. Write the names of geographical locations on cards. Place the cards in a pile face down on a desk in front of the room.

c. Have each student pick a card and write the name in the appropriate place on the map.

4. Talking About Travels

a. Display a large world map.

b. As a class, in pairs, or in small groups, have students tell about places they have traveled. Have students tell . . .

    places they visited
    what they liked and disliked about
        these places
    places they recommend to visit

c. Have students refer to the map if there are questions about any of the geographical locations.

5. Who, What, and Where in the World

a. Collect some information about students in the class. For example:

  places they lived
  places they visited
  languages they speak
  favorite foreign foods
  favorite foreign countries
  favorite foreign cities

b. Put this information in the following form:

Find someone . . .

1. whose favorite city is
   Hong Kong.   _____

2. who speaks French and
   Italian well.   _____

3. whose favorite country is
   Ecuador.   _____

4. who lived in Athens for
   five years.   _____

5. whose favorite food is
   Thai food.   _____

---

c. Have students circulate around the room asking each other questions to identify the above people.

d. The first student to identify all the people wins.

ExpressWays

Have students do the activity individually, in pairs, or as a class. You may want to assign this exercise as homework.

1. France
2. Paris
3. French
4. Kyoto
5. Japan
6. Japanese
7. Korea
8. Seoul
9. Korean
10. Canada
11. Canadian
12. Montreal

CrossTalk

Have pairs of students complete the conversation any way they wish and then present their conversations to the class.

FOCUS

TOPICS

Travel: Accommodations — Checking In
Personal Information: Name

GRAMMAR

1. **Question Formation**

   May I help you?
   What's your last name?

2. **Tense Review**

   I see here you **requested** twin beds.
   I see here you**'re staying** three nights.

FUNCTIONS

1. **Asking for and Reporting Information**

   What's your *last name*?

   Could you spell that, please?
   Could you please spell that?

2. **Correcting**

   Giving Correction
   No, actually not.
   Not really.

VOCABULARY

Travel/Accommodations	Personal Information
American Express card	first name
charge (your) bill	last name
king-size bed	
regular room	
reservation	
room	
suite	
twin beds	

COMMENTARY

1. "May I help you?" is customarily used by salesclerks and service people when they are available to help a customer or client.

2. In line 9, the clerk says "I see here . . .," because he is reading the information on the computer.

3. "No, actually not" (line 10) is a polite expression for correcting someone.

1. Review the alphabet.

   a. Write the letters of the alphabet on the board.

   b. Point to the letters in order, say each one, and have students repeat them after you.

   c. At random, point to different letters and have students say the name of the letter.

2. Practice spelling names.

   a. Model the following conversation:

   > A. What's your last name?
   > B. Garcia.
   > A. Could you spell that, please?
   > B. G-A-R-C-I-A.

   b. Call on pairs of students to create dialogs based on the model, using their own names.

THE MODEL CONVERSATION

1. **Setting the Scene.** Have students look at the model illustration. Set the scene: "Mr. Francovich is checking in to a hotel."

2. **Listening to the Model.** With books closed, have students listen to the model conversation — presented by you, by a pair of students, or on the audiotape.

3. **Class Practice.** With books still closed, model each line and have the whole class repeat in unison.

4. **Reading.** With books open, have students follow along as two students present the model. Ask students if they have any questions, and check understanding of vocabulary.

Culture Note

There are four sizes of beds in the United States: twin bed (or single bed, for one person), double bed (for two people), queen-size bed (larger than a double), and king-size bed (the largest).

5. **Pair Practice.** In pairs, have students practice the model conversation.

6. **Alternative Expressions.** Present to the class each sentence of the dialog containing a footnoted expression. Call on different students to present the same sentence, but replacing the footnoted expression with its alternatives. (You can cue students to do this quickly by asking, "What's another way of saying that?" or "How else could he/she/you say that?")

THE EXERCISES

Examples

1. A. May I help you?
   B. Yes. I have a reservation.
   A. What's your last name?
   B. Holmes.
   A. Could you spell that, please?
   B. Sure. H-O-L-M-E-S.
   A. First name Bruce?
   B. That's right.
   A. I see here you're staying 3 nights.
   B. No, actually not. I'm staying 2 nights.

2. A. May I help you?
   B. Yes. I have a reservation.
   A. What's your last name?
   B. Creighton.
   A. Could you please spell that?
   B. Yes. C-R-E-I-G-H-T-O-N.
   A. First name Emily?
   B. That's correct.
   A. I see here you requested a suite.
   B. Not really. I requested a regular room.

Before doing each exercise, check students' understanding of the vocabulary and introduce any unfamiliar words or phrases. Have students use the footnoted expressions or any of their alternatives as they do the exercises.

Exercise Practice (optional). Have pairs of students simultaneously practice all the exercises.

Exercise Presentations. Call on pairs of students to present the exercises.

Culture Notes

Exercise 2: Most people staying at hotels in the United States stay in a "regular" room, which usually contains one or two beds, a closet, a dresser with a mirror, a television, a telephone, and an adjoining bathroom with a toilet, a sink, and a combination bathtub/shower. A suite is usually larger and more luxurious, and may include an additional sitting room and a small kitchen.

Exercise 5: Many people in the United States have charge accounts and credit cards, such as the American Express card. These accounts and card services enable people to charge bills or purchases and pay for them at a later time.

ORIGINAL STUDENT CONVERSATIONS

Have pairs of students create and present original conversations based on the model. (You may want students to prepare their original conversations as homework, then practice them the next day with another student and present them to the class.)

EXPANSION

1. Telephone

a. Divide the class into large groups. Have each group sit in a circle.

b. Whisper a name and its spelling to one student. For example:

Elizabeth Mitchell Elder
E-L-I-Z-A-B-E-T-H M-I-T-C-H-E-L-L E-L-D-E-R

c. The first student whispers the name and its spelling to the second student, and so forth around the circle.

d. When the name gets to the last student, that person says it aloud and spells it. Is it the same as you started with? The group with the most accurate name and spelling wins.

2. Around the World Spelling Bee

a. On several sets of cards write the names of places around the world. For example:

Marrakech
Nagoya
Prague
Somalia
Antarctica

b. Divide the class into teams and give each team a set of cards.

c. Have students take turns reading the words aloud and spelling them to the team members. All the members of each team must write the words correctly.

d. The first team to correctly spell all the places wins the spelling bee.

3. Information Gap: Checking In to the Riverside Hotel

a. Write the following roles on index cards. Make enough copies for the class.

b. Divide the class into pairs. Give Role A to one member of the pair and Role B to the other.

c. Have students role-play the situations.

1.

Role A: Mr. and Mrs. Thomas Winger

You're checking in to the Riverside Hotel. You'll be staying 3 nights. Your son Peter will be staying with you, and so you requested a cot, a small extra bed, in the room.

Role B:

You work at the Riverside Hotel. According to your computer, Mr. and Mrs. Thomas "Wagner" will be staying 4 nights. They requested a cot, but you don't have any available.

2.

Role A: Debbie Paige

You're checking in to the Riverside Hotel. You'll be staying 6 nights. You requested a room on the top floor.

Role B:

You work at the Riverside Hotel. According to your computer, Debbie "Page" will be staying 6 nights. She requested a room on the top floor. You can give her a room on that floor for only 3 nights.

3.

Role A: Mr. and Mrs. Marvin Travers

You're checking in to the Riverside Hotel. You'll be staying one week. You requested twin beds.

Role B:

You work at the Riverside Hotel. According to your computer, Mr. and Mrs. "Martin Traverson" will be staying one night. They requested a king-size bed.

4.

> Role A: Mr. and Mrs. Walter Knowles
>
> You're checking in to the Riverside Hotel. You'll be staying 2 nights. You don't want a room near the pool. You think it's too noisy there.

> Role B:
>
> You work at the Riverside Hotel. According to your computer, Mr. and Mrs. Walter "Noble" will be staying 2 nights. The only rooms you have available are near the pool.

5.

> Role A: Ms. Beverly Crane
>
> You're checking in to the Riverside Hotel. You'll be staying 5 nights. You requested a room facing the river.

> Role B:
>
> You work at the Riverside Hotel. According to your computer, Beverly Crane will be staying 3 nights. She requested a room facing the park.

4. My Dream Weekend Vacation

a. Have students imagine they can chose any destination and any hotel for a weekend vacation.

b. Have them write about their *dream weekend vacation*, answering the following questions:

Where do you want to go? Why?
Who do you want to go there with?
What will you do there?
What kind of hotel do you want to stay in?
What kind of hotel room will you request?

c. Have them share their writings with each other in pairs, in small groups, or as a class.

Crossed Lines

Have students do the activity individually, in pairs, or as a class. You may want to assign this exercise as homework.

13 No. I'm afraid not.

4 Andersen.

10 No, actually not. I requested a non-smoking room. I'm allergic to smoke.

1 May I help you?

12 You don't?!

7 Is your first name Ingrid?

2 Yes. I have a reservation.

11 I'm afraid we don't have any non-smoking rooms.

5 Could you please spell that?

3 What's your last name?

6 A-N-D-E-R-S-E-N.

9 I see here you requested a smoking room.

8 That's correct.

InterActions

Have pairs of students practice role-playing the activity and then present their role plays to the class.

FOCUS

TOPICS

Personal Information: **Address**
Age
Date of Birth
Name
Occupation
Social Security Number
Telephone Number
Health: Checking In to a Hospital or Clinic

GRAMMAR

1. **Question Formation**

   What's your last name?

   Do you have medical insurance?

2. **Tense Review**

   Before you can see a doctor, we **need** some information.
   I **left** my membership card at home.
   Take a seat over there, and somebody **will see** you in a few minutes.

FUNCTIONS

Asking for and Reporting Information

We need some information.

What's your *last name*?
And your *first name*?

Could you spell that, please?

Address?
   35 Winter Street in *Middletown.*

Telephone number?
   732-4495.

What's your date of birth?
   May 15th, 1975.

Occupation?
   Shoe salesman.

What's your Social Security number?
Do you have *medical insurance*?
Do you know *your I.D. number*?

VOCABULARY

Personal Information

address	membership card	
date of birth	occupation	
first name	road	
I.D. number	Social Security number	
last name	telephone number	

Health

Blue Cross/Blue Shield
doctor
Emergency Room
medical insurance

COMMENTARY

1. "Social Security number." Anyone who earns money in the United States must report his or her earnings to the federal government. Individuals are given Social Security numbers. Social Security taxes are paid to support a national program of life insurance and old-age pension payments.

2. In the statement "I'm sorry. I don't remember" (line 19), "I'm sorry" makes the statement more polite. Similarly, "I'm afraid not" (line 23) is a polite way of answering "No."

3. "Blue Cross/Blue Shield" is a large health insurance company in the United States.

4. "I.D. number" is the abbreviation for "identification number."

5. "That's okay" (line 24) means "Don't worry about it" or "No problem."

GETTING READY

Review dates and telephone numbers.

a. Write several telephone numbers on the board. Have students practice reading the numbers chorally and individually. Make sure students pause after reading the first three numbers. For example, 723-4650 is read "seven two three (pause) four six five zero (or 'oh')."

b. Have students practice saying and reading dates, using one or more of the following:

   (1) Ask students, "What's the date today?" "What was the date yesterday?"

   (2) Ask students about their birthdays. ("When is your birthday?" "When is his/her birthday?")

   (3) Write dates on the board (including a variety of ways of showing the dates) and have students practice reading them.

   (4) Point to different dates on a calendar and ask, "What is the date?"

THE MODEL CONVERSATION

1. **Setting the Scene.** Have students look at the model illustration. Set the scene: "A man is at the Emergency Room of a hospital."

2. **Listening to the Model.** With books closed, have students listen to the model conversation — presented by you, by a pair of students, or on the audiotape.

3. **Class Practice.** With books still closed, model each line and have the whole class repeat in unison.

4. **Reading.** With books open, have students follow along as two students present the model. Ask students if they have any questions and check understanding of vocabulary.

5. **Pair Practice.** In pairs, have students practice the model conversation.

Now have pairs of students create and present original conversations using the model dialog as a guide. Encourage students to be inventive and to use new vocabulary. (You may want to assign this exercise as homework, having students prepare their original conversations, practice them the next day with another student, and then present them to the class.) Students should present their conversations without referring to the written text, but they also should not memorize them. Rather, they should feel free to adapt and expand them any way they wish.

Reflections

Have students discuss the questions in pairs or small groups and then share their ideas with the class.

InterActions

Have pairs of students practice role-playing the activity and then present their role plays to the class.

Possible Answers:

1. What's your name?
2. Could you spell your last name please?
3. What's your address?
4. And your telephone number?
5. What is your Social Security number?
6. Do you have medical insurance?
7. Who is your supervisor?/
   What's your supervisor's name?

Reading: *No More Numbers, Please!*

Preview: Have students discuss the following question:

   What numbers do you use every day?

Then have students read the passage silently, or have them listen to the passage and take notes as you read it or play the audiotape.

Do You Remember?

Have students do the activity individually, in pairs, or as a class. You may want to assign this exercise as homework.

1. a   5. b
2. c   6. b
3. c   7. c
4. c

Yes, No, or Maybe?

Have students do the activity individually, in pairs, or as a class. You may want to assign this exercise as homework.

1. Yes
2. No
3. Maybe
4. Maybe
5. No
6. Maybe
7. No
8. Yes
9. No
10. Yes

Matching Numbers

Have students do the activity individually, in pairs, or as a class. You may want to assign this exercise as homework.

1. e
2. c
3. b
4. d
5. a

Figure It Out!

Do the activity as a class, in pairs, or in small groups. You may want to do the activity as a game with competing teams.

Looking Back

Have students look at the list of expressions. Encourage them to ask you any questions they have about the meaning or pronunciation of any of the words. If students ask for the pronunciation, repeat after the student until the student is satisfied with his or her pronunciation of the word.

Vocabulary Review

To review the vocabulary introduced in the unit, do the following activity.

Association Game

a. Divide the class into several teams.

b. Call out a topic category from the *Looking Back* section on student text page 18.

c. Have students in each group work together to see how many phrases they can associate with that category. For example:

Greeting People: Hi.
Hello.
How do you do?
Nice to meet you.
Nice meeting you.

d. The team with the most items wins.

EXIT 2

OVERVIEW
Student Text
Pages 19–34

Topics	Functions	Grammar

P. 20 What's New with You?

Social Communication:
  Sharing Information
	Initiating a Topic
	Asking for and Reporting
	  Information
	Congratulating
		Past Tense

P. 22 Is Anything Wrong?

Social Communication:
  Sharing Information
	Initiating a Topic
	Asking for and Reporting
	  Information
	Sympathizing
		Past Tense

Pp. 24–25 Can I Ask You a Question?

Social Communication:
  Sharing Information
	Attracting Attention
	Initiating a Topic
	Asking for and Reporting
	  Information
	Certainty/Uncertainty
		Yes/No Questions
		Negative Sentences
		Tense Review

P. 28 What Are You Going to Do This Weekend?

Social Communication: Sharing Information	Intention Surprise–Disbelief Agreement/Disagreement Certainty/Uncertainty Probability/Improbability Leave Taking	Future: Going to Future: Will

P. 30 Tell Me a Little About Yourself

Social Communication:
  Sharing Information
	Asking for and Reporting
	  Information
	Hesitating
		Tense Review
		Question Formation

LOOKING AHEAD

Grammar This Exit

Yes/No Questions

Is our English teacher going to quit?
Are they going to lay off the workers on the
night shift?
Do the bus drivers plan to go on strike?
Does our supervisor want to shorten our
coffee break?
Did the boss fire Fred this morning?
Was our gym teacher in the 1992 Olympics?

Negative Sentences

Our English teacher **isn't** going to quit.
They **aren't** going to lay off the workers on the
night shift.
The bus drivers **don't** plan to go on strike.
Our supervisor **doesn't** want to shorten our
coffee break.
The boss **didn't** fire Fred this morning.
Our gym teacher **wasn't** in the 1992 Olympics.

Question Formation

What do you want to know?
Where are you from?

Are you originally from around here?
Do you have any brothers and sisters?

Simple Present Tense

I **have** a brother and two sisters.
Our supervisor **wants** to shorten our coffee break.

I'm originally from Chicago.
Santa Claus **is** just "make believe!"

Past Tense

I just **passed** my driver's test!

I just **got** a big raise!
My wife **had** a baby girl last week!
My husband and I **won** the state lottery!
My daughter **broke up** with her fiance.
I **was** born there, I **grew** up there, and I **went** to
school there.

You **did**?
I **didn't** get the raise!

Future: Going to

What are you **going to** do this weekend?
  I'm **going to** clean out my attic.
  My husband and I are **going to** repaint our
    kitchen.

Future: Will

I'll probably visit my grandchildren.

Functions This Exit

Asking for and Reporting Information

What's new with you?
What's happening with you?
What's new?
What's happening?
  Nothing much.

How about you?
And you?

Is anything wrong?

Where did you hear that?
Who told you that?

Tell me a little about yourself.

What do you want to know?

What do you do?
Do you have any brothers and sisters?
Are you originally from around here?

Congratulating

That's great!
That's wonderful!
That's fantastic!

Congratulations!

Sympathizing

That's too bad!
That's a shame!
What a shame!

I'm very sorry to hear that.
I'm very sorry.
I'm so sorry.

Intention

Inquiring about . . .

What are you going to do *this weekend*?

Expressing . . .

I'm going to *clean out my attic*.

Attracting Attention

Mohammed?

Agreement/Disagreement

Expressing Agreement

I suppose so.

Certainty/Uncertainty

Expressing Certainty

I'm sure _____.

Expressing Uncertainty

I'm not sure.
I don't know for sure.
I'm not positive.

Surprise–Disbelief

Repaint your kitchen?!

Probability/Improbability

Expressing Probability

I'll probably ⎫
I'll most likely ⎬ *visit my grandchildren.*
I'm pretty sure I'll ⎭

Leave Taking

Have a good weekend!
 You, too.

Initiating a Topic

What's new with you?
What's happening with you?
What's new?
What's happening?

Can I ask you a question?
Can I ask you something?

I have some good news.

You seem upset.

Hesitating

Gee . . . uh.

I don't know where to begin.

Well . . .

PREVIEWING EXIT 2: CHAPTER-OPENING PHOTOS

Have students talk about the people and the situations and, as a class or in pairs, predict what the characters might be saying to each other. Students in pairs or small groups may enjoy practicing role plays based on these scenes and then presenting them to the class.

Text Page 20: What's New with You?

FOCUS

TOPIC

Social Communication: Sharing Information

GRAMMAR

Past Tense

I just **got** a big promotion!
My wife **had** a baby girl last week!
My husband and I **won** the lottery!

FUNCTIONS

1. **Initiating a Topic**

   What's new with you?
   What's happening with you?
   What's new?
   What's happening?

   I have some good news.

2. **Asking for and Reporting Information**

   What's new with you?
   What's happening with you?
   What's new?
   What's happening?
     Nothing much.

3. **Congratulating**

   That's great!
   That's wonderful!
   That's fantastic!

   Congratulations!

COMMENTARY

1. The tone of this dialog suggests the informality common between friends who see each other regularly.

2. "Congratulations!" is the standard expression for congratulating people on a personal accomplishment (such as success in school or a job promotion), a happy turning point in life (such as a marriage or a birth), or a lucky event (such as winning a prize).

GETTING READY

Have students practice using _____ *did?!* to react to and show interest in information about the past.

a. Make up a list of events in the recent past, preferably announcements that may interest your students.

b. Read each one to the class (or have a student read each one). Ask students to respond by saying: "_____ did?!" ("You did?!" "He did?!" "She did?!" "They did?!" "It did?!") For example:

> A. Mrs. Smith had a baby girl two days ago!
> B. She did?!
>
> A. My car broke down on the highway last night!
> B. It did?!
>
> A. The man sitting next to me on the bus this morning fainted!
> B. He did?!
>
> A. My children gave me a new watch for my birthday!
> B. They did?!

THE MODEL CONVERSATION

1. **Setting the Scene.** Have students look at the model illustration. Set the scene: "Two friends are jogging in a park. They see each other, and they start talking."

2. **Listening to the Model.** With books closed, have students listen to the model conversation — presented by you, by a pair of students, or on the audiotape.

3. **Class Practice.** With books still closed, model each line and have the whole class repeat in unison.

4. **Reading.** With books open, have students follow along as two students present the model. Ask students if they have any questions and check understanding of vocabulary.

5. **Pair Practice.** In pairs, have students practice the model conversation.

6. **Alternative Expressions.** Present to the class each sentence of the dialog containing a footnoted expression. Call on different students to present the same sentence, but replacing the footnoted expression with its alternatives. (You can cue students to do this quickly by asking, "What's another way of saying that?" or "How else could he/she/you say that?")

THE EXERCISES

Examples

> 1. A. What's new with you?
>   B. Nothing much. How about you?
>   A. Well, actually, I have some good news.
>   B. Really? What?
>   A. I just passed my driver's test!
>   B. You did? That's great! Congratulations!
>
> 2. A. What's happening with you?
>   B. Nothing much. How about you?
>   A. Well, actually, I have some good news.
>   B. Really? What?
>   A. My wife had a baby girl last week!
>   B. She did? That's wonderful! Congratulations!

Before doing each exercise, check students' understanding of the vocabulary and introduce any unfamiliar words or phrases. Have students use the footnoted expressions or any of their alternatives as they do the exercises.

Exercise Practice (optional). Have pairs of students simultaneously practice all the exercises.

Exercise Presentations. Call on pairs of students to present the exercises.

Culture Notes

Exercise 1: "Driver's test." To get a driver's license, drivers in the United States must take a written test and a road (driving) test. States typically require that applicants take a driver's education course and be at least 16 years old.

Exercise 3: In the United States, some states have state-operated lotteries, or gambling games, for which tickets are sold and daily and weekly winners are awarded money. These lotteries enable states to raise public funds.

Exercise 4: Young adults in the United States usually move out of their parents' home soon after completion of their high school or college education or career training. For most young people, this move coincides with getting a job, graduating from college, or getting married. Speaker A is happy that his 32-year-old son has finally moved away from home.

ORIGINAL STUDENT CONVERSATIONS

Have pairs of students create and present original conversations based on the model. (You may want students to prepare their original conversations as homework, then practice them the next day with another student and present them to the class.)

EXPANSION

1. *Extend the Conversation*

a. Divide the class into pairs.

b. Have each pair select one of the situations on page 20 of the student text and role-play a continuation of the conversation between the two characters.

c. Have students present their role plays to the class.

2. *Telephone*

a. Divide the class into large groups. Have each group sit in a circle.

b. *Invent* a news story with many details, and whisper it to one student.

c. That student whispers the story to the second student, and so forth around the circle.

d. When the story gets to the last student, that person says it aloud or writes it on the board. Is it the same story you started with? The group with the most accurate story wins.

3. *Appropriate and Inappropriate News*

The amount and type of news that people share with each other varies from culture to culture.

a. Have students draw two columns on a piece of paper. Have students write Appropriate at the top of one column and Inappropriate at the top of the other.

b. Tell the students that they are going to decide what is appropriate and what is inappropriate for two co-workers to talk about during a break at work.

c. Call out different pieces of news, and have students write them under either one of the columns. For example:

> "I just got engaged."
> "I lost six pounds on my new diet."
> "My brother just got married."
> "I just got a raise of $3.50 an hour."

d. Have students compare their lists.

4. *Chain Story: A Fantastic Day*

a. Begin by saying, "Today was a special day. This morning I had breakfast in bed."

b. Student 1 repeats what you said and adds another item. For example: "This morning I had breakfast in bed. The sun was shining, and the weather was wonderful."

c. Continue around the room in this fashion, with each student repeating what the previous one said and adding another sentence.

d. Do the activity again, beginning and ending with different students.

If the class is large, you can divide students into groups to give students more practice with past tense.

5. *You Did?! She Did?!*

a. Have students sit in a circle and toss a beanbag back and forth. The student who throws the beanbag makes a statement about something good that happened. The student to whom the beanbag is tossed must react with the appropriate phrase and intonation. For example:

> Student 1: This morning I found ten dollars on the street!
> [*tosses the beanbag to Student 2*]
>
> Student 2: [*catches the beanbag and reacts to the good news*]
> You did?! That's great!
> My sister won the lottery yesterday!
> [*tosses the beanbag to Student 3*]
>
> Student 3: [*catches the beanbag and reacts to the good news*]
> She did?! That's wonderful!

b. Continue until everyone has had a turn.

ExpressWays

Have students do the activity individually, in pairs, or as a class. You may want to assign this exercise as homework.

1. left
2. got
3. found
4. gave
5. won
6. left

CrossTalk

Have students first work in pairs and then share with the class what they talked about.

FOCUS

TOPIC

Social Communication: Sharing Information

GRAMMAR

Past Tense

I **got** a ticket for speeding on my way to work this morning!
I **didn't get** the raise I was hoping for!

FUNCTIONS

1. **Initiating a Topic**

   You seem upset.

2. **Asking for and Reporting Information**

   Is anything wrong?

3. **Sympathizing**

   That's too bad!
   That's a shame!
   What a shame!

   I'm very sorry to hear that.
   I'm very sorry.
   I'm so sorry.

COMMENTARY

1. "You seem upset." This personal comment on Speaker B's appearance, along with the question "Is anything wrong?," suggests that Speaker A knows speaker B well.

2. "As a matter of fact" is the equivalent of "Now that you mention it." Speaker B uses this expression to introduce the bad news.

GETTING READY

Have students practice using _____ *didn't?!* to react to and show interest in negative statements about the past.

   a. Make up a list of events in the recent past involving a negative statement, preferably announcements that may interest your students.

   b. Read each one to the class (or have a student read each one). Ask students to respond by saying: "_____ didn't?!" ("You didn't?!" "He didn't?!" "She didn't?!" "They didn't?!" "It didn't?!") For example:

   A. You know what happened at my apartment last night? The electricity didn't work!
   B. It didn't?!

   A. Yesterday I saw a man drive through a red light. There was a police officer right there, and he didn't do anything about it!
   B. He didn't?!

   A. This morning I was in a hurry, and I didn't lock my front door!
   B. You didn't?!

A. My sister lost her wedding ring yesterday. She looked everywhere, but she didn't find it!
B. She didn't?!

THE MODEL CONVERSATION

1. **Setting the Scene.** Have students look at the model illustration. Set the scene: "Two people are at work. They work together every day. Right now, one of them is upset."

2. **Listening to the Model**. With books closed, have students listen to the model conversation — presented by you, by a pair of students, or on the audiotape.

3. **Class Practice.** With books still closed, model each line and have the whole class repeat in unison.

4. **Reading.** With books open, have students follow along as two students present the model. Ask students if they have any questions and check understanding of vocabulary.

5. **Pair Practice.** In pairs, have students practice the model conversation.

6. **Alternative Expressions.** Present to the class each sentence of the dialog containing a footnoted expression. Call on different students to present the same sentence, but replacing the footnoted expression with its alternatives. (You can cue students to do this quickly by asking, "What's another way of saying that?" or "How else could he/she/you say that?")

THE EXERCISES

Examples

1. A. You seem upset. Is anything wrong?
   B. Yes, as a matter of fact, there is.
   A. Oh? What?
   B. My son wrecked the car last night!
   A. He did? That's too bad! I'm very sorry to hear that.

2. A. You seem upset. Is anything wrong?
   B. Yes, as a matter of fact, there is.
   A. Oh? What?
   B. I didn't get the raise I was hoping for!
   A. You didn't? That's a shame! I'm very sorry.

Before doing each exercise, check students' understanding of the vocabulary and introduce any unfamiliar words or phrases. Have students use the footnoted expressions or any of their alternatives as they do the exercises.

Exercise Practice (optional). Have pairs of students simultaneously practice all the exercises.

Exercise Presentations. Call on pairs of students to present the exercises.

Language Note

Exercise 3: The expression "broke up" (break up) means that the girl and boy have stopped dating.

Culture Notes

Exercise 4: Many people in the United States use plants to decorate their homes.

Exercise 5: Valentine's Day is celebrated each year on February 14th. On this day, people express their affection for friends, classmates, and loved ones by sending valentine cards. Special friends or loved ones also may exchange gifts, such as chocolate candy. Red hearts are the common symbol of Valentine's Day.

ORIGINAL STUDENT CONVERSATIONS

Have pairs of students create and present original conversations based on the model. (You may want students to prepare their original conversations as homework, then practice them the next day with another student and present them to the class.)

EXPANSION

1. You Did?! She Did?!

a. Have students sit in a circle and toss a beanbag back and forth. The student who throws the beanbag makes a statement about something bad that happened. The student to whom the beanbag is tossed must react with the appropriate phrase and intonation. For example:

Student 1: This morning my car broke down!
[*tosses the beanbag to Student 2*]

Student 2: [*catches the beanbag and reacts to the bad news*]
It did?! That's too bad!
This morning I slipped on some ice!
[*tosses the beanbag to Student 3*]

Student 3: [*catches the beanbag and reacts to the bad news*]
You did?! That's a shame!

b. Continue until everyone has had a turn.

2. Good News and Bad News in Our Class

a. Collect information about recent events in students' lives. Make sure each student in the class tells you a piece of news — either good or bad.

b. Put this information in the following form:

> Find someone . . .
>
> 1. who just got a new job.   _____
> 2. who just bought a new house.   _____
> 3. whose brother wrecked the family car.   _____
> 4. who just had a bicycle accident.   _____

c. Have students circulate around the room, taking with each other about the recent events in their lives, using the model conversations on pages 20 and 22 of the student text as a guide. As students identify the people on the worksheet, they should write their names on the blank lines.

d. The first student to identify all the people wins.

3. Telephone

a. Divide the class into large groups. Have each group sit in a circle.

b. *Invent* a detailed news story and whisper it to one student.

c. That student whispers the story to the second student, and so forth around the circle.

d. When the story gets to the last student, that person says it aloud or writes it on the board. Is it the same story you started with? The group with the most accurate story wins.

4. Listen Carefully!

a. Tell the class a short story in the past tense.

b. After you finish telling the story, make several statements in the past tense about the story. Some of the statements should be true, and some should be false.

c. Students listen to the statements and decide if they are true or false. If a statement is false, have them correct it. For example:

> Teacher: The little girl walked to the playground.
> Student: False. She didn't walk. She rode her bicycle.

Variation: This activity can be done as a game with two competing teams. The teams take turns deciding whether the statements are true or false.

5. What Really Happened?

a. Find two articles from two different newspapers about the same news event. Give each student a copy of both articles.

b. Have students read the articles and compare them, working as a class, in pairs, or in small groups. For example, students might say:

> "In this article it says he didn't see the robber."
> "In this article it says he identified the robber."

6. Comparing Newspapers

a. Tell students to find several news articles about the same event from different newspapers.

b. Have them compare the quality of coverage, by answering the following questions:

> How were the articles different?
> Which article did you like the most? Why?
> Which article did you like the least? Why?
> Which article gave the most information?
> Which one do you trust the most? Why?

c. Have students discuss their findings as a class, in pairs, or in small groups.

Fill It In!

Have students do the activity individually, in pairs, or as a class. You may want to assign this exercise as homework.

1. didn't get
2. bought
3. didn't find
4. saw
5. wrote
6. didn't eat
7. didn't win
8. went
9. didn't take
10. made
11. had, woke

Listen

Listen and choose the most appropriate response.

1. I got the raise I was hoping for!
2. My husband wrecked our car last weekend!
3. My daughter broke up with her fiancé last week.
4. My wife got a big promotion!
5. Our next-door neighbor's apartment was robbed last night!
6. I'm really enjoying my classes.
7. I didn't pass my driver's test.
8. I had a wonderful time on my vacation.
9. My wife had a baby last night!

Answers

1. a	4. b	7. a
2. b	5. a	8. b
3. b	6. b	9. a

Community Connections

Have students do the activity in pairs or in small groups and then report back to the class.

FOCUS

TOPIC
Social Communication: Sharing Information

GRAMMAR

1. **Yes/No Questions**

   Is our English teacher going to quit?
   Are they going to lay off the workers on the night shift?
   Do the bus drivers plan to go on strike at midnight?
   Did the boss fire Fred this morning?

2. **Negative Sentences**

   Our English teacher **isn't** going to quit.
   They **aren't** going to lay off the workers on the night shift.
   The bus drivers **don't** plan to go on strike at midnight.
   The boss **didn't** fire Fred this morning.

3. **Tense Review**

   Our supervisor **wants** to shorten our coffee break!
   The people across the hall **are getting** a divorce!
   Mr. Davis **canceled** our final exam!
   They**'re going** to lay off the workers on the night shift!
   Our gym teacher **was** in the 1992 Olympics!

FUNCTIONS

1. **Attracting Attention**

   Mohammed?

2. **Initiating a Topic**

   Can I ask you a question?
   Can I ask you something?

3. **Asking for and Reporting Information**

   Where did you hear that?
   Who told you that?

4. **Certainty/Uncertainty**

   Expressing Certainty
   I'm sure _____.

VOCABULARY

Community

bus stop
laundromat

Occupations

accountant
bookkeeper
bus driver
secretary
security guard

Education

English teacher
final exam
gym teacher
locker room
student
teacher

Places of Work

corporation
office

Places on the Job

cafeteria
elevator

Additional Employment Vocabulary

boss
coffee break
fire (v.)
lay off
night shift
pay
quit
strike (n.)
supervisor
union meeting
worker

COMMENTARY

1. Calling a person's name is a very common way of getting his or her attention.

2. "Can I ask you a question?" is commonly used to preface a question.

3. "Where did you hear that?" (line 7) is commonly asked when people want to know the source of hearsay information.

GETTING READY

1. Introduce the names of occupations students will be practicing in this lesson. (See the Vocabulary above.) For each occupation, ask students, "What do _____s do?" For example:

    Accountant: What do accountants do?

    They work with numbers.
    They prepare tax forms.
    They make financial plans and handle money.

2. Introduce the terms *lay off, fire,* and *quit.* Check students' understanding of these ways in which people leave their jobs:

    a. An employer can *lay off* an employee. This usually means that the job will not exist anymore. (We say the person *got laid off.*) Often the job ends because the company is having financial problems or is reorganizing.

    b. An employer can *fire* an employee. (We say the person *got fired.*) If an employee does not or cannot do a satisfactory job, he or she risks getting fired.

c. An employee can *quit* or can choose to leave his or her job.

THE MODEL CONVERSATION

1. **Setting the Scene.** Have students look at the model illustration. Set the scene: "Two students are talking. One of them is asking about something she overheard."

2. **Listening to the Model.** With books closed, have students listen to the model conversation — presented by you, by a pair of students, or on the audiotape.

3. **Class Practice.** With books still closed, model each line and have the whole class repeat in unison.

4. **Reading.** With books open, have students follow along as two students present the model. Ask students if they have any questions and check understanding of vocabulary.

5. **Pair Practice.** In pairs, have students practice the model conversation.

6. **Alternative Expressions.** Present to the class each sentence of the dialog containing a footnoted expression. Call on different students to present the same sentence, but replacing the footnoted expression with its alternatives. (You can cue students to do this quickly by asking, "What's another way of saying that?" or "How else could he/she/you say that?")

THE EXERCISES

Examples

> 1. A. Jimmy?
>   B. Yes?
>   A. Can I ask you a question?
>   B. Sure. What?
>   A. Did the boss fire Fred this morning?
>   B. No. The boss didn't fire Fred this morning. Where did you hear that?
>   A. I heard it in the cafeteria.
>   B. Well, I can't believe it's true. I'm sure it's just a rumor.
>
> 2. A. Carla?
>   B. Yes?
>   A. Can I ask you something?
>   B. Sure. What?
>   A. Do the bus drivers plan to go on strike at midnight?
>   B. No. The bus drivers don't plan to go on strike at midnight. Who told you that?
>   A. Someone mentioned it at the bus stop.
>   B. Well, I can't believe it's true. I'm sure it's just a rumor.

Before doing each exercise, check students' understanding of the vocabulary and introduce any unfamiliar words or phrases. Have students use the footnoted expressions or any of their alternatives as they do the exercises.

Exercise Practice (optional). Have pairs of students simultaneously practice all the exercises.

Exercise Presentations. Call on pairs of students to present the exercises.

Language Note

Exercise 9: "To have to take a cut in pay" means to be forced to accept a lower salary.

Culture Notes

Exercise 7: "Coffee break." Employers in the United States usually give their employees a fifteen-minute "break," or rest time, in the morning and in the afternoon. Employers also usually give workers a lunch break. Most workers get a one-hour lunch break, or "lunch hour."

Exercise 11: "Santa Claus." Many young children in the United States believe that "Santa Claus" brings them presents on the night before Christmas. Many

companies use the image and story of Santa Claus in their advertising around Christmas time. Also, most large department stores hire people to "be Santa" and talk to children as they shop with their parents.

ORIGINAL STUDENT CONVERSATIONS

Have pairs of students create and present original conversations based on the model. (You may want students to prepare their original conversations as homework, then practice them the next day with another student and present them to the class.)

EXPANSION

1. Twenty Questions

a. Divide the class into groups of three or four.

b. One student in each group thinks of something in one of the following categories:

> a location at work
> a location in the community
> a location in the school
> an occupation

c. The other students in the group then try to guess the answer by asking yes/no questions. For example:

> [*thinking of the school library*]
>
> Student 1: I'm thinking of a location in our school.
> Student 2: Do you go there every day?
> Student 1: No.
> Student 3: Do you like to go there?
> Student 1: Yes.
> Student 2: Are you going to go there today?
> Student 1: Yes.
> Student 3: Do we go there together as a class?
> Student 1: Yes.
> Student 2: Is it the school library?
> Student 1: Yes.

d. Have the remaining students in each group take their turn thinking of something for the others to guess.

2. Tic Tac News

a. Draw a tic tac grid on the board, and fill it with auxiliary verbs. For example:

Is	Are	Will
Do	Did	Am
Does	Was	Were

b. Divide the class into teams. Give each team a mark — X or O.

c. Have each team ask a question that begins with one of the question words and then provide the answer to that question. If the question and answer are correct, the team puts its mark in that space. For example:

> X Team: Does the president plan to run for reelection?
> Yes, he does.

Is	Are	Will
Do	Did	Am
X	Was	Were

d. The first team to mark out three boxes in a straight line — horizontally, vertically, or diagonally — wins.

3. *Class Discussion: Rumors*

a. Divide the class into small groups.

b. Have each group discuss the following questions:

> How do rumors usually begin?
> Why do people start rumors?
> How do rumors spread?
> What kinds of rumors are most common at work?
> What kinds of rumors are most common at school?
> What kinds of rumors are most common in a neighborhood?
> How can rumors hurt people?

c. Have the groups tell the whole class about their discussion.

Variation: Have students interview other students in the school about their attitudes towards rumors. Have students share their findings with the class and write up a summary, which can be submitted to the school newspaper or other publication.

Rumors

Have students do the activity individually, in pairs, or as a class. You may want to assign this exercise as homework.

1. Is Bill going to move to
2. Did they get married
3. Does the boss plan to lay off
4. Are the teachers going to go
5. Does Alice want to
6. Did the Apex Company buy
7. Are we going to have to
8. Did Mr. Miller

More Rumors

Have students do the activity individually, in pairs, or as a class. You may want to assign this exercise as homework.

1. didn't hear
2. didn't fire
3. don't have to shorten
4. aren't going to lay off
5. didn't get married
6. weren't talking
7. doesn't want to
8. isn't getting
9. it isn't/it's not

CrossTalk

Have each student write down one rumor. Then have students sit in a circle and take turns whispering their rumors. Several rumors can move through the circle at the same time, as long as the last person writes down the final version. When everyone has stopped whispering, they should compare the original and final versions.

FOCUS

TOPIC

Social Communication: Sharing Information

GRAMMAR

1. **Future: Going to**

    What are you **going to** do this weekend?
       My husband and I are **going to** repaint our kitchen.

2. **Future: Will**

    I**'ll** probably visit my grandchildren.

FUNCTIONS

1. **Intention**

    Inquiring about . . .
    What are you going to do *this weekend*?

    Expressing . . .
    I'm going *to clean out my attic.*

2. **Surprise–Disbelief**

    Clean out your attic?!

3. **Agreement/Disagreement**

    Expressing Agreement
    I suppose so.

4. **Certainty/Uncertainty**

    Expressing Uncertainty
    I'm not sure.
    I don't know for sure.
    I'm not positive.

5. **Probability/Improbability**

    Expressing Probability
    I'll probably
    I'll most likely   } *visit my grandchildren.*
    I'm pretty sure I'll

6. **Leave Taking**

    Have a good weekend!
       You, too.

VOCABULARY

Housing	Recreation and Entertainment
attic	beach
chores	Brownie troop
kitchen	circus
	garden
	movie
	TV

COMMENTARY

1. General questions about weekend plans are appropriate in friendly, informal conversations, or "small talk". Other common topics of small talk are the weather, local sports events, and popular entertainment, such as movies, TV shows, and popular music.

2. "Repaint your kitchen?!" It is common to express surprise or disbelief by repeating information using question (rising) intonation.

3. "I suppose so" (line 6) expresses agreement in a way that downplays or reduces the importance of the information. In this situation, Speaker B is expressing modesty about the large amount of work she is going to do on the weekend.

4. "What are YOUR plans?" (line 7). Capitalization of the word "YOUR" shows that this word is emphasized, or said more loudly.

5. "Well, have a good weekend!" (line 10). Here, "well" signals that speaker B is closing the conversation.

6. "You, too" (line 11) means "I hope you have a good weekend, too."

THE MODEL CONVERSATION

1. **Setting the Scene.** Have students look at the model illustration. Set the scene: "It's Friday. Two employees are asking each other about their plans for the weekend."

2. **Listening to the Model.** With books closed, have students listen to the model conversation — presented by you, by a pair of students, or on the audiotape.

3. **Class Practice.** With books still closed, model each line and have the whole class repeat in unison.

4. **Reading.** With books open, have students follow along as two students present the model. Ask students if they have any questions and check understanding of vocabulary.

5. **Pair Practice.** In pairs, have students practice the model conversation.

6. **Alternative Expressions.** Present to the class each sentence of the dialog containing a footnoted expression. Call on different students to present the same sentence, but replacing the footnoted expression with its alternatives. (You can cue students to do this quickly by asking, "What's another way of saying that?" or "How else could he/she/you say that?")

THE EXERCISES

Examples

1. A. What are you going to do this weekend?
   B. I'm going to clean out my attic.
   A. Clean out your attic?!
   B. Yes.
   A. You're certainly going to be busy!
   B. I suppose so. How about you? What are YOUR plans for the weekend?
   A. I'm not sure. I'll probably go to the beach.
   B. Well, have a good weekend!
   A. You, too.

2. A. What are you going to do this weekend?
   B. I'm going to finish three term papers.
   A. Three term papers?! You're certainly going to be busy!
   B. I suppose so. How about you? What are YOUR plans for the weekend?
   A. I don't know for sure. I'll most likely see a movie.
   B. Well, have a good weekend!
   A. You, too.

Before doing each exercise, check students' understanding of the vocabulary and introduce any unfamiliar words or phrases. Have students use the footnoted expressions or any of their alternatives as they do the exercises.

Exercise Practice (optional). Have pairs of students simultaneously practice all the exercises.

Exercise Presentations. Call on pairs of students to present the exercises.

Language Note

Exercise 2: A "term paper" is a lengthy, formal report for a school subject, usually containing footnotes and a bibliography. In some high school and college courses, a term paper may take the place of a final exam.

Culture Notes

Exercise 3: "Christmas shopping" refers to buying Christmas gifts. Many people in the United States exchange gifts with family members and close friends at Christmas.

Exercise 4: This situation is unusual because a typical birthday party for a young child would not include as many as thirty children.

Exercise 5: "Brownie troop." The younger members of the "Girl Scouts" organization are "Brownies" and are organized into small groups, or troops. The Girl Scouts, like the Boy Scouts, are clubs that usually focus on nature, camping, arts and crafts, and community service.

ORIGINAL STUDENT CONVERSATIONS

Have pairs of students create and present original conversations based on the model. (You may want students to prepare their original conversations as homework, then practice them the next day with another student and present them to the class.)

EXPANSION

1. Find Someone Who . . .

a. Collect some information about students' vacation plans.

b. Put this information in the following form:

```
Find someone who . . .

1. will probably go to Greece.      _____

2. is going to stay home
   and relax.                       _____

3. is going to study for the
   TOEFL.                           _____

4. is going to go to New York.      _____

5. will probably clean the
   house.                           _____
```

c. Have students circulate around the room asking each other questions about vacation plans to identify the above people.

d. The first student to identify all the people wins.

2. Our Weekend Plans

a. Have students draw a column down the middle of a page and label the columns with the headings Certain Plans and Probable Plans. In the left column have them write three things they're *certain* they're going to do this weekend. In the right column have them write three things they think they'll *probably* do this weekend. Make sure they contrast the future with *going to* and the future with *will*. For example:

> Certain Plans
> I'm going to study English.
> I'm going to clean my attic.
>
> Probable Plans
> I'll probably go to a movie.
> I'll most likely go out for dinner.

b. Have students compare their lists and talk about their weekend plans.

3. Role Play: A Tour of the City

a. Have students pretend to be tour guides who are taking groups of tourists on an all-day bus tour of their town or city. In their role plays, students should include the names of real places in the area where they live.

b. Write the following on the board or on a handout for students to use as a basis for their tour descriptions:

```
Welcome to    (city)   . This
morning we're going to see many
interesting sights. We're going to visit
_____, _____, and _____. Then,
we're going to have lunch at _____.
I'm sure you'll enjoy it. The food
there is excellent!

This afternoon we're going too see
_____, _____, and _____. And
this evening, if the weather is nice,
we'll _____. If it rains, we'll
_____.

I'm sure you'll all have a wonderful
time today on our tour of _____.
```

ExpressWays

Have students do the activity individually, in pairs, or as a class. You may want to assign this exercise as homework.

1. I'll finish
2. I'm going to write
3. I'll tell
4. you'll have to take
5. We're going to see
6. You're going to get
7. will come
8. She's going to take
9. I'll be

CrossTalk

Have students first work in pairs and then share with the class what they talked about.

FOCUS

TOPIC

Social Communication: Sharing Information

GRAMMAR

1. **Tense Review**

   I**'m** originally from Chicago.
   I **have** a brother and two sisters.
   I **was** born there, I **grew** up there, and I **went** to school there.

2. **Question Formation**

   Are you originally from around here?
   Do you have any brothers and sisters?

   Where are you from?
   What do you do?

FUNCTIONS

1. **Asking for and Reporting Information**

   Tell me a little about yourself.

   What do you want to know?

   What do you do?
   Do you have any brothers and sisters?
   Are you originally from around here?

   How about you?

2. **Hesitating**

   Gee . . . uh.

   I don't know where to begin.

   Well . . .

VOCABULARY

Education	Occupations	Personal Information	Family
high school	dentist	born	brother
school	journalist	grew up	sister

COMMENTARY

1. In line 1, "So" implies that the speakers have already been talking and are now switching to a new topic of conversation. The overall tone and style of this conversation suggest that the speakers are just getting acquainted. Questions about place of birth, place of residence, and place of work are very appropriate topics in this context.

2. "Gee . . . uh" (line 2) is an expression speakers use when they wish to hesitate.

3. "How about _____?" is a convenient way of introducing a new topic and moving a conversation along. "How about you?" (line 7).

4. "By the way" (line 17) is used to introduce a new topic of conversation or signal a change in the conversation.

5. "What do you do?" (line 17) means "What profession or type of work do you do?"

6. "That's interesting" (line 20) shows that the new information has been heard and understood. Because it is routine, it does not carry much meaning. The speaker may or may not really find the information interesting.

GETTING READY

1. Have students use a map of the United States to locate these cities: Chicago, Illinois; Los Angeles, California; San Diego, California; and Cleveland, Ohio.

2. Introduce the expressions *was born, originally from, grew up,* and *live in*. You might do this by telling about yourself or someone you know and then asking students about themselves. For example:

    "I was born in San Diego, California. I grew up there. I came to Los Angeles to go to college. Now I live in Los Angeles, but as I said, I'm originally from San Diego."

    a. Ask students about themselves:

    Where were you born?
    (I was born in _____.)
    Where did you grow up?
    (I grew up in _____.)
    Where do you live now?
    (I live in _____.)

    b. Ask about other students:

    Where was _____born?
    Where did he/she grow up?
    Where does he/she live now?
    Where is he/she from originally?

THE MODEL CONVERSATION

1. **Setting the Scene.** Have students look at the model illustration. Set the scene: "Two people are talking at a party."

2. **Listening to the Model.** With books closed, have students listen to the model conversation — presented by you, by a pair of students, or on the audiotape.

3. **Class Practice.** With books still closed, model each line and have the whole class repeat in unison.

4. **Reading.** With books open, have students follow along as two students present the model. Ask students if they have any questions and check understanding of vocabulary.

5. **Pair Practice.** In pairs, have students practice the model conversation.

Now have pairs of students create and present original conversations using the model dialog as a guide. Encourage students to be inventive and to use new vocabulary. (You may want to assign this exercise as homework, having students prepare their original conversations, practice them the next day with another student, and then present them to the class.) Students should present their conversations without referring to the written text, but they also should not memorize them. Rather, they should feel free to adapt and expand them any way they wish.

InterView

Have students circulate around the room to conduct their interviews, or have students interview people outside the class. Students should then report back to the class about their interviews.

Reflections

Have students discuss the questions in pairs or small groups and then share their ideas with the class.

Listen

Listen and choose the correct answer.

1. A. Are you from Los Angeles?
   B. No, I'm from Denver.
2. A. What do you do?
   B. I'm a gym teacher.
3. A. I'm going to get a raise!
   B. Me, too!
4. A. I just passed my driver's test!
   B. Congratulations!
5. A. So, what's new?
   B. All my employees plan to go on strike soon.
6. A. Is Fred going to quit?
   B. Not as far as I know.
7. A. What did you do in Vancouver?
   B. I went to college there.

8. A. Where are you from?
   B. I was born in Taipei and lived there until I finished high school.
9. A. What did you do in England?
   B. I was a journalist.
10. A. Do you have any children?
    B. Yes. I have a boy and a girl.

Answers

1. b	6. a
2. b	7. b
3. a	8. a
4. b	9. a
5. a	10. b

Matching Lines

Have students do the activity individually, in pairs, or as a class. You may want to assign this exercise as homework.

1. b
2. d
3. a
4. f
5. c
6. g
7. e

Reading: *The Weekend*

Preview: Have students discuss the following question:

> What do you do on the weekend?

Then have students read the passage silently, or have them listen to the passage and take notes as you read it or play the audiotape.

True or False?

Have students do the activity individually, in pairs, or as a class. You may want to assign this exercise as homework.

1. False
2. True
3. False
4. True
5. True
6. True
7. False

Do You Remember?

Have students do the activity individually, in pairs, or as a class. You may want to assign this exercise as homework.

1. b
2. c
3. a
4. b
5. b
6. c

Cultural Intersections

Have students do the activity as a class, in pairs, or in small groups.

Looking Back

Have students look at the list of expressions. Encourage them to ask you questions about the meaning or pronunciation of any of the words. If students ask for the pronunciation, repeat after the student until the student is satisfied with his or her pronunciation of the word.

Review Activities

To review the language introduced in the unit, do the following activities.

1. Association Game

a. Divide the class into several teams.

b. Call out a topic category from the *Looking Back* section on student text page 34.

c. Have students in each group work together to see how many phrases they can associate with that category. For example:

    Congratulating: That's great!
                         That's wonderful!
                         That's fantastic!

d. The team with the most items wins.

2. Create a Conversation!

a. Divide the class into pairs of students.

b. Tell each pair they have three minutes to make up a conversation using one item from each category from the *Looking Back* section on page 34 of the student text.

c. Have students present their conversations to the class.

3. Famous People Party

a. Have students choose a living person whom they admire. Have them do a little research into that person's life and find out some basic facts, such as the person's home, family, occupation, hobbies, and attitudes.

b. Have the class role-play a party scene. Have students take on the *persona* of the celebrity they chose but not disclose that person's identity. To focus the student's language use, have them review the *Looking Back* section of Exits 1 and 2 before beginning the role play.

c. At the end of the party, ask students how many *celebrities* they could identify.

EXIT TWO   59

EXIT 3

OVERVIEW
Student Text
Pages 35–54

Topics	Functions	Grammar

P. 36 Directory Assistance

Telephone: Directory Assistance	Asking for and Reporting Information Apologizing Certainty/Uncertainty Hesitating	Question Formation

P. 38 I Guess I Dialed the Wrong Number

Telephone: Wrong Numbers	Greeting People Asking for and Reporting Information Apologizing	Negative Sentences

P. 40 Does This Train Go to the Bronx?

Transportation: Modes of Transportation, Route Information	Attracting Attention Asking for and Reporting Information Checking and Indicating Understanding Gratitude	Simple Present Tense

P. 42 When Is the Next Flight to Chicago?

Transportation: Schedules	Attracting Attention Asking for and Reporting Information Surprise–Disbelief Obligation Hesitating	Declarative Sentences with Question Intonation Have to/Have Got to Question Formation

Topics	Functions	Grammar

Pp. 44–45 Can You Tell Me How to Get to City Hall?

Getting Around Town	Attracting Attention	Imperatives
	Asking for and Reporting	
	Information	
	Instructing	
	Directions–Location	
	Asking for Repetition	
	Checking and Indicating	
	Understanding	

Pp. 48–49 I'm Lost!

Getting Around Town	Greeting People	Imperatives
	Directions–Location	Past Tense
	Checking and Indicating	
	Understanding	
	Instructing	
	Asking for Repetition	

LOOKING AHEAD

Grammar This Exit

Question Formation

How do you spell that?
Where can I get the 8:30 flight to Chicago?
When is the next flight?

Are you sure you have the correct address?
Will that get you to Chicago in time for your brother's wedding?

Negative Sentences

Is this 965-0231?
No, it **isn't**.

Simple Present Tense

Does this train **go** to the Bronx?
No, it **doesn't**.

It **goes** to Queens.

Past Tense

I **went** north on Union Boulevard.
I **turned** right and **drove** to Washington Avenue.
I **took** the parkway south and **got off** at Exit 14.

You **were** supposed to get off at Exit 15.

Imperatives

Go to the next corner.
Walk three blocks to Second Avenue and **turn** right.

Have to/Have Got to

I **have to** get to my brother's wedding.

I**'ve got to** get to my brother's wedding.

Declarative Sentences with Question Intonation

I missed the flight?!

Functions This Exit

Asking for and Reporting Information

Can you tell me _____?
Could you tell me _____?
Do you know _____?

Tell me, _____?

I'd like the number of *Carlos Ramirez*.

How do you spell that?
Can you spell that?

What *city*?
What *street*?

Is this *965-0231*?

Does this *train* go to *the Bronx*?

Where can I get the *8:30 flight* to *Chicago*?
When is the next *flight*?

Instructing

First, . . .
Then . . .
After that, . . .

Attracting Attention

Excuse me.
Pardon me.

Directions–Location

Asking for Directions
Can you tell me how to get to _____?

Giving Directions
Go to _____.
Turn left (_____).
Turn right (_____).
You'll see _____ on the left/right.
Take a left/right (at _____).
Take the first right/left after the _____.
Walk _____ blocks (to _____).
Drive *about five or six blocks*.
Drive down _____ until _____.
Follow *Main Street*.
Walk down _____.
Walk along _____.
You'll come to a _____.
Go about _____ miles.
You'll see a sign (_____).
Take the *interstate north* to Exit *11*.

Greeting People

Hello.

Hello, *Bob*?

This is *Larry*.

Apologizing

I apologize.
Excuse me.
I'm sorry.

I'm sorry, but _____.

Gratitude

Expressing . . .

Thank you.
Thanks.
Thank you very much
Thanks very much.

Certainty/Uncertainty

Inquiring about . . .

Are you sure
Are you certain } *you have the correct address?*
Are you positive

Expressing Certainty

I think so.
I'm pretty sure.

Correcting

Giving Correction

No.

This isn't *Joe.*

Surprise–Disbelief

Oh, no!

I missed the flight?!

I don't believe it!
I can't believe it!

Obligation

Expressing . . .

I've got to }
I have to } *get to my brother's wedding.*
I need to }

Checking and Indicating Understanding

Checking Another Person's Understanding

Are you with me so far?
Okay so far?
Are you following me so far?

Have you got that?

Checking One's Own Understanding

The Number 4 train?

Indicating Understanding

Yes.
Uh-húh.
Um-hḿm.
That's right.
Okay.

I'm following you.
I understand.
I'm with you.

Now I've got it.
Now I understand.

Asking for Repetition

(I'm sorry.) I didn't follow you.
(I'm sorry.) I didn't get that.

Could you please repeat that?
Could you please say that again?

Could you repeat the last part?

Hesitating

Hmm.

Let me see.
Let's see.

PREVIEWING EXIT 3: CHAPTER-OPENING PHOTOS

Have students talk about the people and the situations and, as a class or in pairs, predict what the characters might be saying to each other. Students in pairs or small groups may enjoy practicing role plays based on these scenes and then presenting them to the class.

Text Page 36: Directory Assistance

FOCUS

TOPIC

Telephone: Directory Assistance

GRAMMAR

Question Formation

What city?
How do you spell that?

FUNCTIONS

1. **Asking for and Reporting Information**

   I'd like the number of *Carlos Ramirez*.

   How do you spell that?
   Can you spell that?

   What *city*?
   What *street*?

2. **Apologizing**

   I'm sorry.

3. **Certainty/Uncertainty**

   Inquiring about . . .
   Are you sure
   Are you certain } *you have the correct address*?
   Are you positive

   Expressing Certainty
   I think so.
   I'm pretty sure.

4. **Hesitating**

   Hmm.

VOCABULARY

Telephone

directory assistance
number
operator

COMMENTARY

1. Most people in the United State use telephone books to get phone number information for the areas where they live. (Everyone who has a telephone receives a telephone book for his or her area.) For numbers in other areas, people call "directory assistance." Telephone numbers are listed by city or town; within each city, numbers are organized in an alphabetical list of the last names; the street address is also listed.

2. "Directory assistance. What city?" (line 1) is used to ask, "What city does the person live in?" Similarly, in line 5, "What street?" means "What street does the person live on?"

3. "Miami. I'd like the number of Carlos Ramirez" (line 2). It is common to answer the question "What city?" with the name of the city and the name of the person whose number is needed.

4. "I'm sorry" (line 7) is often used as a polite expression for introducing negative information.

5. "I don't have a Carlos Ramirez . . ." (lines 7–8). The operator means that she doesn't have a listing for a person named Carlos Ramirez in her directory.

6. "Hmm" (line 10) is used for hesitating, especially when the speaker needs time to think about a question or new information.

7. In the expression "I'm pretty sure" (an alternative expression for "I think so" in line 10), "pretty" is used to mean "almost."

8. "I'd better (I had better) check" (line 10) means "I should check."

9. "Operator" (line 11) is one of the few job titles that can be used as a form of address. Others are "Doctor" and "Nurse."

GETTING READY

1. Introduce the term *directory assistance*.

   a. If possible, bring a U.S. telephone book to class.

   b. Have students look at the book to see how names and numbers are listed. (See note 1 above.)

   c. Find out if your students know about directory assistance. Do they know how to dial directory assistance? Tell them that in this lesson they are going to practice calling directory assistance.

2. Use a map of the United States to introduce the following cities in this lesson:

   Miami, Florida
   Cincinnati, Ohio
   Boston, Massachusetts
   San Francisco, California
   Dallas, Texas
   Chicago, Illinois

THE MODEL CONVERSATION

1. **Setting the Scene.** Have students look at the model illustration. Set the scene: "Someone is calling directory assistance."

2. **Listening to the Model.** With books closed, have students listen to the model conversation — presented by you, by a pair of students, or on the audiotape.

3. **Class Practice.** With books still closed, model each line and have the whole class repeat in unison.

4. **Reading.** With books open, have students follow along as two students present the model. Ask students if they have any questions, and check understanding of vocabulary.

5. **Pair Practice.** In pairs, have students practice the model conversation.

6. **Alternative Expressions.** Present to the class each sentence of the dialog containing a footnoted expression. Call on different students to present the same sentence, but replacing the footnoted expression with its alternatives. (You can cue students to do this quickly by asking, "What's another way of saying that?" or "How else could he/she/you say that?")

THE EXERCISES

Examples

---

1. A. Directory assistance. What city?
   B. Cincinnati. I'd like the number of Michael Wittler.
   A. How do you spell that?
   B. W-I-T-T-L-E-R.
   A. What street?
   B. Madison Road.
   A. Just a moment . . . I'm sorry, but I don't have a Michael Wittler on Madison Road. Are you sure you have the correct address?
   B. Hmm. I think so, but I'd better check. Thank you, Operator.

2. A. Directory assistance. What city?
   B. Boston. I'd like the number of Cathy Flanigan.
   A. Can you spell that?
   B. F-L-A-N-I-G-A-N.
   A. What street?
   B. Dorchester Avenue.
   A. Just a moment . . . I'm sorry, but I don't have a Cathy Flanigan on Dorchester Avenue. Are you certain you have the correct address?
   B. Hmm. I'm pretty sure, but I'd better check. Thank you, Operator.

Before doing each exercise, check students' understanding of the vocabulary and introduce any unfamiliar words or phrases. Have students use the footnoted expressions or any of their alternatives as they do the exercises.

Exercise Practice (optional). Have pairs of students simultaneously practice all the exercises.

Exercise Presentations. Call on pairs of students to present the exercises.

ORIGINAL STUDENT CONVERSATIONS

Have pairs of students create and present original conversations based on the model. (You may want students to prepare their original conversations as homework, then practice them the next day with another student and present them to the class.)

EXPANSION

1. Spelling Game: Telephone

a. Divide the class into large groups. Have each group sit in a circle.

b. Whisper a name and its spelling to one student. For example:

> Janet MacGregor Kerr
> J-A-N-E-T M-A-C-G-R-E-G-O-R K-E-R-R

c. The first student whispers the name and its spelling to the second student, and so on around the circle.

d. When the message gets to the last student, that person says it aloud. Is it the same message you started with? The group with the most accurate message wins.

2. Name Dictation

a. Have students ready with pen and paper.

b. Rapidly call out several names—both familiar ones and *unusual* ones.

c. At the end of each reading, write the correct name on the board so students have the opportunity to correct their spelling.

3. Information Gap: Calling Directory Assistance

a. Divide the class into pairs. Have one person in each pair role-play a telephone operator. Have the other student role-play a person who is calling directory assistance.

b. Give all the operators a one-page *telephone directory*. This page could be a copy of a real page from a directory or it could be a page you have created containing telephone numbers of your choice.

c. Give the other student in each pair a list of names (no numbers) from the telephone directory that you gave the operators.

d. Have each student with the list of names *call* the operator to get the numbers and write them down.

e. Have the students compare their lists, checking for errors. Which pair completed the role play first? Which pair had the fewest errors?

4. Home Assignment: Calling Directory Assistance

a. Give students the names and addresses of several people and businesses. Make sure that at least one address is incorrect.

b. As a homework assignment, have students call directory assistance to get the phone numbers for these people and businesses. Have students take notes on the conversations that took place.

c. Have students compare their conversations and telephone numbers in class.

Listen 1

Listen and complete the sentence.

1. My friend is living . . .
2. Did he stop . . . ?
3. Please . . .
4. I put the cars . . .
5. Let's work . . .
6. Did you take him . . . ?
7. Do you have any plans . . . ?
8. Let's clean the kitchen . . .
9. Do you know who . . . ?

Answers

1. a	4. b	7. b
2. a	5. b	8. b
3. a	6. b	9. b

Listen 2

Listen to the conversation and circle the word you hear.

1. A. I'd like the number of David Yu.
   B. How do you spell that?
   A. Y-U.
2. A. How do you spell Flanigan?
   B. F-L-A-N-I-G-A-N.
3. A. What street?
   B. Beech Road.
   A. B-E-E-C-H?
   B. Yes.
4. A. Can you spell that?
   B. Sure. W-I-T-T-L-E-R.
5. Just a moment. I'd better check the spelling. Yes, it's K-R-I-Z-I-C-K.
6. A. How do you spell Rio de Janeiro?
   B. R-I-O D-E J-A-N-E-I-R-O.
7. A. Did you say H-E-N-L-E-Y?
   B. Yes.
8. A. Do you spell Ramirez with a "z" or an "s"?
   B. With a "z."

Answers

1. b
2. a
3. a
4. b
5. a
6. b
7. b
8. a

Community Connections

Have students do the activity individually, in pairs, or in small groups.

FOCUS

TOPIC

Telephone: Wrong Numbers

GRAMMAR

Negative Sentences

No, it **isn't.**

FUNCTIONS

1. **Greeting People**

   Hello.

   Hello, *Joe?*

2. **Asking for and Reporting Information**

   Is this *965-0231?*

3. **Apologizing**

   I apologize.
   Excuse me.
   I'm sorry.

VOCABULARY

Telephone

dial
wrong number

COMMENTARY

1. In line 2, Speaker B responds "Hello, *Joe?*" because she thinks "Joe" has answered the phone.

2. "Oh. I apologize" (line 7). It is polite to apologize for dialing a wrong number.

THE MODEL CONVERSATION

1. **Setting the Scene.** Have students look at the model illustration. Set the scene: "A woman is trying to call her friend Joe."

2. **Listening to the Model.** With books closed, have students listen to the model conversation — presented by you, by a pair of students, or on the audiotape.

3. **Class Practice.** With books still closed, model each line and have the whole class repeat in unison.

4. **Reading.** With books open, have students follow along as two students present the model. Ask students if they have any questions and check understanding of vocabulary.

5. **Pair Practice.** In pairs, have students practice the model conversation.

68 EXIT THREE

6. **Alternative Expressions.** Present to the class the sentence of the dialog containing the footnoted expression. Call on different students to present the same sentence, but replacing the footnoted expression with its alternatives. (You can cue students to do this quickly by asking, "What's another way of saying that?" or "How else could he/she/you say that?")

THE EXERCISES

Examples

---

1. A. Hello.
   B. Hello, Lucy?
   A. I'm sorry. There's nobody here by that name.
   B. Is this 439-2185?
   A. No, it isn't.
   B. Oh, I apologize. I guess I dialed the wrong number.

2. A. Hello.
   B. Hello, Irving?
   A. I'm sorry. There's nobody here by that name.
   B. Is this 972-1138?
   A. No, it isn't.
   B. Oh. Excuse me. I guess I dialed the wrong number.

Before doing each exercise, check students' understanding of the vocabulary and introduce any unfamiliar words or phrases. Have students use the footnoted expression or any of its alternatives as they do the exercises.

Exercise Practice (optional). Have pairs of students simultaneously practice all the exercises.

Exercise Presentations. Call on pairs of students to present the exercises.

ORIGINAL STUDENT CONVERSATIONS

Have pairs of students create and present original conversations based on the model. (You may want students to prepare their original conversations as homework, then practice them the next day with another student and present them to the class.)

EXPANSION

1. Number Dictation

a. Have students get ready with pen and paper.

b. Rapidly call out several telephone numbers.

c. At the end of each reading, write the correct number on the board so students can check their answers.

2. Discussion: Phone Etiquette

Have students discuss the following questions in pairs, in small groups, or as a class:

In your country, what do people say when they answer the phone?

In your country, what do people say when they get the wrong number?

In your experience, are people usually friendly when you call a wrong number?

Did you ever call a wrong number? What happened?

3. Role Play: Call and Find Out

a. Make a list of businesses or institutions that your students might need to call for information. The list might include a restaurant, a car repair shop, a bookstore, a hardware store, and a pharmacy.

b. Create a telephone call cue card for each of the places on the list. For example:

CALL: Joe's Bookstore

REASON: sell/Spanish-English dictionaries?
how late/open/tonight?

CALL: Wilson's Department Store

REASON: sell/stereos?
open/Sunday?

CALL: Harry's Garage

REASON: what time/close today?
when/open/tomorrow?

CALL: Bell Pharmacy

REASON: how late/open tonight?
sell/Taylor's Aspirin?

CALL: Apex Hardware

REASON: sell/"Marvel" electric saws?

Make enough cards for all the students in the class.

c. Have students work in pairs. Give one person in each pair the cue card and have the other student *answer the telephone* at the particular business.

d. Ask for volunteers to present their role plays to the class. For example:

A. Hello. Joe's Bookstore.
B. Hello. Do you sell Spanish-English dictionaries?
A. Yes, we do.
B. And how late are you open tonight?
A. Until eight o'clock.
B. Until eight o'clock? Thank you very much.
A. You're welcome. Good-bye.
B. Bye.

ExpressWays

Have students do the activity individually, in pairs, or as a class. You may want to assign this exercise as homework.

1. it isn't
2. I don't
3. you didn't
4. she wasn't
5. he doesn't
6. they aren't
7. you didn't
8. they weren't
9. it isn't

Listen

Listen to the conversation and choose the number you hear.

1. A. I'd like the number of Bob Williams.
   B. Just a moment. The number is 539-7899.
2. A. Is this 592-8622?
   B. Yes, it is.
3. A. I guess I dialed the wrong number.
   B. What number did you dial?
   A. 832-5660.
4. A. Did you dial 860-5439?
   B. Yes, I did.
5. A. What's your telephone number?
   B. 834-5935.
6. A. Are you sure this is the correct number?
   B. Let me check. 648-2341. Yes, that's it.

Answers

1. b
2. b
3. b
4. a
5. b
6. a

InterActions

Have pairs of students practice role-playing the activity and then present their role plays to the class.

FOCUS

TOPICS

Transportation: Modes of Transportation
Route Information

GRAMMAR

Simple Present Tense

Does this train **go** to the Bronx?
   No, it **doesn't.** It **goes** to Queens.

FUNCTIONS

1. **Attracting Attention**

   Excuse me.
   Pardon me.

2. **Asking for and Reporting Information**

   Does this *train* go to *the Bronx*?

3. **Checking and Indicating Understanding**

   Checking One's Own Understanding

   The Number 4 Train?

   Indicating Understanding

   Yes.
   Uh-húh.
   Um-hmm.
   That's right.

4. **Gratitude**

   Expressing . . .

   Thank you.
   Thanks.
   Thank you very much.
   Thanks very much.

VOCABULARY

Transportation

bus	gate	plane	track
express	monorail	platform	train
flight	pier	ship	

COMMENTARY

"Excuse me" is a polite expression for getting someone's attention before requesting assistance or information.

GETTING READY

Identify the following places from this lesson. If possible, use a map of North America and talk about where each place is located.

In the United States

> The Bronx, New York (part of New York City)
> Queens, New York (part of New York City)
> Atlanta, Georgia
> Palm Beach, Florida
> Las Vegas, Nevada
> Seattle, Washington

Outside the United States

> Toronto, Canada
> Montreal, Canada
> Jamaica
> Bermuda

THE MODEL CONVERSATION

1. **Setting the Scene.** Have students look at the model illustration. Set the scene: "This conversation takes place in a subway station in New York City. A man is looking for the train to the Bronx."

2. **Listening to the Model.** With books closed, have students listen to the model conversation — presented by you, by a pair of students, or on the audiotape.

3. **Class Practice.** With books still closed, model each line and have the whole class repeat in unison.

4. **Reading.** With books open, have students follow along as two students present the model. Ask students if they have any questions and check understanding of vocabulary.

Culture Note

"The Bronx" and "Queens" are parts of New York City. "Times Square" (shown on the subway sign in the illustration) is a major entertainment district in the center of New York City. Many subway lines have connections at the Times Square subway station.

5. **Pair Practice.** In pairs, have students practice the model conversation.

6. **Alternative Expressions.** Present to the class each sentence of the dialog containing a footnoted expression. Call on different students to present the same sentence, but replacing the footnoted expression with its alternatives. (You can cue students to do this quickly by asking, "What's another way of saying that?" or "How else could he/she/you say that?")

THE EXERCISES

Examples

---

1. A. Excuse me. Does this bus go to Palm Beach?
   B. No, it doesn't. It goes to Atlanta. You want the Florida bus.
   A. The Florida bus?
   B. Yes.
   A. Where can I get it?
   B. It's at gate 9.
   A. Thank you.

2. A. Pardon me. Does this train go to Las Vegas?
   B. No, it doesn't. It goes to Seattle. You want the Nevada Express.
   A. The Nevada Express?
   B. Uh-húh.
   A. Where can I get it?
   B. It's on track 7.
   A. Thanks.

Before doing each exercise, check students' understanding of the vocabulary and introduce any unfamiliar words or phrases. Have students use the footnoted expressions or any of their alternatives as they do the exercises.

Exercise Practice (optional). Have pairs of students simultaneously practice all the exercises.

Exercise Presentations. Call on pairs of students to present the exercises.

Culture Note

Exercise 5: The people in this exercise are at Disney World, a family amusement park and resort outside Orlando, Florida. Monorails (elevated trains) are used for transportation inside Disney World. The Magic Kingdom is the area where many of the main attractions and rides are.

ORIGINAL STUDENT CONVERSATIONS

Have pairs of students create and present original conversations based on the model. (You may want students to prepare their original conversations as homework, then practice them the next day with another student and present them to the class.)

EXPANSION

1. Local Transportation Guessing Game

a. Write on the board four different local bus or train lines that you are sure your students are familiar with. For example:

```
Bus Number 29
Riverside Drive
Main Street
Taylor Square

The Number 9 Train
Washington Avenue
Pine Street
Waterville

Bus Number 52
Appleton Road
Century Avenue
The Airport

The Number 38 Train
Thompson Boulevard
48th Street
Greenway Avenue
```

b. Divide the class into pairs. On the back of each student, tape the number of one of the transportation lines.

c. Have students ask each other yes/no questions in order to identify the number of the line on their back. For example:

Student 1: Does it stop on Riverside Drive?
Student 2: No, it doesn't.
Student 1: Does it stop on Appleton Road?
Student 2: Yes, it does.
Student 1: Is it Bus Number 52?
Student 2: Yes, it is.

2. Local Transportation Contest

a. Have students carefully study a local transportation map.

b. Prepare questions about the local transportation system. Use only yes/no questions. For example:

Does the A Train go to Riverside?
Does Bus Number 19 stop on Broadway?
Is the A Train an express?

c. Divide the class into groups, and have the groups take turns answering your questions about the local transportation system. The group that gives the most correct answers wins.

3. Out-of-Class Survey: A Long-Distance Vacation

a. Have students choose two possible destinations for a week-long class vacation.

b. Brainstorm with students some of the questions they will need to ask about transportation to those destinations.

c. Have students actually call the airlines, bus station, or train station to get the information they need.

d. Have students report their findings to the class and then vote on the best way to get to their vacation spot.

Fill It In!

Have students do the activity individually, in pairs, or as a class. You may want to assign this exercise as homework.

1. a   5. a
2. a   6. a
3. b   7. b
4. a   8. b

Transportation Survey

Have students write the questions in groups and then conduct their interviews individually. Have students report the results of their surveys to the class and compare what they found out.

FOCUS

TOPIC

Transportation: Schedules

GRAMMAR

1. **Declarative Sentences with Question Intonation**

   I missed the flight?!

2. **Have to/Have Got to**

   I **have to** get to my brother's wedding.
   I **'ve got to** get to my brother's wedding.

3. **Question Formation**

   Where can I get the 8:30 flight to Chicago?
   When is the next flight?

FUNCTIONS

1. **Attracting Attention**

   Excuse me.

2. **Asking for and Reporting Information**

   Where can I get the *8:30 flight to Chicago*?
   When is the next *flight*?

3. **Surprise–Disbelief**

   Oh, no!

   I missed the flight?!

   I don't believe it!
   I can't believe it!

4. **Obligation**

   Expressing . . .

   I've got to
   I have to } *get to my brother's wedding.*
   I need to

5. **Hesitating**

   Let me see.
   Let's see.

VOCABULARY

Family Members	Transportation	Education
aunt	bus	graduation
nephew	ferry	high school reunion
	flight	interview
	train	university

COMMENTARY

1. "I missed the flight?!" (line 5). Speaker A is checking that he has understood correctly and is at the same time, expressing dismay.

2. In line 6, "I'm afraid you did" is an expression for politely and sympathetically confirming bad news.

3. In lines 7–8, when Speaker A states "I've got to get to my brother's wedding," it is clear that he is very upset, since it is unusual for a passenger to talk to a ticket agent about anything other than the ticket or the flight.

4. "Let me see" (line 10) indicates that the person is hesitating while she checks the information.

GETTING READY

1. Have students practice reading and telling time using digital time expressions.

   a. Write times such as those below on the board or on cue cards.

8:45	9:30	7:20	12:15	6:50	7:25
1:19	3:10	1:42	10:23	4:40	2:19

   b. Point to each time and ask, "What time is it?" Have students answer chorally and individually.

2. Practice using intonation to change a statement to a question and to express surprise.

   a. Write several statements on the board. For example:

   It's twelve thirty.
   John is getting married tomorrow.
   The meeting is in ten minutes.
   The plane is going to be late.

   b. Read the first sentence using three different kinds of intonation. Have students guess whether you are asking a question, making a statement, or expressing surprise. For example:

   "It's twelve thirty." (*falling intonation for a statement*)
   "It's twelve thirty?" (*rising intonation for using a statement to ask a question*)
   "It's TWELVE THIRTY?!" (*strong emphasis on certain information to imply surprise*)

   c. Have students read the other sentences and change the meaning by changing their intonation.

3. Practice *have to, have got to,* and *need to.* Have students listen as you describe one or more situations, and then have students answer questions. For example:

   "Mrs. Jones lives in North Dakota. That's in the midwestern part of the United States. In the winter it's cold and it snows a lot. The snow is beautiful, but it makes extra work for Mrs. Jones. What does she have to do when it snows?"

   (She has to wear warm clothing.)
   (She's got to drive carefully.)
   (She needs to shovel the snow.)

   "Bob and Mary Jackson both go to work every day. They have two small children. Early morning is a very busy time in their house. Why? What do they have to do?"

   (They have to get up early.)
   (They've got to make breakfast.)
   (They need to make lunch for their children.)

THE MODEL CONVERSATION

1. **Setting the Scene.** Have students look at the model illustration. Set the scene: "A man is talking to a ticket agent at the airport."

2. **Listening to the Model**. With books closed, have students listen to the model conversation — presented by you, by a pair of students, or on the audiotape.

3. **Class Practice.** With books still closed, model each line and have the whole class repeat in unison.

4. **Reading.** With books open, have students follow along as two students present the model. Ask students if they have any questions and check understanding of vocabulary.

5. **Pair Practice.** In pairs, have students practice the model conversation.

6. **Alternative Expressions**. Present to the class each sentence of the dialog containing a footnoted expression. Call on different students to present the same sentence, but replacing the footnoted expression with its alternatives. (You can cue students to do this quickly by asking, "What's another way of saying that?" or "How else could he/she/you say that?")

THE EXERCISES

Examples

1. A. Excuse me. Where can I get the 9:00 bus to New Haven?
   B. I'm sorry, but the 9:00 bus to New Haven just left.
   A. Oh, no! I missed the bus?!
   B. I'm afraid you did.
   A. I don't believe it! I've got to get to my interview at Yale University. When is the next bus?
   B. Let me see. It's at 10:00. Will that get you to New Haven in time for your interview at Yale University?
   A. I hope so.

2. A. Excuse me. Where can I get the 7:00 ferry to Manhattan?
   B. I'm sorry, but the 7:00 ferry to Manhattan just left.
   A. Oh, no! I missed the ferry?!
   B. I'm afraid you did.
   A. I can't believe it! I have to get to my high school reunion. When is the next ferry?
   B. Let's see. It's at 7:30. Will that get you to Manhattan in time for your high school reunion?
   A. I hope so.

Before doing each exercise, check students' understanding of the vocabulary and introduce any unfamiliar words or phrases. Have students use the footnoted expressions or any of their alternatives as they do the exercises.

Exercise Practice (optional). Have pairs of students simultaneously practice all the exercises.

Exercise Presentations. Call on pairs of students to present the exercises.

Culture Notes

Exercise 1: Colleges and universities commonly suggest that applicants living within reasonable traveling distance visit the school for a personal interview. A few institutions actually require an interview, but this is not very common.

Exercise 2: Many high school and college classes hold reunions to celebrate the anniversary of their graduation, often every five or ten years after the graduation.

ORIGINAL STUDENT CONVERSATIONS

Have pairs of students create and present original conversations based on the model. (You may want students to prepare their original conversations as homework, then practice them the next day with another student and present them to the class.)

EXPANSION

1. Telephone

a. Divide the class into large groups. Have each group sit in a circle.

b. Whisper some information about a transportation schedule to one student. For example:

"Bill has to catch the 7:30 flight leaving from gate 17. If he misses that, he'll need to catch the 8:15 flight leaving from gate 34."

c. The first student whispers the information to the second student, and so forth around the circle.

d. When the message gets to the last student, that person says it aloud. Is it the same message you started with? The group with the most accurate message wins.

2. Listen Carefully!

a. Tell students a short *transportation* story. For example:

"Erica is going to her first day of work downtown. Today is her first commute.

From her street, she has to catch the 7:18 bus to get to the train station by 7:45. The train leaves at 7:50. When she arrives downtown, she needs to catch the 8:25 bus, which will get her to work at 8:45."

b. Make several statements about the story. Some statements should be true and others false.

c. Tell students to listen carefully to the statements to determine if they are true or false. If a statement is false, have students correct it. For example:

Teacher: She has to catch the 8:17 bus to get to the train station.
Student: False. She has to catch the 7:18 bus.

Variation: This activity can be done as a game with two competing teams. The teams take turns deciding whether the statements are true or false.

3. Information Gap: Transportation Schedules

a. Find a real bus, subway, or train schedule that your students will be interested in studying, and make enough copies for half of the class.

b. Prepare a list of questions or problems related to the schedule, and make enough copies for the other half of the class. The transportation questions should include *asking for facts* ("What time does the bus for _____ leave?") and *asking for interpretation of the schedule* ("How long is the ride from _____ to _____?/How many buses to _____ are there?/How many stops are there between _____ and _____?/Can you go from _____ to _____?")

c. Divide the class into pairs. Give one student the schedule and the other student the list of questions or problems. As you introduce the activity, give students a few minutes to preview the schedule and the list of questions. Check understanding and pronunciation of any new vocabulary. (You may wish to have students switch roles halfway through the activity.)

d. After the various pairs have completed asking and answering the list of questions, have them compare their answers.

4. Extend the Situation

a. Divide the class into pairs.

b. Have each pair select one of the situations on page 42 of the student text and think up a possibility for the rest of the story. What happened? Did the person arrive on time?

c. Have students present their stories to the class.

5. Discussion: Comparing Cultures

With students working as a class, in pairs, or in small groups, have students compare their attitudes towards schedules and punctuality by answering the following questions:

Do buses and trains run on schedule in your country? Why or why not?
Do people get upset or worried when a train or bus is running late? Why or why not?
How do people react when they miss a train or a bus?
Look at the various situations on page 42 of the student text. How would people react to your being late in each of those situations?

Variation: Students may also want to interview people outside of class to get a broader spectrum of attitudes about schedules and punctuality.

Listen

Listen to the announcements. Which words do you hear?

1. The bus for Las Vegas is now leaving from gate thirteen.
2. Attention . . . passengers for New York and New Haven . . . your bus is at gate eleven.
3. Attention, passengers. The nine-thirty bus is now boarding at gate five.
4. Your attention, please. The three o'clock bus to Philadelphia is now boarding.
5. Attention, please. The eleven forty-five bus to Kansas City is now leaving from gate seventeen.
6. Attention . . . passengers for San Francisco. Your bus is now boarding at gate twelve.
7. Passengers going to Chicago . . . Your bus will leave at ten thirty from gate two.
8. Your attention, please. The next bus to Baltimore will leave from gate eight.

Answers

1. a
2. b
3. a
4. a
5. b
6. a
7. b
8. b

ExpressWays

Have students do the activity individually, in pairs, or as a class. You may want to assign this exercise as homework.

1. Where is the 7:15 train to Philadelphia?
2. When is the next flight to London?
3. Where can I buy a ticket?
4. When does the next ferry to Manhattan leave?
5. Why is the flight from Detroit late?

CrossTalk

Have students first work in pairs and then share with the class what they talked about.

FOCUS

TOPIC

Getting Around Town

GRAMMAR

Imperatives

Go to the next corner and **turn** left onto Center Street.
Walk three blocks to Second Avenue and **turn** right.

FUNCTIONS

1. **Attracting Attention**

   Excuse me.

2. **Asking for and Reporting Information**

   Can you tell me
   Could you tell me ⎬ *how to get to City Hall?*
   Do you know

3. **Instructing**

   First, . . .
   Then . . .

4. **Directions–Location**

   Asking for Directions

   Can you tell me how to get to *City Hall?*

   Giving Directions

   Go to *the next corner.*
   Turn left *(onto Center Street).*
   Turn right *(onto Center Street).*
   You'll see *City Hall* on the left/right.
   Take a left/right (at *the next intersection).*
   Take the first right/left after the
      supermarket.
   Walk *three* blocks (to *Second Avenue).*
   Drive *about five or six blocks.*
   Drive down *this road* until *you get to the
      first traffic light.*
   Follow *Main Street.*
   Walk down *this street.*
   Walk along *Park Avenue.*
   You'll come to a *big supermarket.*

   Go about *two* miles.
   You'll see a sign (*for the interstate*).
   Take the *interstate north* to *Exit 7.*

5. **Asking for Repetition**

   (I'm sorry.) I didn't follow you.
   (I'm sorry.) I didn't get that.

   Could you please repeat that?
   Could you please say that again?

6. **Checking and Indicating Understanding**

   Checking Another Person's Understanding

   Are you with me so far?
   Okay so far?
   Are you following me so far?

   Have you got all that?

   Indicating Understanding

   Yes.
   Uh-húh.
   Um-hmm.
   Okay.

   I'm following you.
   I understand.
   I'm with you.

   Now I've got it.
   Now I understand.

VOCABULARY

Community	Driving
City Hall	block
library	drive
supermarket	exit
zoo	intersection
	interstate
	mile
	sign
	traffic light

COMMENTARY

1. When asking strangers for assistance, the polite form "Can you tell me _____?" is more appropriate than a direct question such as "How do you get to _____?"

2. "I didn't follow you" (line 5) is commonly used to indicate confusion about new information, particularly a set of directions or instructions.

3. "Okay" (line 6) is a friendly way to say "yes" to a request.

4. In line 7, "Uh-húh" is an expression used by the listener to show that he has understood. By using this expression, the listener is encouraging the other speaker to continue.

5. "Are you with me so far?" (line 8) and "Have you got all that?" (line 10) are used to check whether the listener has understood what was said — particularly when a long set of directions or instructions is being given.

GETTING READY

Practice giving directions.

   a. Draw a simple street map on the board or on a large piece of paper. Include three or four streets that intersect and a number of community locations (hospital, supermarket, school, gas station, library).

   b. Point to a location on the map and ask for directions from there to another place on the map. For example:

   Teacher: I'm here (point to a location), and I want to go to the library. Can you tell me how to get there?

   Student: Yes. Walk down Green Street to River Avenue. Turn left on River Avenue. Follow River Avenue and you'll see the library on the right.

THE MODEL CONVERSATION

1. **Setting the Scene.** Have students look at the model illustration. Set the scene: "Someone is asking for directions to City Hall."

2. **Listening to the Model.** With books closed, have students listen to the model conversation — presented by you, by a pair of students, or on the audiotape.

3. **Class Practice.** With books still closed, model each line and have the whole class repeat in unison.

4. **Reading.** With books open, have students follow along as two students present the model. Ask students if they have any questions and check understanding of vocabulary.

5. **Pair Practice.** In pairs, have students practice the model conversation.

6. **Alternative Expressions.** Present to the class each sentence of the dialog containing a footnoted expression. Call on different students to present the same sentence, but replacing the footnoted expression with its alternatives. (You can cue students to do this quickly by asking, "What's another way of saying that?" or "How else could he/she/you say that?")

THE EXERCISES

Examples

1. A. Excuse me. Can you tell me how to get to the Acme Furniture Company?
   B. Yes. Take a left at the next intersection. Drive about five or six blocks to Main Street and turn right. Follow Main Street all the way to the end, and you'll see the Acme Furniture Company on the left.

A. I'm sorry. I didn't follow you. Could you please repeat that?

B. Okay. First, take a left at the next intersection.

A. Uh-húh.

B. Then drive about five or six blocks to Main Street and turn right. Are you with me so far?

A. Yes. I'm following you.

B. Then follow Main Street all the way to the end, and you'll see the Acme Furniture Company on the left. Have you got all that?

A. Yes. Now I've got it. Thanks very much.

2. A. Excuse me. Could you tell me how to get to the library?

B. Yes. Walk down this street to Park Avenue and turn right. Walk along Park Avenue a few blocks, and you'll come to a big supermarket. Take the first right after the supermarket, and you'll see the library in the middle of that block.

A. I'm sorry. I didn't get that. Could you please say that again?

B. Sure. First, walk down this street to Park Avenue and turn right.

A. Um-hḿm.

B. Then walk along Park Avenue a few blocks, and you'll come to a big supermarket. Okay so far?

A. Yes. I understand.

B. Then take the first right after the supermarket, and you'll see the library in the middle of that block. Have you got all that?

A. Yes. Now I understand. Thanks very much.

Before doing each exercise, check students' understanding of the vocabulary and introduce any unfamiliar words or phrases. Have students use the footnoted expressions or any of their alternatives as they do the exercises.

Exercise Practice (optional). Have pairs of students simultaneously practice all the exercises.

Exercise Presentations. Call on pairs of students to present the exercises.

Culture Note

Exercise 3: In this situation, a group of students is going on a "field trip" to the zoo. It is common for school groups to go on one or more trips during the school year, often to museums, historical places, or government institutions.

Language Note

Exercise 3: An "interstate" is a highway that crosses state lines.

ORIGINAL STUDENT CONVERSATIONS

Have pairs of students create and present original conversations based on the model. (You may want students to prepare their original conversations as homework, then practice them the next day with another student and present them to the class.)

EXPANSION

1. Telephone: Directions

a. Divide the class into large groups. Have each group sit in a circle.

b. Whisper to one student a set of directions to a well-known place in your community.

c. The first student whispers the directions to the second student, and so forth around the circle. The student listening may ask for clarification by saying, "I'm sorry. Could you please repeat that?" The student speaking can also check for understanding by saying, "Are you with me so far?"

d. When the message gets to the last student, that person says it aloud. Is it the same set of directions you started with? The group with the most accurate message wins.

2. Name That Place!

a. Divide the class into pairs or small groups.

b. Have students look at the map at the top of page 46 of the student text and take turns writing directions to one of the places on the map from the perspective of the two characters in the bottom left corner of the map.

c. The others should follow along on the map while they listen and tell the letter where the place is located.

3. Class Survey: Asking for and Giving Directions to Places Around Town

a. Prepare a set of cue cards with one card for each student. On each card write the name of a well-known place in the community: the public library, the bus or subway station, a restaurant, park, store, or a nearby town center. (If you wish, you can name a form of transportation, such as *by car, by bus, by subway,* or *on foot.*)

b. Give a card to each student. Have students ask several people in the class for directions to the location and write down the directions. Set an appropriate time limit for this part of the activity, such as 10–15 minutes.

c. Then, ask each student to choose the best directions and present them to the class. Encourage the class to agree or disagree and to suggest better ways to go there.

4. Writing Assignment: Someone Is Coming to Dinner!

Have students imagine that an English-speaking guest from out of town is coming to dinner. Ask each student to write directions for the visitor, explaining how to get to his or her home (from the airport/bus station/train station) by car or public transportation. Provide students with a street map and public transportation maps of your area for reference.

Listen

Listen and follow the directions to different places. Write the letter of the place people are talking about in each conversation.

1. A. Excuse me. Could you please tell me how to get to the library?
   B. Okay. Walk down Fourth Street to Broad Street and turn left. Walk one block, and you'll see the library on the corner of Third and Broad.
   A. Thanks.

2. A. Can you tell me how to get to the laundromat?
   B. Sure. Walk down Oak Street to Third Street and make a right. You'll see the laundromat in the middle of the block.
   A. Thanks very much.

3. A. Excuse me. How do I get to the zoo?
   B. Follow Fourth Street to Broad Street. Make a left on Broad Street and go three more blocks to First Street. You'll see the zoo on the left, at the intersection of First and Broad.
   A. Thanks very much.

4. A. Pardon me. Do you know how to get to Max's Supermarket?
   B. Uh-húh. Follow Fourth Street all the way to the end and make a left. Go one block, and you'll see it on the left.
   A. Thank you.

5. A. Excuse me. Could you possibly tell me how to get to River City High School?
   B. Uh-húh. Go down Fourth Street two blocks and make a left onto Broad Street. Go two more blocks and make a right on Second Street. You'll see the school on your right.
   A. Thank you very much.

6. A. Excuse me. Is there a parking lot nearby?
   B. Yes. Follow Fourth Street all the way to the end. You'll see it on the left.
   A. Thanks.

7. A. Pardon me. Where's City Hall?
   B. Follow Oak Street two blocks and make a right onto Second Street. Walk two more blocks, and you'll see City Hall at the intersection of Broad and Second.
   A. Thanks very much.

8. A. I'm looking for the bus station. Can you help me?
   B. Sure. Walk down Fourth Street and make a left on Main Street. Follow Main Street to Second Street. You'll see the bus station on the left.
   A. Thank you.

9. A. Pardon me. Do you by any chance know where the bank is?
   B. Yes. Go down Fourth to Main and make a left. Go two blocks and make a right. The bank is in the middle of the block on the right.
   A. Thank you very much.

Answers

1. F
2. J
3. B
4. G
5. H
6. I
7. A
8. C
9. E

Reflections

Have students discuss the questions in pairs or small groups and then share their ideas with the class.

Matching Lines

Have students do the activity individually, in pairs, or as a class. You may want to assign this exercise as homework.

1. b
2. c
3. a
4. e
5. d
6. f

Choose the Right Way

Have students do the activity individually, in pairs, or as a class. You may want to assign this exercise as homework.

1. c	5. b
2. b	6. a
3. b	7. a
4. c	8. b

Listen

Listen to the conversation. Did the person understand the directions?

1. A. Take Exit 15.
   B. I'm following you.

2. A. Go north.
   B. Could you please repeat that?

3. A. Turn left at Second Avenue.
   B. I didn't get that.

4. A. Take the first right, and you'll see a sign.
   B. I understand.

5. A. Go to the next corner and turn right.
   B. I didn't follow you.

6. A. Drive through three traffic lights and make a right.
   B. I'm with you.

7. A. Turn left at the light, go about a mile, and you'll see a sign.
   B. I've got it.

8. A. Take the second left after the intersection.
   B. All right.

9. A. Take a right and go about seven blocks.
   B. I didn't get that.

Answers

1. a	4. a	7. a
2. b	5. b	8. a
3. b	6. a	9. b

Figure It Out!

Divide the class into pairs. Have them write and practice their role plays and then present them to the class.

FOCUS

TOPIC

Getting Around Town

GRAMMAR

1. **Imperatives**

   Go to the corner and **turn** right at Station Street.
   Follow Station Street about seven blocks.

2. **Past Tense**

   I **went** north on Union Boulevard.
   Then I turn**ed** right and **drove** to Washington Avenue.

   You **were** supposed to get off at Exit 15.

FUNCTIONS

1. **Greeting People**

   Hello.

   Hello, *Bob*?

   This is *Larry*.

2. **Directions–Location**

   Giving Directions
   Go to *the corner*.
   Turn right *(at Station Street)*.
   You'll see *my house* on the left/right.

3. **Checking and Indicating Understanding**

   Checking Another Person's Understanding
   Have you got that?

   Indicating Understanding
   Yes.
   Uh-húh
   Um-hmm.
   That's right.
   Okay.

4. **Instructing**

   Then . . .
   After that, . . .

5. **Asking for Repetition**

   Could you repeat the last part?

VOCABULARY

Driving

directions
exit
parkway

COMMENTARY

1. In line 2, when Speaker B says "Hello, Bob?," he thinks Bob has answered the phone and he wants to check to make sure.

2. In line 3, Speaker A asks, "Where ARE you?" The stress on *are* gives emphasis to the question and indicates that Speaker A has been expecting him for some time.

3. In line 12, Speaker A says "Um-hḿm" to indicate that he is listening and to encourage Speaker B to continue.

4. A "parkway" (line 13) is a wide highway with grass and trees planted either on a strip in the middle or on the sides.

5. "Uh-oh!" in line 14 signals a problem or error.

6. In line 21, Speaker B begins to review and repeat the directions part by part. This is a common way of checking understanding. After each part, Speaker A indicates understanding by responding "Uh-húh" (line 22) and "Um-hḿm" (line 24).

GETTING READY

1. Practice vocabulary for giving directions. Give directions and have the class tell you the opposite. For example:

   A. Go *north* on Main Street.
   B. Go *south* on Main Street.

   A. Turn *left* at the light.
   B. Turn *right* at the light.

   A. Take a *right* after the supermarket.
   B. Take a *left* after the supermarket.

   A. Get *on* interstate 93.
   B. Get *off* interstate 93.

   A. Go *down* Parker Road to the *first* house on your *right*.
   B. Go *up* Parker Road to the *last* house on your *left*.

2. Practice the past-tense forms of verbs commonly used in giving directions. Have the class imagine that you are checking to find out if they followed directions correctly. Ask questions such as those below, and have students respond with *yes* answers and past-tense forms. For example:

   A. Did you drive to Union Boulevard?
   B. Yes, we drove to Union Boulevard.

   A. Did you take a right on Circuit Road?
   B. Yes, we took a right on Circuit Road.

   Other questions:

   1. Did you follow Main Street all the way to the end?
   2. Did you go down Park Avenue and turn right on East Street?
   3. Did you see the sign for the interstate on your left?
   4. Did you drive down Station Street all the way to the interstate?
   5. Did you turn left at the library?
   6. Did you come to a big furniture store on your right?
   7. Did you get to the traffic light on Colonial Road?
   8. Did you take the second left onto Center Street?
   9. Did you see the phone booth at the corner of Second Avenue and Vine Street?
   10. Did you get off the expressway at Exit 14?

THE MODEL CONVERSATION

1. **Setting the Scene.** Have students look at the model illustration. Set the scene: "Larry is going to a party at Bob's house. He's lost. He's calling Bob to get directions."

2. **Listening to the Model.** With books closed, have students listen to the model conversation — presented by you, by a pair of students, or on the audiotape.

3. **Class Practice.** With books still closed, model each line and have the whole class repeat in unison.

4. **Reading.** With books open, have students follow along as two students present the model. Ask students if they have any questions, and check understanding of vocabulary.

5. **Pair Practice.** In pairs, have students practice the model conversation.

Now have pairs of students create and present original conversations using the model dialog as a guide. Encourage students to be inventive and to use new vocabulary. (You may want to assign this exercise as homework, having students prepare their conversations, practice them the next day with another student, and then present them to the class.) Students should present their conversations without referring to the written text, but they also should not memorize them. Rather, they should feel free to adapt and expand them any way they wish.

Reading: *Honk! Honk!*

Preview: Have students discuss the following questions:

> When is rush hour in your city?
> What kinds of transportation do most people use in your city?

Then have students read the passage silently, or have them listen to the passage and take notes as you read it or play the audiotape.

True or False?

Have students do the activity individually, in pairs, or as a class. You may want to assign this exercise as homework.

1. False
2. True
3. False
4. True
5. False
6. False

Do You Remember?

Have students do the activity individually, in pairs, or as a class. You may want to assign this exercise as homework.

1. b
2. a
3. b
4. c
5. c
6. b

Your Turn

Have students discuss the activity as a class, in pairs, or in small groups. Then have students write their responses at home, share their written work with other students, and discuss in class.

Looking Back

Have students look at the list of expressions. Encourage them to ask you any questions about the meaning or pronunciation of any of the words. If students ask for the pronunciation, repeat after the student until the student is satisfied with his or her pronunciation of the word.

Review Activities

To review the language introduced in the unit, do the following activities.

1. Association Game

a. Divide the class into several teams.

b. Call out a topic category from the *Looking Back* section on student text page 52.

c. Have students in each group work together to see how many phrases they can associate with that category. For example:

Asking for
Information: Can you tell me . . . ?
Do you know . . . ?
Could you tell me . . . ?

d. The team with the most items wins.

2. Create a Conversation!

a. Divide the class into pairs of students.

b. Tell each pair they have three minutes to make up a conversation using one item from each category from the *Looking Back* section on page 52 of the student text.

c. Have students present their conversations to the class.

Have students talk about the people and the situations, and then present role plays based on the scenes. Students may refer back to previous lessons as a resource, but they should not simply reuse specific conversations. (You may want to assign these exercises as written homework, having students prepare their conversations, practice them the next day with another student, and then present them to the class.)

1. **FOCUS: Social Communication: Meeting People**
   Housing: Relations with Neighbors

   Two neighbors are introducing themselves.

2. **FOCUS: Social Communication: Meeting People**

   A man is introducing someone at the office.

3. **FOCUS: Personal Information: Address, Age, Date of Birth, Name, Occupation, Social Security Number, Telephone Number. Health: Checking In to a Hospital or Clinic**

   A woman who is going to have a baby is checking in to a hospital with her husband.

4. **FOCUS: Social Communication: Sharing Information**

   Two people at work are talking about plans for the weekend.

5. **FOCUS: Social Communication: Sharing Information**

   Two people are talking at a party.

6. **FOCUS: Telephone: Directory Assistance**

   Someone is calling directory assistance.

7. **FOCUS: Transportation: Modes of Transportation, Route Information**

   A man is trying to find the right bus.

8. **FOCUS: Getting Around Town**

   A gas station attendant is giving directions to a driver who is lost.

EXIT 4

OVERVIEW
Student Text
Pages 55–74

Topics	Functions	Grammar

Pp. 56–57 Looking for an Apartment

Housing: Obtaining Housing	Want–Desire Hesitating Asking for and Reporting Information Directions–Location Describing Asking for and Reporting Additional Information Permission	Adjectives Singular/Plural

Pp. 60–61 Could You Do Me a Favor?

Food: Food Items	Requests Want–Desire Hesitating Gratitude	Count/Non-Count Nouns Partitives

P. 64 It's in the Dairy Section, Aisle B

Supermarket: Locating Items	Attracting Attention Directions–Location Correcting Gratitude	Count/Non-Count Nouns

P. 66 It's Amazing How Little You Can Buy!

Supermarket: Purchasing Items Money: Paying for Goods and Services	Surprise–Disbelief Certainty/Uncertainty Agreement/Disagreement	Count/Non-Count Nouns

Topics	Functions	Grammar

P. 68 Mmm! These Are Delicious!

Food: Describing Food
Social Communication:
   Compliments

Complimenting
Checking and Indicating
   Understanding
Describing
Hesitating

Count/Non-Count Nouns
Adjectives
Pronoun Review

Pp. 70–71 Could I Ask You for the Recipe?

Food: Recipes

Complimenting
Requests
Instructing
Checking and Indicating
   Understanding
Asking for Repetition
Gratitude

Imperatives
Partitives

LOOKING AHEAD

Grammar This Exit

Adjectives

It's very **safe.**
It has a **brand new** refrigerator.
We're looking for a **two-bedroom** apartment.

These are **delicious.**
They're a **popular Mexican** dish.

Singular/Plural

It has **a** brand new refrigerator.

You don't find many two-bedroom apartment**s** with brand new refrigerator**s.**

Count/Non-Count Nouns

Count

We need **a few** oranges.
How **many**?

Lamb chop**s**?
They're in the Frozen Food Section.

The vitamins **were** six ninety-four.

These are delicious! What **are they**?
They're enchiladas.
What's in **them**?
A few tomato**es.**

Non-Count

We need **some** sugar.
How **much**?

Yogurt?
It's in the Dairy Section.

The skim milk **was** a dollar.

This is excellent! What **is it**?
It's borscht.
What's in **it**?
A little sour cream.

Partitives

a **bag of** sugar
a **bottle of** mineral water
a **box of** rice
a **bunch of** bananas
a **can of** tuna fish
a **container of** yogurt
a **dozen** eggs
a **gallon of** milk
a **head of** lettuce
a **jar of** peanut butter
a **loaf of** bread
a **pint of** ice cream
a **pound of** coffee
a **quart of** orange juice
a **six-pack of** soda

a **stick of** butter
a **tube of** toothpaste

half a dozen eggs
half a pound of Swiss cheese
a **half gallon of** milk
a **pound and a half of** ground beef

a **cup of** bread crumbs
half a cup of milk
a **teaspoon of** salt

Pronoun Review

What are **they**?
They're enchiladas.
What's in **them**?

What is **it**?
It's borscht.
What's in **it**?

Imperatives

Mix together one egg, two teaspoons of salt, and two pounds of ground beef.

Functions This Exit

Want–Desire

Inquiring about . . .

What do you want me to *get*?

How much do you want me to *get*?

Expressing . . .

We're looking for _____.

We need _____.
We're out of _____.

Asking for and Reporting Information

What kind of *neighborhood is it*?
How much *is the rent*?

What can you tell us (about _____)?

Asking for and Reporting Additional Information

Another question.

Directions–Location

Inquiring about Location

Where is it?

Where can I find _____?

Giving Location

It's on *Dixon Street*.

It's in the *Dairy* Section, Aisle *B*.

Describing

It's (very) *safe/convenient/clean/ quiet/friendly/desirable*.

It has (a) brand new _____.

They're *a popular Mexican dish*.

Certainty/Uncertainty

Inquiring about Certainty

Are you sure that's right?

Complimenting

Expressing Compliments

Mmm!

This is/These are
- delicious!
- excellent!
- wonderful!
- superb!
- fantastic!

Your _____ was/were *delicious*!

It was/They were *excellent*!

Responding to Compliments

Oh, did you really like it/them?

Thank you for saying so.

Instructing

First, . . .
Then . . .
Next, . . .
After that, . . .

Surprise–Disbelief

Twelve dollars and forty-nine cents?!

How about that!
How do you like that!
Isn't that something!

It's amazing (_____)!

Permission

Inquiring about Permissibility

Are _____ allowed?

Indicating Permissibility

Yes, I believe they are.

Requests

Direct, Polite

Could you do me a favor?

Could you _____?

Could I ask you _____?

Responding to Requests

Sure.
Certainly.
All right.
Okay.

Gratitude

Expressing . . .

Thanks.
Thanks very much.
Thank you.
Thank you very much.
Thanks a lot.

Responding to . . .

You're welcome.
My pleasure.
Any time.

Agreement/Disagreement

Expressing Agreement

You're right.
That's true.
[*less formal*]
I'll say!
You can say THAT again!

Asking for Repetition

I didn't get the last step.

Could you repeat that part?

Checking and Indicating Understanding

Checking Another Person's Understanding

Are you with me so far?

Checking One's Own Understanding

Enchiladas?

Did you say _____?
Was that _____?

Indicating Understanding

That's right.

I'm with you.
Now I've got it.

Hesitating

Hmm.

Let's see . . .
Let me see . . .
Let me think . . .

Uh . . .

PREVIEWING EXIT 4: CHAPTER-OPENING PHOTOS

Have students talk about the people and the situations and, as a class or in pairs, predict what the characters might be saying to each other. Students in pairs or small groups may enjoy practicing role plays based on these scenes and then presenting them to the class.

------- Text Pages 56–57: Looking for an Apartment -------

FOCUS

TOPIC

Housing: Obtaining Housing

GRAMMAR

1. **Adjectives**

   It's very **safe.**
   The apartment has a **brand new** refrigerator.
   We're looking for a **two-bedroom** apartment.

2. **Singular/Plural**

   It has **a** brand new refrigerator.
   You don't find many two-bedroom
   apartment**s** with brand-new refrigerator**s.**

FUNCTIONS

1. **Want–Desire**

   Expressing . . .
   We're looking for *a two-bedroom apartment.*

2. **Hesitating**

   Hmm.

3. **Asking for and Reporting Information**

   What kind of *neighborhood is it?*
   How much is *the rent?*

   What can you tell us *about the apartment?*

4. **Directions–Location**

   Inquiring about Location
   Where is it?

   Giving Location
   It's on *Dixon Street.*

5. **Describing**

   It's (very) *safe/convenient/clean/quiet/*
   friendly/desirable.
   It has (a) brand new *refrigerator.*

6. **Asking for and Reporting Additional Information**

   Another question.

7. **Permission**

   Inquiring about Permissibility
   Are *dogs* allowed?

   Indicating Permissibility
   Yes, I believe they are.

VOCABULARY

Describing	**Housing**		**Transportation**
brand new	bedroom	microwave oven	airport
clean	building	neighborhood	bus line
convenient	cabinet	parking fee	public
desirable	dishwasher	pet	transportation
friendly	dues	public	
quiet	electricity	transportation	
reasonable	garbage disposal	refrigerator	
safe	gas	rent	
	health club	stove	
	heat	utilities	
	landlord		

COMMENTARY

1. A real estate agent, or realtor, assists people in locating houses or apartments to buy or rent, usually for a fee. Many people use the want ads in the back of their local newspaper to locate houses and apartments.

2. "How can I help you?" (line 1) is a conversation opener commonly used in business to address a customer.

3. In line 3, Speaker A says "Hmm," because he is hesitating in order to think.

4. "What kind of neighborhood is it?" (line 7). People who are apartment hunting in the United States usually want to know whether a neighborhood is considered safe, and which services (such as public transportation, laundromats, restaurants) and facilities (such as parks and libraries) are available.

5. "Brand new" (line 10) indicates very new or never used.

6. "And believe me" (line 10) prefaces a strong statement. Speaker A would like B to consider this apartment.

7. In line 13, Speaker B uses the phrase "Another question" to introduce his next question.

8. "Utilities" (line 17) are costs for fuel (usually oil or gas) and electricity. These costs are usually paid monthly and are sometimes included in the rent.

9. In line 18, Speaker A replies to a question with a short phrase, "Everything except gas." Shortened sentences carrying essential information are common in everyday conversation.

GETTING READY

1. Talk to your class about rent prices where you live and costs that may or may not be included in the rent. Write some typical rent prices on the board, and have students practice reading them chorally and individually. For example:

   $500 a month plus gas
   $650 a month plus heat
   $400 a month plus electricity
   $550 a month plus the parking fee
   $1100 a month plus utilities

2. Check students' knowledge of names of household furnishings and appliances, such as *kitchen cabinets, a refrigerator, a garbage disposal, a stove, a microwave oven,* and *a dishwasher.* Use magazine pictures or your own visuals to introduce and practice new vocabulary.

THE MODEL CONVERSATION

1. **Setting the Scene.** Have students look at the model illustration. Set the scene: "A family is looking for an apartment. They're talking to a real estate agent."

2. **Listening to the Model.** With books closed, have students listen to the model conversation — presented by you, by a pair of students, or on the audiotape.

3. **Class Practice.** With books still closed, model each line and have the whole class repeat in unison.

4. **Reading.** With books open, have students follow along as two students present the model. Ask students if they have any questions and check understanding of vocabulary.

Culture Note

Dogs (line 13) are not allowed in many apartment buildings in the United States.

5. **Pair Practice.** In pairs, have students practice the model conversation.

THE EXERCISES

Examples

1. A. How can I help you?
   B. We're looking for a two-bedroom apartment near the airport.
   A. Hmm. A two-bedroom apartment near the airport. I think I have just what you are looking for.
   B. Oh, good. Where is it?
   A. It's on Jefferson Parkway.
   B. What kind of neighborhood is it?
   A. I think you'll like the neighborhood. It's very convenient.
   B. That sounds good. What can you tell us about the apartment?
   A. Well, you'll love the kitchen! It has a brand new garbage disposal. And believe me, you don't find many two-bedroom apartments near the airport with brand new garbage disposals!
   B. Hmm. Another question. Are cats allowed in the building?
   A. Cats? Yes, I believe they are.
   B. How much is the rent?
   A. $650 a month.
   B. Does that include utilities?
   A. Everything except heat. Would you like to see the apartment?
   B. Yes, I think so.

2. A. How can I help you?
   B. We're looking for a three-bedroom apartment near public transportation.
   A. Hmm. A three-bedroom apartment near public transportation. I think I have just what you are looking for.
   B. Oh, good. Where is it?
   A. It's on Forest Avenue.
   B. What kind of neighborhood is it?
   A. I think you'll like the neighborhood. It's very clean.

   B. That sounds good. What can you tell us about the apartment?
   A. Well, you'll love the kitchen! It has brand new cabinets. And believe me, you don't find many three-bedroom apartments near public transportation with brand new cabinets!
   B. Hmm. Another question. Are pets allowed in the building?
   A. Pets? Yes, I believe they are.
   B. How much is the rent?
   A. $550 a month.
   B. Does that include utilities?
   A. Everything except the parking fee. Would you like to see the apartment?
   B. Yes, I think so.

Before doing each exercise, check students' understanding of the vocabulary and introduce any unfamiliar words or phrases.

Exercise Practice (optional). Have pairs of students simultaneously practice all the exercises.

Exercise Presentations. Call on pairs of students to present the exercises.

Language Note

Exercise 1: A "garbage disposal" is an electrical appliance installed in the drain of a kitchen sink. Garbage disposals grind up food waste.

Culture Notes

Exercise 2: Some city apartments have private parking lots, where spaces can be rented for a monthly parking fee.

Exercise 4: Some apartment buildings do not allow pianos.

Exercise 5: Some expensive apartment buildings have health clubs, which residents may join by paying monthly dues or charges.

Exercise 5: Waterbeds are water-filled plastic mattresses. Some apartment buildings do not allow them because they are very heavy or because they may cause damage if they break.

ORIGINAL STUDENT CONVERSATIONS

Have pairs of students create and present original conversations based on the model. (You may want students to prepare their original conversations as homework, then practice them the next day with another student and present them to the class.)

EXPANSION

1. Practice Reading Apartment Ads from the Newspaper

a. Clip ads for apartments from the newspaper.

b. Divide the class into pairs or small groups and give each pair or group an ad.

c. Have students practice reading the ads, and then write them on the board. Have students then explain the ads to the class, including the important information about the apartments and any abbreviations used in the ads.

d. Have the class ask questions about the ads.

Check students' understanding of all the abbreviations. Have one student make a list of all abbreviations found in the ads. Later, make a copy of the list for everyone in the class.

2. Draw, Write, and Read

Have students draw a picture of their house or apartment. Then have them write a description to accompany the picture. In pairs, have students describe their homes as they show their pictures. As students describe their homes, they may wish to add more details, which they should also add to their drawing and their writing.

3. Whose Home Is It?

a. Have each student draw a picture of his or her home.

b. Divide the class into groups of four or five students. Have the group scramble the pictures so no one knows which picture belongs to whom.

c. Have students take turns describing their homes. The group must listen and identify each student's picture.

Variation: Have students draw a picture of their home and write a description to accompany it. The group members then read the descriptions and attempt to match them with the corresponding pictures.

4. Drawing Game

a. Write on two sets of cards descriptions of different kinds of apartments. For example:

> Two-bedroom, two-bathroom apartment with balcony. Pets allowed. Brand new refrigerator.

> Three-bedroom apartment with kitchen, dining room, and living room. Brand new cabinets in the kitchen.

> Four-bedroom apartment near the airport. Air conditioning, garbage disposal, dishwasher, and microwave oven. No pets allowed.

> Studio apartment with balcony. Downtown. Close to public transportation.

b. Place the two piles of cards on a table or desk in the front of the room. Also place a pad of paper and pencil next to each team's set of cards.

c. Divide the class into two teams. Have each team sit together in a different part of the room.

d. When you say "Go!," a person from each team comes to the front of his or her team, picks a card from the pile, and draws the home described. The rest of the team then guesses the description. Remind students that they are not allowed to gesture while drawing.

e. When a team correctly guesses the description, another team member picks a card and draws the apartment described on that card.

f. Continue until each team has guessed all the cards in their pile.

5. Role Play: I'm Calling About Your Ad in Today's Paper

a. Cut out newspaper ads for apartments for rent, or make up your own (using common abbreviations). For example:

> Fairfield — 2-BR. apt., Spring St. $450/mo. plus elec. and gas. No pets. Avail. 8/15. Call 874-9233.

> Sullivan Hills — 1 BR., $350/mo., off-street pkg., quiet area, refs. reqd., no smokers. Call after 8 P.M. 239-7711.

Newcastle — Queen St. 4 BR., 2
baths, $850/mo. plus heat, avail.
immed. Call 978-5561 (9–5) or
978-3476 (after 5).

Taylorville—sunny 4th-fl. studio with
dishwasher and a.c., reas. rent. Call
231-5548 after 5:30 P.M.

b. Divide the class into pairs and give each pair
one or more ads.

c. Have students role-play calling for additional
information about the apartments.
Encourage students to improvise questions
and create any information they wish about
the apartments. Since apartments are often
rented very quickly, have students ask, "Is
the apartment still available?" If it's still
available, they may want to arrange an
appointment to see the apartment.

d. Have volunteers perform their role play for
the class.

6. Class Discussion: Our Neighborhoods

With students working in pairs, in small
groups, or as a class, have students discuss the
following questions:

What do you like about your neighborhood?
What don't you like about your
neighborhood?
What is most important to you — a
neighborhood that is safe, clean,
convenient, or desirable?
What are other aspects to a neighborhood
that you look for? (For example: good
schools, good shops, diversity, or parks
nearby?)
If you could afford to live in any
neighborhood in your city, which one
would you choose? Why?

7. My Dream Home

Have students write a description of their
dream home. Have them then share their
writing with a partner. Encourage the partners
to ask each other questions to clarify the text.
Have students rewrite their descriptions
according to their partners' feedback. Then
have students share their final version with the
class.

8. Price Investigation

a. Make up a worksheet such as the one below
and distribute it to students. Have students
interview each other or others in the
community, asking people what they think
the average costs of the following are:

How much is . . . ?

rent for a one-bedroom
apartment   _____

rent for a two-bedroom
apartment   _____

rent for a three-bedroom
apartment   _____

gas   _____

electricity   _____

heat   _____

the parking fee   _____

b. Have students report their findings to the
class and compare the results.

Variation: Have students investigate the average
rent costs in different neighborhoods and then
compare their findings.

Fill It In!

Have students do the activity individually, in pairs, or as a class. You may want to assign this exercise as homework.

1. b
2. b
3. b
4. a
5. b
6. a
7. b
8. b

Apartment Match

Have students do the activity individually, in pairs, or as a class. You may want to assign this exercise as homework.

1. c	7. d
2. f	8. l
3. j	9. i
4. a	10. k
5. e	11. b
6. h	12. g

Which Apartment?

Have students do the activity individually, in pairs, or as a class. You may want to assign this exercise as homework.

1. C
2. A
3. C
4. D
5. A
6. B
7. D
8. B
9. D

InterActions

Have pairs of students practice role-playing the activity and then present their role plays to the class.

FOCUS

TOPIC

Food: Food Items

GRAMMAR

1. Count/Non-Count Nouns

Count

We need **a few** oranges.
How **many**?

Non-Count

We need **some** sugar.
How **much**?

2. Partitives

a bag of sugar
a bottle of mineral water
a box of rice
a bunch of bananas
a can of tuna fish
a container of yogurt
a dozen eggs
a gallon of milk
a head of lettuce
a jar of peanut butter
a loaf of bread
a pint of ice cream
a pound of coffee
a quart of orange juice
a six-pack of soda
a stick of butter
a tube of toothpaste

half a dozen eggs
half a pound of Swiss cheese
a half gallon of milk
a pound and a half of ground beef

FUNCTIONS

1. Requests

Direct, Polite

Could you do me a favor?

Could you *pick up some sugar*?

Responding to Requests

Sure.
Certainly.
All right.
Okay.

2. Want–Desire

Inquiring about . . .

What do you want me to *get*?
How much do you want me to *get*?

Expressing . . .

We need *a few things*.
We're out of *milk*.

3. Hesitating

Let's see . . .
Let me see . . .
Let me think . . .

4. Gratitude

Expressing . . .

Thanks.
Thanks very much.
Thank you.
Thank you very much.
Thanks a lot.

Responding to . . .

My pleasure.

VOCABULARY

Food Items

apple
avocado
banana
beef
  ground beef
bread
  white bread
butter
cheese
  Swiss cheese
coffee
egg
green pepper
ice cream
  chocolate ice cream
lemon
lettuce
mayonnaise
milk
mineral water
onion
orange
orange juice
peanut butter
potato
rice
soda
  orange soda
sugar
tuna fish
yogurt

Food Units

bag
bottle
box
bunch
can
container
dozen
gallon
half a dozen
half a pound
half gallon
head
jar
liter
loaf–loaves
pint
pound
quart
six-pack
stick

COMMENTARY

1. "Could you do me a favor?" (line 1) is used to politely signal a request.

2. When Speaker B replies, "Sure. What is it?," he is telling Speaker A to go ahead.

3. "Run over to" in line 3 means "go to" and implies that it is not very far and that it's an easy task. By using this expression, Speaker A is minimizing the favor that he is asking.

4. "Pick up" (line 5) means "get" or "buy."

5. Shortened questions and answers, such as "How much?" (line 6) and "A small bag" (line 7), are common in everyday conversation.

6. "Let's see . . . " (line 9) indicates hesitating in order to think.

7. "We're out of milk" (line 11) means "We don't have any more milk."

8. "Is that everything?" (line 14) means "Is that everything I should get at the supermarket?"

GETTING READY

1. Use *ExpressWays Picture Cards* 59–77 and 190–197 or your own visuals to review food vocabulary. Practice naming the foods. For count nouns, such as *apples* and *bananas,* have students say the singular and plural forms. For non-count nouns, such as *beef* and *bread,* have students say a food unit (partitive) expression — for example: "apple"—"apples," "milk"—"a gallon of milk."

2. Practice *much* and *many.*

   a. Write on the board:

   > How much _____ do you want?
   >
   > How many _____ do you want?

   b. Have the class listen as you name different foods from the vocabulary list. Call on a student to form the correct sentence, and then have the class repeat. For example:

   "butter" (How much butter do you want?)
   "eggs" (How many eggs do you want?)

3. Read the following incomplete sentences, or write them on cue cards and have students read them. Have the class provide one or more correct food items to finish each sentence. Examples:

   I have a bag of _____. (*cookies, crackers, lemons, apples, potatoes, rice*)

   I need a box of _____. (*rice, crackers, sugar, raisins*)

   Where did I put the can of _____? (*coffee, tuna fish, soup, tomatoes*)

   Please get a half gallon of _____. (*milk, orange juice*)

   Here's a head of _____. (*lettuce, cabbage*)

   I need a loaf of _____. (*bread, white bread*)

This is a pound of _____. (*butter, margarine, beef, cheese, coffee*)

Can you give me a pint of _____? (*milk, ice cream*)

I want a jar of _____. (*peanut butter, jelly, jam, mayonnaise*)

Did you get a quart of _____? (*milk, orange juice*)

THE MODEL CONVERSATION

1. **Setting the Scene.** Have students look at the model illustration. Set the scene: "A father is asking his son to buy a few things at the store."

2. **Listening to the Model.** With books closed, have students listen to the model conversation — presented by you, by a pair of students, or on the audiotape.

3. **Class Practice.** With books still closed, model each line and have the whole class repeat in unison.

4. **Reading.** With books open, have students follow along as two students present the model. Ask students if they have any questions and check understanding of vocabulary.

5. **Pair Practice.** In pairs, have students practice the model conversation.

6. **Alternative Expressions.** Present to the class each sentence of the dialog containing a footnoted expression. Call on different students to present the same sentence, but replacing the footnoted expression with its alternatives. (You can cue students to do this quickly by asking, "What's another way of saying that?" or "How else could he/she/you say that?")

THE EXERCISES

Examples

1. A. Could you do me a favor?
   B. Sure. What is it?
   A. Could you run over to the store? We need a few things.
   B. All right. What do you want me to get?
   A. Well, could you pick up some peanut butter?
   B. Okay. How much?
   A. A big jar. I guess we also need a few potatoes.
   B. How many?
   A. Let's see . . . How about three?

   B. Anything else?
   A. Yes. We're out of orange juice.
   B. Okay. How much do you want me to get?
   A. I think one quart will be enough.
   B. Is that everything?
   A. I think so.
   B. Okay. So that's a big jar of peanut butter, three potatoes, and one quart of orange juice.
   A. That's right. Thanks. I really appreciate it.
   B. My pleasure.

2. A. Could you do me a favor?
   B. Certainly. What is it?
   A. Could you run over to the store? We need a few things.
   B. Okay. What do you want me to get?
   A. Well, could you pick up some coffee?
   B. Okay. How much?
   A. A pound. I guess we also need a few eggs.
   B. How many?
   A. Let me see . . . How about half a dozen?
   B. Anything else?
   A. Yes. We're out of chocolate ice cream.
   B. Okay. How much do you want me to get?
   A. I think one pint will be enough.
   B. Is that everything?
   A. I think so.
   B. Okay. So that's a pound of coffee, half a dozen eggs, and a pint of chocolate ice cream.
   A. That's right. Thanks very much. I really appreciate it.
   B. My pleasure.

Before doing each exercise, check students' understanding of the vocabulary and introduce any unfamiliar words or phrases.

Exercise Practice (optional). Have pairs of students simultaneously practice all the exercises.

Exercise Presentations. Call on pairs of students to present the exercises.

Language Note

Exercise 6: "Six-pack" refers to a package of six items, most often soda or juice.

ORIGINAL STUDENT CONVERSATIONS

Have pairs of students create and present original conversations based on the model. (You may want students to prepare their original conversations as homework, then practice them the next day with another student and present them to the class.)

EXPANSION

1. Quantities of Food

a. On separate cards, write out the names of different food items you have introduced in class. Give each student one card.

b. Call out a category, such as: *a pound of, a gallon of, a box of, a jar of.*

c. Have all the students whose food can be measured in that category go to the left side of the room and then call out their foods.

2. Fill That Container!

Call out the name of a container or quantity and have students repeat it, adding an appropriate noun. For example:

Teacher: jar
Student: a jar of mustard

Teacher: quart
Student: a quart of milk

This activity can also be done as a game with competing teams.

3. Chain Game: We Need to Pick Up . . .

a. Begin the game by saying, "We need to pick up a few things from the supermarket. We need a loaf of bread."

b. The first student repeats what you said and adds another item. For example: "We need a loaf of bread and a bottle of ketchup."

c. Continue around the room in this fashion, with each student repeating what the previous one said and adding another item.

d. Play the game again, beginning and ending with different students.

If the class is large, you can divide students into groups to give students more container and quantity practice.

4. Identifying Foods and Prices

Bring a variety of foods and/or empty food containers (cereal boxes, cans, or jars) to class. Arrange the containers on a desk or shelf.

a. Have each student create a *shopping list* of four or five of the items on display.

b. Have students take turns *shopping* (finding and collecting the items) as a classmate reads his or her shopping list aloud. Replace the items before each turn.

c. Use the containers to practice locating and reading the prices that are marked on them. Create math problems based on the containers. For example: "You need a box of cereal, two cans of tuna fish, and a can of soup. How much will it cost?" Write the problems on the board, and have students work in small groups to solve them.

5. Estimating Quantities

Present situations such as those below, and have the class estimate quantities of food needed. Encourage students to explain their estimates.

a. There will be a party for six people at Fran's house tonight. Fran wants to have ice cream for dessert. How much does she need?

b. My neighbor's daughter is getting married. There will be fifty people at the wedding reception. They're going to serve orange juice punch. How many oranges or cans of frozen orange juice do they need?

c. Bill is having a cookout in his backyard tonight. He's going to cook chicken on the grill for fifteen people. How much chicken should he buy?

d. Mrs. Martinetti is preparing a spaghetti dinner. She wants to serve salad before the meal. There are five people in Mrs. Martinetti's family, and she has invited seven guests. How much salad should she make? How many cucumbers, tomatoes, and heads of lettuce does she need?

6. What Did You Buy at the Supermarket?

In pairs or in small groups, have students tell what they bought the last time they went to a supermarket. Make sure they specify a container or quantity with each item.

7. Name the Dish

a. Divide the class into groups.

b. Have each group think of a dish to prepare and make a list of foods they would need to buy.

c. Have students take turns reading their group's shopping list as others listen and guess the dish. For example:

> a dozen eggs
> an onion
> a pint of milk
> a pound of mushrooms
> half a pound of cheese
>
> [*Answer: a mushroom, cheese, and onion omelet*]

8. *What Do We Need?*

a. Divide the class into several groups.

b. Call out the name of a dish, and have each group tell you what you need to buy in order to make that dish. For example:

> "tuna fish sandwiches"

c. Compare the different groups' suggestions.

> [*possible ingredients*]
> a loaf of bread
> a can of tuna fish
> a jar of mayonnaise

Shopping Lists

Have students do the activity individually, in pairs, or as a class. You may want to assign this exercise as homework.

Students can decide on the amounts of each item. The following is a list of the foods and their corresponding *containers*.

1. can of tuna fish
   bag of potato chips
   box of crackers
   pound of cheese
   liter/gallon of mineral water

2. loaf of bread
   bunch/pound of grapes
   six-pack of soda
   jar of mayonnaise
   stick/pound of butter

3. gallon of milk
   jar of peanut butter
   loaf of white bread
   tube of toothpaste
   box/bag of cookies

4. dozen eggs
   pound/bag of sugar
   gallon of vanilla ice cream
   pound/container of margarine
   container of yogurt

Fill It In!

Have students do the activity individually, in pairs, or as a class. You may want to assign this exercise as homework.

1. a few
2. a few
3. some
4. some
5. much
6. some
7. a
8. some
9. a few
10. a few
11. some
12. a few

Listen

Listen and complete the sentence.

1. I need a dozen . . .
2. Could you pick up a quart of . . . ?
3. We have to get a jar of . . .
4. Did you get a tube of . . . ?
5. Can you do me a favor and get a box of . . . ?
6. I've got to get a head of . . .
7. I need a stick of . . .
8. Could you buy a few . . . ?

Answers

1. a		5. b	
2. b		6. a	
3. b		7. a	
4. b		8. a	

FOCUS

TOPIC

Supermarket: Locating Items

GRAMMAR

Count/Non-Count Nouns

Count

Lamb chop**s**?
They're in the Frozen Food Section.

Non-Count

Yogurt?
It's in the Dairy Section.

FUNCTIONS

1. **Attracting Attention**

   Excuse me.
   Pardon me.

2. **Directions-Location**

   Inquiring about Location
   Where can I find *yogurt*?

3. **Checking and Indicating Understanding**

   Checking One's Own Understanding

   Did you say ⎫
   Was that ⎬ *Aisle D?*

4. **Correcting**

   No. *"B."*

5. **Gratitude**

   Expressing . . .
   Thanks very much.

   Responding to . . .
   You're welcome.
   My pleasure.
   Any time.

VOCABULARY

Food Items

apple cider
lamb chop
taco shell
yogurt

COMMENTARY

1. Supermarkets in the United States organize food into large sections, such as "Dairy," "Meat," "Produce," and "Frozen Foods." Most supermarkets have aisles of canned or packaged goods that are designated by a number or letter. Each aisle has a sign listing the types of food located there.

2. "I'm sorry" in line 3 is a polite way of prefacing Speaker A's question.

3. In line 5, Speaker A says "Oh" to indicate that he has understood.

GETTING READY

Have students practice listening discrimination and pronunciation of similar sounds.

a. Write the following pairs of similar sounding letters and numbers on the board:

1	2
A	H
N	M
17	70
3	C
4	40
14	40
H	8
J	A
Q	U

b. Point to a pair and say just one of the numbers or letters.

c. Ask students to respond "1" if they heard you say the item in column 1, and "2" if they heard you say the number or letter in column 2.

d. Have the class practice saying the letters and numbers chorally and individually.

e. Have students take turns testing the class's listening skills as you did in step b.

THE MODEL CONVERSATION

1. **Setting the Scene.** Have students look at the model illustration. Set the scene: "A customer is talking to a clerk in the supermarket."

2. **Listening to the Model.** With books closed, have students listen to the model conversation — presented by you, by a pair of students, or on the audiotape.

3. **Class Practice.** With books still closed, model each line and have the whole class repeat in unison.

4. **Reading.** With books open, have students follow along as two students present the model. Ask students if they have any questions and check understanding of vocabulary.

5. **Pair Practice**. In pairs, have students practice the model conversation.

6. **Alternative Expressions.** Present to the class each sentence of the dialog containing a footnoted expression. Call on different students to present the same sentence, but replacing the footnoted expression with its alternative. (You can cue students to do this quickly by asking, "What's another way of saying that?" or "How else could he/she/you say that?")

THE EXERCISES

Examples

1. A. Excuse me. Where can I find lamb chops?
   B. Lamb chops? They're in the Frozen Food Section, Aisle J.
   A. I'm sorry. Did you say Aisle A?
   B. No. "J."
   A. Oh. Thanks very much.
   B. You're welcome.

2. A. Pardon me. Where can I find apple cider?

   B. Apple cider? It's in the Produce Section, Aisle M.

   A. I'm sorry. Was that Aisle N?

   B. No. "M."

   A. Oh. Thanks very much.

   B. My pleasure.

Before doing each exercise, check students' understanding of the vocabulary and introduce any unfamiliar words or phrases. Have students use the footnoted expressions or any of their alternatives as they do the exercises.

Exercise Practice (optional). Have pairs of students simultaneously practice all the exercises.

Exercise Presentations. Call on pairs of students to present the exercises.

ORIGINAL STUDENT CONVERSATIONS

Have pairs of students create and present original conversations based on the model. (You may want students to prepare their original conversations as homework, then practice them the next day with another student and present them to the class.)

EXPANSION

1. Categorize It!

a. Make one or more sets of cue cards by writing the names of a variety of different foods and household items on cards or strips of paper.

b. Have the class or small groups sort the cards into logical groups and discuss in which sections of the supermarket they would find the items.

2. Dictating Lists

Have each student write a shopping list of 8 to 10 items and then dictate the list to a partner. Have partners compare their lists for accuracy and spelling.

3. Food Spelling

a. Divide the class into large groups. Have each group sit in a circle.

b. Whisper the spelling of a long food word to one student. For example:

   "C-H-O-C-O-L-A-T-E I-C-E C-R-E-A-M"

c. The first student whispers the spelling to the second student, and so forth around the circle. The student listening may ask for clarification by saying,

   "I'm sorry. Did you say 'E'?"

d. When the message gets to the last student, that person says it aloud. Is it the same spelling you started with? The group with the most accurate spelling wins.

4. Kinds of Food

a. On separate cards, write out the names of different supermarket items you have introduced in class. Give each student one card.

b. Call out a category, such as: *diary, meat, produce, household supplies, imported foods, frozen foods, snack foods.*

c. Have all the students whose supermarket item belongs to that category go to the left side of the room and then call out their words.

5. Association Game

a. Divide the class into several teams.

b. Call out a category such as in Exercise 4 above.

c. Have the students in each group work together to see how many supermarket items they can associate with that category. For example:

   dairy: skim milk/ice cream/chocolate milk/cheese/yogurt

d. The team with the most items wins.

6. Supermarket Knowledge Contest

a. Brainstorm with students the names of all the different sections in a supermarket. Write their ideas on the board.

b. Prepare questions about the location of various items in a supermarket. For example:

   Where can I find yogurt?
   Where can I find napkins?
   Where can I find soy sauce?
   Where can I find ice cream?

c. Divide the class into groups and have the groups take turns answering your questions. The group that gives the most correct answer wins.

Variation: Have students write the questions for the game.

7. *Store Design*

Today's stores are designed to encourage shoppers to buy more. This activity gets students to think about how stores display their products so that shoppers will buy them.

a. Have students draw a map of the supermarket they use most often.

b. Have pairs or small groups of students discuss the similarities and differences of the supermarket designs. Also have them discuss the following questions:

> Where are sale items placed?
> What is the quality of products that are placed on the higher shelves?
> What is the quality of products that are placed on the lower shelves?
> Where are the frozen foods located? How is that location convenient for shoppers?
> What kinds of items are next to the cashier? Why are these items placed there?
> Where are sweets and cakes displayed?
> How is produce displayed?
> Are the shelves ever empty? Why not?

c. Have the groups share their ideas with the class.

Match and Practice

Have students do the activity individually, in pairs, or as a class. You may want to assign this exercise as homework.

1. c
2. a
3. e
4. b
5. f
6. d

Then have students practice conversations based on the conversational model below the exercise.

Listen

Listen and choose the letter or number you hear.

1. Excuse me. Did you say Aisle 3?
2. Sorry. Did you say H Street?
3. Is this Aisle J?
4. You can find it in Aisle 8.
5. Do you spell that with a D?
6. I'm sorry. I said G.
7. We need fourteen.
8. Pardon me. Is this N Street?
9. What number is this? Seventy?
10. Sorry. Did you say Aisle F?

Answers

1. a
2. b
3. b
4. a
5. b
6. a
7. b
8. b
9. a
10. b

Community Connections

Have students do the activity individually, in pairs, or in small groups and then report back to the class.

FOCUS

TOPICS

Supermarket: Purchasing Items
Money: Paying for Goods and Services

GRAMMAR

Count/Non-Count Nouns

Count

The **vitamins** were six ninety-four.

Non-Count

The **skim milk** was a dollar seventeen.

FUNCTIONS

1. **Surprise–Disbelief**

   Twelve dollars and forty-nine cents?!

   How about that!
   How do you like that!
   Isn't that something!

   It's amazing *how little you can buy*!

2. **Certainty/Uncertainty**

   Inquiring about Certainty

   Are you sure that's right?

3. **Agreement/Disagreement**

   Expressing Agreement

   You're right.
   That's true.
   [*less formal*]
   I'll say!
   You can say THAT again!

VOCABULARY

Food Items

artichokes	garlic	potato chips
baked beans	hot dogs	pretzels
bean sprouts	ice cream	prunes
cat food	mushrooms	skim milk
coffee	mustard	soda
cookies	pie	diet soda
chocolate	apple pie	spaghetti
chip cookies	popcorn	tea
crackers	potatoes	vitamins

COMMENTARY

1. The cashier has just finished ringing up the total amount of the purchase on the cash register. By saying "Okay," he is attracting the customer's attention before he announces the price.

2. In line 3, Speaker B repeats the total price with a question intonation: "Twelve dollars and forty-nine cents!?" This intonation is a way of expressing surprise. She wants to check the accuracy of this figure, so she asks the cashier, "Are you sure that's right?" She expresses doubt about the amount by saying, "That seems a little high to me." In general, it is considered appropriate for customers to request clarification and check accuracy of prices when they have a question.

3. In line 7, Speaker A is using the short way of reading the numbers. He reads the dollar number and then the cents number, as in "six ninety-four." When the price is one dollar and some cents, he says "a dollar _____" as in lines 7–8, "a dollar seventeen."

GETTING READY

Practice reading prices.

a. Write a variety of prices on the board. For example:

$1.19	$6.49	$54.22
$2.21	$12.50	$78.14
$1.17	$29.99	$82.55
$1.86	$67.36	$99.99

b. Point out that amounts beginning with the number 1 can be read *a* or *one*. For example:

   $1.19—"one dollar and nineteen cents" or "a dollar and nineteen cents"
   $100—"one hundred dollars" or "a hundred dollars"

c. Practice reading the prices using full forms. For example:

   $2.21—"two dollars and twenty-one cents"
   $1.17—"one/a dollar and seventeen cents"

d. Practice reading the prices using reduced forms. For example:

   $2.21—"two twenty-one"
   $1.17—"one seventeen" or "a dollar seventeen"

e. Dictate several prices to the class, and then have each student dictate one price to the class. Write the prices on the board, and have students check their answers.

THE MODEL CONVERSATION

1. **Setting the Scene.** Have students look at the model illustration. Set the scene: "A cashier and customer are talking in a supermarket. The customer is very surprised at the total price of the groceries."

2. **Listening to the Model.** With books closed, have students listen to the model conversation — presented by you, by a pair of students, or on the audiotape.

3. **Class Practice.** With books still closed, model each line and have the whole class repeat in unison.

4. **Reading.** With books open, have students follow along as two students present the model. Ask students if they have any questions, and check understanding of vocabulary.

Culture Note

"Diet soda" (line 9) is a soft drink sweetened with an artificial sweetener. The prevalence of diet soda and diet food in the United States reflects the national obsession with dieting.

5. **Pair Practice.** In pairs, have students practice the model conversation.

6. **Alternative Expressions.** Present to the class each sentence of the dialog containing a footnoted expression. Call on different students to present the same sentence, but replacing the footnoted expression with its alternatives. (You can cue students to do this quickly by asking, "What's another way of saying that?" or "How else could he/she/you say that?")

THE EXERCISES

Examples

1. A. Okay. That comes to thirteen dollars and thirty-seven cents.
   B. Thirteen dollars and thirty-seven cents?! Are you sure that's right? That seems a little high to me.
   A. Well, let's see. The hot dogs were six dollars. The baked beans were a dollar eighty-nine. The mustard was

was ninety-eight cents. And the apple pie was four fifty. That comes to a total of thirteen dollars and thirty-seven cents.

B. Hmm. How about that! It's amazing how little you can buy these days for thirteen dollars and thirty-seven cents!

A. You're right.

2. A. Okay. That comes to eleven dollars and ninety-three cents.

B. Eleven dollars and ninety-three cents!? Are you sure that's right? That seems a little high to me.

A. Well, let's see. The pretzels were a dollar fifty-eight. The potato chips were ninety-nine cents. The popcorn was a dollar thirty-eight. And the soda was seven ninety-eight. That comes to a total of eleven dollars and ninety-three cents.

B. Hmm. How do you like that! It's amazing how little you can buy these days for eleven dollars and ninety-three cents!

A. That's true.

Before doing each exercise, check students' understanding of the vocabulary and introduce any unfamiliar words or phrases. Have students use the footnoted expressions or any of their alternatives as they do the exercises.

Exercise Practice (optional). Have pairs of students simultaneously practice all the exercises.

Exercise Presentations. Call on pairs of students to present the exercises.

ORIGINAL STUDENT CONVERSATIONS

Have pairs of students create and present original conversations based on the model. (You may want students to prepare their original conversations as homework, then practice them the next day with another student and present them to the class.)

EXPANSION

1. Reading Supermarket Receipts

Have students practice reading the information on supermarket receipts. (Some receipts, produced by electronic cash registers, now include the name of the item, the quantity, and the unit price.)

a. Collect several supermarket receipts. Number them and make copies for the class.

b. Create a questionnaire or ask students questions they can answer based on the receipts, such as, "What was the total price?" "How many things did the customer buy?" "What did the customer buy?" "What was the date of purchase?" Have students work in pairs or small groups to answer the questions.

2. Reading Newspaper Advertisements for Sales and Specials

a. Make copies of supermarket ads from the newspaper.

b. On the board, write a list of 10 food items that are prominently advertised as being on sale.

c. Divide the class into small groups and give each group a copy of supermarket ads from two or more stores. Ask students to work together to locate the food items in the ads and decide which store they should go to to buy them. Have students make a chart to compare the prices. For example:

	Supermarket A	Supermarket B	Supermarket C
Item	$	$	$
Item			
Item			

d. As a class, discuss which supermarket offers the best prices in general.

3. Class Discussion: Unit Pricing

a. Bring in examples of food labels that include unit pricing information, or write the following on the board:

```
Swiss cheese

You pay:      Unit Price:
$1.46         $4.75 per pound
```

```
1 qt. milk

You pay:      Unit Price:
$1.05         $4.20/gal.
```

veal	Sell by MAR 12
price per pound $1.85 price	total price $1.58

b. Discuss unit pricing with students, using these examples. Ask:

> How much does the item cost per pound/gallon/ . . . ?
> What is the actual price of the item?

c. If you wish, discuss with students how it is usually more economical to buy food products in larger sizes.

4. More for Your Money

a. Bring to class a variety of supermarket advertisements.

b. Divide the class into pairs or small groups and distribute the supermarket ads.

c. Tell the groups that they must feed a family of four a healthy diet for one week for as little money as possible. Have each group write a grocery list with food items that are both economical and nutritious.

d. Have groups present their plans to the class.

5. What's the Price?

a. Bring in pictures of food items from newspaper advertisements and fliers. Delete the prices.

b. Divide the class into two teams.

c. Show the class an advertisement for a food item, and have both teams guess the price.

d. The team with the guess closest to the actual price wins a point.

e. The team with the most points wins the game.

6. My Favorite Places to Shop

a. Divide the class into groups.

b. Have the groups discuss and then write down the three best places to buy groceries. In making their decision, tell students to consider the following:

> the prices
> the variety of products
> the freshness of produce and meats
> the quality of the food
> the service
> the organization of the store
> the lighting and cleanliness
> the variety of services available (for example — bank machine, flowers, film developing)

c. Have the groups compare their lists and compile a final class list of recommendations.

Listen

What prices do you hear?

1. That comes to thirteen dollars and fifteen cents.
2. The total is eighteen dollars and ten cents.
3. Your change is seven dollars and forty cents.
4. It's hard to believe how little you can buy for sixteen dollars and forty-three cents.
5. Fifteen dollars and seventy-six cents? That's unbelievable!
6. How about that! It's only thirty dollars and fifty-eight cents.
7. That'll be twenty-two dollars and eleven cents.
8. Nineteen dollars and eighty-eight cents, please.
9. Nine dollars and ninety-eight cents? That's cheap!

Answers

1. b	4. a	7. a
2. b	5. b	8. b
3. b	6. a	9. a

CrossTalk

Have students first work in pairs and then share with the class what they talked about.

Comparison Shopping

Have students do their price estimates and supermarket investigations in groups. Then have them report their findings to the class.

FOCUS

TOPICS

Food: Describing Food
Social Communication: Compliments

GRAMMAR

1. **Count/Non-Count Nouns**

    Count

    These are delicious! What **are they**?
    They're enchiladas.
    What's in **them**?
    A few tomato**es**.

    Non-Count

    This is excellent! What **is it**?
    It's borscht.
    What's in **it**?
    A little sour cream.

2. **Adjectives**

    These are **delicious**!
    They're a **popular Mexican** dish.

3. **Pronoun Review**

    What are **they**?
    They're enchiladas.
    What's in **them**?

    What is **it**?
    It's borscht.
    What's in **it**?

FUNCTIONS

1. **Complimenting**

    Expressing Compliments
    Mmm!

    This is/These are { delicious!
    excellent!
    wonderful!
    superb!
    fantastic! }

2. **Checking and Indicating Understanding**

    Checking One's Own Understanding
    Enchiladas?

3. **Describing**

    They're *a popular Mexican dish.*

4. **Hesitating**

    Let's see . . .
    Let me see . . .
    Let me think . . .

VOCABULARY

Describing	Food Items		Nationalities
delicious	bean sprouts	enchiladas	mushrooms	American
difficult	beets	flour	onions	Chinese
excellent	borscht	ground beef	pork	Greek
fantastic	cabbage	manicotti	sour cream	Italian
superb	cheese	milk	tomato sauce	Mexican
wonderful	egg rolls	moussaka	waffles	Russian
	eggplants	M.S.G.	water	
	eggs			

COMMENTARY

1. "Mmm" is an appreciative sound. Speaker A is enjoying food she has never eaten before.

2. In line 7, as Speaker B is naming the ingredients, she pauses, saying "and . . . uh," and then names one last item, "oh yes, a little ground beef."

GETTING READY

If possible, bring a homemade cake or bread to share with the class.

a. Have students taste it and then try to guess what the ingredients are.

b. Write their guesses on the board, and then tell what the real ingredients are. When you tell the ingredients, use the expressions *a little* (for non-count nouns such as *flour*) and *a few* (for count nouns such as *eggs*).

c. Review count and non-count nouns by pointing to the ingredients listed on the board and asking the class "A little?" or "A few?" and having them choose the correct expression.

THE MODEL CONVERSATION

1. **Setting the Scene.** Have students look at the model illustration. Set the scene: "A woman is eating dinner at the home of a friend."

2. **Listening to the Model.** With books closed, have students listen to the model conversation — presented by you, by a pair of students, or on the audiotape.

3. **Class Practice.** With books still closed, model each line and have the whole class repeat in unison.

4. **Reading.** With books open, have students follow along as two students present the model. Ask students if they have any questions and check understanding of vocabulary.

5. **Pair Practice.** In pairs, have students practice the model conversation.

6. **Alternative Expressions.** Present to the class each sentence of the dialog containing a footnoted expression. Call on different students to present the same sentence, but replacing the footnoted expression with its alternatives. (You can cue students to do this quickly by asking, "What's another way of saying that?" or "How else could he/she/you say that?")

THE EXERCISES

Examples

1. A. Mmm! This is excellent! What is it?
   B. It's borscht.
   A. Borscht?
   B. Yes. It's a popular Russian dish.
   A. Well, wonderful! What's in it?
   B. Let's see . . . a little water, a few beets, a little sour cream, and . . . uh, oh yes, a few onions.
   A. Is it difficult to make?
   B. No, not at all. I'll be happy to give you the recipe.
   A. Thanks.

2. A. Mmm! These are wonderful! What are they?
   B. They're waffles.
   A. Waffles?
   B. Yes. They're a popular American dish.
   A. Well, they're superb! What's in them?

> B. Let me see . . . a little flour, a little water, a few eggs, and . . . uh, oh yes, a little milk.
> A. Are they difficult to make?
> B. No, not at all. I'll be happy to give you the recipe.
> A. Thanks.

Before doing each exercise, check students' understanding of the vocabulary and introduce any unfamiliar words or phrases. Have students use the footnoted expressions or any of their alternatives as they do the exercises.

Culture Note

Exercise 5: Monosodium Glutamate is a flavor enhancer that is commonly used in Chinese restaurant food. Since many people are allergic to this additive, restaurant menus often specify which dishes have it as an ingredient.

Exercise Practice (optional). Have pairs of students simultaneously practice all the exercises.

Exercise Presentations. Call on pairs of students to present the exercises.

ORIGINAL STUDENT CONVERSATIONS

Have pairs of students create an present original conversations based on the model. (You may want students to prepare their original conversations as homework, then practice them the next day with another student and present them to the class.)

EXPANSION

1. Expert Tasters

   a. Bring to class various prepared or processed foods. For example:

   a candy bar
   macaroni salad
   fruit punch
   sesame sticks
   muffins
   cole slaw
   pretzels

   b. Have groups of students sample the foods and try to guess the ingredients.

   c. Have the groups share their ideas with the class.

2. An Imaginary Potluck Supper

The *pot luck* supper is a U.S. tradition. Friends or members of an organization (church, club, volunteer group, or school group) may celebrate an occasion by having a dinner party to which each person brings a food of his or her choice.

   a. Have your students create an imaginary pot luck supper by writing the name of a favorite dish on a card.

   b. Collect the cards and put them into a box.

   c. Have students draw cards from the box, make a comment about how good that particular dish is, and ask who made it. The student who wrote that dish on the card should then explain the recipe.

   d. If possible, have a real pot luck supper or lunch. Have students prepare a favorite dish to share with other students. During the meal, have students make comments about the food and exchange recipes.

3. Name the Dish

   a. Divide the class into groups.

   b. Have each group think of a common dish and make a list of its ingredients.

   c. Have students read their list of ingredients to the class as everyone listens and tries to guess the dish. For example:

   some ground beef
   a few spices
   some bread crumbs
   a few eggs

   [*Answer: meat loaf*]

4. Class Investigation: Food Ingredients

   a. Bring some food packages to class and show students how to read ingredient lists on the side of the package. Explain that ingredients are listed in order of their quantity.

   b. Have students visit food stores individually or in pairs and identify five foods that have healthy ingredients.

   c. Have students make a list of the ingredients of these foods and report their findings to the class.

ExpressWays

Have students do the activity individually, in pairs, or as a class. You may want to assign this exercise as homework.

1. it	8. them
2. A few	9. a little
3. a little	10. a little
4. a little	11. a few
5. a few	12. a little
6. a little	13. a few
7. a little	14. a little

Listen

Listen and decide what the people are talking about.

1. These aren't difficult to make.
2. It's really delicious!
3. I think it's really convenient.
4. It has a brand new kitchen.
5. It's very complicated.
6. It's within walking distance of the school.

Answers

1. a
2. a
3. b
4. a
5. a
6. a

CrossTalk

Have students first work in pairs and then share with the class what they talked about.

FOCUS

TOPIC

Food: Recipes

GRAMMAR

1. **Imperatives**

   First, **mix** together . . .
   Then **add** . . .
   Next, **put** the mixture into a greased
   baking pan.
   After that, **bake** an hour and fifteen
   minutes at 350 degrees.

2. **Partitives**

   a cup of bread crumbs
   half a cup of milk
   two pounds of ground beef
   two teaspoons of salt

FUNCTIONS

1. **Complimenting**

   Expressing Compliments

   Your _____ was/were *delicious!*
   It was/They were *excellent!*

   Responding to Compliments

   Oh, did you really like it/them?

   Thank you for saying so.

2. **Requests**

   Direct, Polite

   Could I ask you *for the recipe?*

   Responding to Requests

   Sure.

3. **Instructing**

   First, . . .
   Then . . .
   Next, . . .
   After that, . . .

4. **Checking and Indicating Understanding**

   Checking Another Person's Understanding

   Are you with me so far?

   Indicating Understanding

   I'm with you.
   Now I've got it.

5. **Asking for Repetition**

   I didn't get the last step.

   Could you repeat that part?

6. **Gratitude**

   Expressing . . .

   Thanks very much.

   Responding to . . .

   My pleasure.

VOCABULARY

Food Items	Food Units	Recipes
bread crumbs	cup	add
ground beef	half a cup	bake
meat loaf	teaspoon	baking pan
milk		350 degrees
salt		greased
		mix together
		mixture

COMMENTARY

1. In line 12, Speaker A interrupts Speaker B ("Wait a minute!") because she didn't understand the previous direction.

2. In line 14, Speaker A asks "Is that it?," meaning "Is that all (of the recipe)?"

3. "That's it!" (line 15) signals that a task is completed. Speaker B indicates that she has explained the whole recipe.

GETTING READY

1. Bring a variety of packaged foods to class. Have students read the package labels to find the ingredients and the quantity and/or weight of the contents.

2. Discuss the different ways of measuring liquid and dry ingredients for a recipe. If possible, bring measuring spoons and cups to class. Have students identify a teaspoon and a tablespoon and read the marks on a measuring cup (1/4 — one fourth, 1/3 — one third, 1/2 — one half, 2/3 — two thirds, and 3/4 — three fourths).

THE MODEL CONVERSATION

1. **Setting the Scene.** Have students look at the model illustration. Set the scene: "A mother is having dinner at her daughter's house. She really enjoyed the dinner, and she's asking for a recipe."

2. **Listening to the Model.** With books closed, have students listen to the model conversation — presented by you, by a pair of students, or on the audiotape.

3. **Class Practice.** With books still closed, model each line and have the whole class repeat in unison.

4. **Reading.** With books open, have students follow along as two students present the model. Ask students if they have any questions and check understanding of vocabulary.

5. **Pair Practice.** In pairs, have students practice the model conversation.

Now have pairs of students create and present original conversations using the model dialog as a guide. Encourage students to be inventive and to use new vocabulary. (You may want to assign this exercise as homework, having students prepare their original conversations, practice them the next day with another student, and then present them to the class.) Students should present their conversations without referring to the written text, but they also should not memorize them. Rather, they should feel free to adapt and expand them any way they wish.

Your Turn

Have students write out their favorite recipe and then share it with the class. If you wish, you can collect all the recipes and *publish* a book of *Favorite Recipes* and distribute it to the whole class.

Reflections

Have students discuss the questions in pairs or small groups and then share their ideas with the class.

Reading: *Food Markets*

Preview: Have students discuss the following questions:

> Where do you buy your groceries?
> What do you like about the store you use?

Then have students read the passage silently, or have them listen to the passage and take notes as you read it or play the audiotape.

True or False?

Have students do the activity individually, in pairs, or as a class. You may want to assign this exercise as homework.

1. True
2. True
3. False
4. True
5. False

Do You Remember?

Have students do the activity individually, in pairs, or as a class. You may want to assign this exercise as homework.

1. b
2. a
3. b
4. c
5. b
6. a
7. b
8. c

Cultural Intersections

Have students do the activity as a class, in pairs, or in small groups.

Looking Back

Have students look at the list of expressions. Encourage them to ask you any questions about the meaning or pronunciation of any of the words. If students ask for the pronunciation, repeat after the student until the student is satisfied with his or her pronunciation of the word.

Review Activities

To review the language introduced in the unit, do the following activities.

1. Association Game

a. Divide the class into several teams.

b. Call out a topic category from the *Looking Back* section on student text page 74.

c. Have students in each group work together to see how many phrases they can associate with that category. For example:

Expressing Gratitude: Thanks.
Thanks very much.
Thank you.
Thank you very much.

d. The team with the most items wins.

2. Create a Conversation!

a. Divide the class into pairs of students.

b. Tell each pair they have three minutes to make up a conversation using one item from each category from the *Looking Back* section on page 74 of the student text.

c. Have students share their conversations with the class.

EXIT 5

OVERVIEW
Student Text
Pages 75–92

Topics	Functions	Grammar

P. 76 What Position Do You Have Open?

Employment: Applying for a Job	Asking for and Reporting Information Want–Desire Gratitude	Present Perfect Tense

Pp. 78–79 Has Bob Gone to the Bank Yet?

Employment/On the Job: Describing Procedures	Asking for and Reporting Information	Present Perfect Tense Present Perfect vs. Past Tense Time Expressions

P. 82 Have You Ever Flown a 747?

Employment/Getting a Job: Stating Skills and Qualifications Personal Information: Work Experience	Asking for and Reporting Information Certainty/Uncertainty Ability/Inability	Present Perfect Tense Able to Could

P. 84 Have You Given Out the Paychecks Yet?

Employment/On the Job: Making and Fulfilling Requests	Intention Requests Obligation Apologizing	Present Perfect Tense Past Continuous to Express Future Intention

Topics	Functions	Grammar

P. 86   Do You Know How to Use a Word Processor?

Employment/Getting a
   Job: Stating Skills and
   Qualifications
Personal Information:
   Work Experience
	Ability/Inability
	Hesitating
	Checking and Indicating
	   Understanding
	Agreement/Disagreement
		Present Perfect
		   Continuous Tense
		Since/For
		Can
		Able to

P. 88   Can You Tell Me a Little More About the Position?

Employment/Getting a
   Job: Inquiring about
   Job Responsibilities
	Asking for and Reporting
	   Additional Information
	Asking for and Reporting
	   Information
	Ability/Inability
	Certainty/Uncertainty
	Checking and Indicating
	   Understanding
		Present Perfect
		   Continuous Tense
		Present Perfect vs.
		   Past Tense

LOOKING AHEAD

Grammar This Exit

Present Perfect Tense

Have you **written** obituaries
 before?
 Yes, I **have.**

I**'ve written** obituaries in my
 last two jobs.

Has Bob **gone** to the bank yet?
 Yes, he **has.**
 He**'s** already **gone** there.

Has Barbara **spoken** to her
 supervisor yet?
 Yes, she **has.**
 She**'s** already **spoken** to her.

Have you **seen** the top secret
 report yet?
 Yes, we **have.**
 We**'ve** already **seen** it.

Have the employees **worn** their
 new uniforms yet?
 Yes, they **have.**
 They**'ve** already **worn** them.

Have you ever **flown** a 747?
 No, I **haven't.**

Present Perfect vs. Past Tense

While I **haven't done** the
 payroll in my current position,
 I **did** the payroll in the job I
 had before that.

go-went-gone
He**'s** already **gone** there.
He **went** there this morning.

speak-spoke-spoken
She**'s** already **spoken** to her.
She **spoke** to her this afternoon.

see-saw-seen
We**'ve** already **seen** it.
We **saw** it a few minutes ago.

wear-wore-worn
They**'ve** already **worn** them.
They **wore** them today.

do-did-done
He**'s** already **done** them.
He **did** them a little while ago.

give-gave-given
She**'s** already **given** it.
She **gave** it yesterday afternoon.

take-took-taken
They**'ve** already **taken** it.
They **took** it last week.

drive-drove-driven
I**'ve** already **driven** it.
I **drove** it today.

meet-met-met
I**'ve** already **met** her.
I **met** her this morning.

read-read-read
She**'s** already **read** it.
She **read** it last night.

get-got-gotten
They**'ve** already **gotten** them.
They **got** them yesterday.

sing-sang-sung
He**'s** already **sung** it.
He **sang** it a few minutes ago.

eat-ate-eaten
I**'ve** already **eaten** there.
I **ate** there at lunchtime.

write-wrote-written
He**'s** already **written** it.
He **wrote** it an hour ago.

Present Perfect Continuous Tense

I**'ve been using** word
 processors since 1990.

Past Continuous to Express Future Intention

I **was planning** to give them out
 this afternoon.

Able to

I'm confident I'd **be able** to
 learn.

Could

I'm confident I **could** learn.

Can

Can you use a word processor?

Time Expressions

He went there **this morning.**
 this afternoon.
 today.
 yesterday.
 yesterday
 afternoon.
 last night.
 last week.
 the other day.
 a few minutes
 ago.
 an hour ago.
 a little while
 ago.

Asking for and Reporting Information

Have you ever *flown a 747*?
  No, I haven't, but I've *flown a DC-10*.

Can you tell me a little more about *the position*?
Can you tell me anything more about *the position*?
Can you tell me anything else about *the position*?

What would you like to know?

What exactly are the *bookkeeper's* responsibilities?

Has *Bob gone to the bank* yet?
  Yes, he has.
  He's already *gone there*.
  He *went there this morning*.

Has *Barbara spoken to her supervisor* yet?
  Yes, she has.
  She's already *spoken to her*.
  She *spoke to her this afternoon*.

Have you *seen the top secret report* yet?
  Yes, we have.
  We've already *seen it*.
  We *saw it a few minutes ago*.

Have *the employees worn their new uniforms* yet?
  Yes, they have.
  They've already *worn them*.
  They *wore them today*.

What position *do you have open*?

Have you *taken inventory* before?
  Yes, I have.

Asking for and Reporting Additional Information

Can you tell me a little more (about *the position*)?
Can you tell me anything more (about *the position*)?
Can you tell me anything else (about *the position*)?

Ability/Inability

Inquiring about . . .

Do you know how to *use a word processor*?
Can you *use a word processor*?
Are you able to *use a word processor*?

Do you think you'd be able to *handle those responsibilities*?
Do you think you could *handle those responsibilities*?

Expressing Ability

I'm confident I'd be able to *learn*.
I'm confident I could *learn*.

I've been *using word processors* { for *a long time*. / since *1990*. }

Certainty/Uncertainty

Inquiring about . . .

Are you sure about that?
Are you positive about that?
Are you certain about that?
Do you really think so?

Expressing . . .

I'm positive.
I'm sure.
I'm certain.
I'm a hundred percent sure.

Absolutely!
Definitely!
Positively!

Intention

I was planning to *give them out*.
I was going to *give them out*.

I'll *do it* right away.

Requests

Direct, Polite

Please *do it as soon as possible*.
Can you please *do it as soon as possible*?
Will you please *do it as soon as possible*?

Would you please *do it as soon as possible*?
I'd like you to *do it as soon as possible*.

Want–Desire

Expressing . . .

We're looking for *a reporter*.

I'd like to *apply*.

Obligation

The *paychecks* are supposed to *be given out before lunch hour*.

Apologizing

I'm sorry. I didn't know that.
I'm sorry. I didn't realize that.
I'm sorry. I wasn't aware of that.

Checking Understanding

Checking One's Own Understanding

Since *1990*?

Indicating Understanding

I see.

Gratitude

Expressing . . .

Thank you.

Agreement/Disagreement

I guess I do.

Hesitating

Well, let me see . . .

PREVIEWING EXIT 5: CHAPTER-OPENING PHOTOS

Have students talk about the people and the situations and, as a class or in pairs, predict what the characters might be saying to each other. Students in pairs or small groups may enjoy practicing role plays based on these scenes and then presenting them to the class.

----- Text Page 76: What Position Do You Have Open? -----

FOCUS

TOPIC

Employment/On the Job: Applying for a Job

GRAMMAR

Present Perfect Tense

Have you **written** obituaries before?
Yes, I **have.**

I've written obituaries in my last two jobs.

FUNCTIONS

1. **Asking for and Reporting Information**

    What position *do you have open*?

    Have you *taken inventory* before?

2. **Want–Desire**

    Expressing . . .
    We're looking for *a reporter*.

    I'd like to *apply*.

3. **Gratitude**

    Expressing . . .
    Thank you.

VOCABULARY

Getting a Job	Job Procedures and Skills	Occupations
application form	do *engine tune-ups*	assistant chef
apply	drive *a van*	dance instructor
job	give *tango lessons*	delivery person
open (adj.)	make *sandwiches*	mechanic's assistant
position	take inventory	reporter
sign	write *obituaries*	stock clerk

COMMENTARY

1. Many small businesses post signs in their windows to advertise job openings. Jobs advertised this way are usually for entry-level positions, such as clerk, assistant chef, or delivery person.

2. In line 5, Speaker B asks, "Have you ever written obituaries before?" Employers always ask job applicants about their previous work experience.

3. In line 8, Speaker B says, "Okay. Here's an application form." He has decided the applicant is qualified enough to apply for the job.

4. In lines 8–9, Speaker B says, "You can sit over there and fill it out." In entry-level positions, it is customary to complete the application immediately and not take it home to complete it. Often the manager will then review the completed application and set up a time for an interview.

GETTING READY

1. Introduce the employment vocabulary from student text page 76.

   a. Write on the board and go over the meaning of the following work skills:

      > write advertisements
      > take inventory
      > drive a truck
      > give dance lessons
      > do engine tune-ups
      > make salads

   b. Ask students about their ability to do these work skills. For example:

      Teacher: Can you drive a truck?
      Student A: Yes, I can.

      Teacher: Can you do engine tune-ups?
      Student B: No, I can't.

2. Introduce the present perfect tense.

   a. Write the following verb forms on the board:

I write	I wrote	I've written
I take	I took	I've taken
I drive	I drove	I've driven
I give	I gave	I've given
I do	I did	I've done
I make	I made	I've made

   b. Model each verb form and have students repeat after you. For example:

      > I write
      > I wrote
      > I've written
      >
      > I take
      > I took
      > I've taken

   c. Write the following conversational framework on the board:

      > A. Have you _____ before?
      > B. Yes, I have. I've _____ in my last two jobs.

   d. Model conversations with each of the phrases and have students repeat. For example:

      A. Have you written advertisements before?
      B. Yes, I have. I've written advertisements in my last two jobs.

      A. Have you taken inventory before?
      B. Yes, I have. I've taken inventory in my last two jobs.

      A. Have you driven a truck before?
      B. Yes, I have. I've driven a truck in my last two jobs.

e. Tell students that this is their introduction to the present perfect tense. The word after *I've* is called the past participle. Tell them that the past participle is sometimes irregular (as in *I've written, I've taken, I've given*) and sometimes the same as the past tense (as in *I've made, I've worked, I've cooked, I've cleaned*).

THE MODEL CONVERSATION

1. **Set the Scene.** "Someone wants to apply for a job in a newspaper office."
2. **Listen to the Model.**
3. **Class Practice.**
4. **Read.**
5. **Pair Practice.**

THE EXERCISES

Examples

---

1. A. I saw your sign in the window. What position do you have open?
   B. We're looking for a stock clerk.
   A. I'd like to apply.
   B. Have you taken inventory before?
   A. Yes, I have. I've taken inventory in my last two jobs.
   B. Okay. Here's an application form. You can sit over there and fill it out.
   A. Thank you.

2. A. I saw your sign in the window. What position do you have open?
   B. We're looking for a delivery person.
   A. I'd like to apply.
   B. Have you driven a van before?
   A. Yes, I have. I've driven a van in my last two jobs.
   B. Okay. Here's an application form. You can sit over there and fill it out.
   A. Thank you.

Before doing each exercise, check students' understanding of the vocabulary and introduce any unfamiliar words or phrases.

Culture Note

Exercise 1: To "take inventory" is to review what merchandise has and has not been sold.

Exercise Practice (optional). Have pairs of students simultaneously practice all the exercises.

Exercise Presentations. Call on pairs of students to present the exercises.

ORIGINAL STUDENT CONVERSATIONS

Have pairs of students create and present original conversations based on the model. (You may want students to prepare their original conversations as homework, then practice them the next day with another student and present them to the class.)

EXPANSION

1. Pair Interviews

a. Divide the class into pairs.

b. Have students interview each other about their work experience.

c. Have the pairs report back to the class.

2. Find Someone Who . . .

a. Collect some information about students' work experience.

b. Put this information in the following form:

Find a classmate who has done the following:

1. work as a waiter
   Have you _____ before?
   Name: _____

2. take inventory
   Have you _____ before?
   Name: _____

3. write articles for a newspaper
   Have you _____ before?
   Name: _____

4. give math lessons
   Have you _____ before?
   Name: _____

5. drive a truck
   Have you _____ before?
   Name: _____

---

c. Have students write out the correct questions and then circulate around the room asking each other the questions to identify the above people.

d. The first student to identify all the people correctly wins.

3. Mystery Job Interviews

a. Divide the class into pairs.

b. Have students write a conversation between a manager and a job applicant. Tell them NOT to mention the name of the position.

c. Have students take turns presenting their conversations. The class must listen and guess the position. For example:

    A. Have you used a cash register before?
    B. Yes, I have. I've used a cash register in my last two jobs.
    A. Have you taken inventory before?
    B. Yes, I have. I've taken inventory in my last two jobs.
    A. Have you closed up shop before?
    B. Yes, I have. I closed up shop in my last job.
    A. Finally, have you supervised other clerks?
    B. Yes, I have. I've supervised two other clerks.
    A. Great! You've got the job!

[*shop manager*]

4. Guess the Job!

a. Write each of the following occupations on a separate card:

architect	baker	bilingual secretary
chef	delivery person	mechanic
security guard	teacher	writer

b. Distribute the cards to pairs of students. Have the pairs brainstorm *the perfect applicant* for that position and write a description of that person's experience.

c. Have students read their description of the perfect applicant aloud, and have the class listen and identify what the job is.

ExpressWays

Have students do the activity individually, in pairs, or as a class. You may want to assign this exercise as homework.

1. drive/drove/drive/I've driven
2. do/did/do/I've done
3. write/wrote/write/I've written
4. take/took/take/I've taken
5. make/made/make/I've made
6. give/gave/give/I've given

FOCUS

TOPIC

Employment/On the Job: Describing Job Procedures

GRAMMAR

1. **Present Perfect Tense**

    Has Bob **gone** to the bank yet?
      Yes, he **has.**
      He**'s** already **gone** there.

2. **Present Perfect vs. Past Tense**

      go-went-gone
    He**'s** already **gone** there.
    He **went** there this morning.

      speak-spoke-spoken
    She**'s** already **spoken** to her.
    She **spoke** to her this afternoon.

      see-saw-seen
    We**'ve** already **seen** it.
    We **saw** it a few minutes ago.

      wear-wore-worn
    They**'ve** already **worn** them.
    They **wore** them today.

      do-did-done
    He**'s** already **done** them.
    He **did** them a little while ago.

      give-gave-given
    She**'s** already **given** it.
    She **gave** it yesterday afternoon.

      take-took-taken
    They**'ve** already **taken** it.
    They **took** it last week.

      drive-drove-driven
    I**'ve** already **driven** it.
    I **drove** it today.

      meet-met-met
    I**'ve** already **met** her.
    I **met** her this morning.

      read-read-read
    She**'s** already **read** it.
    She **read** it last night.

      get-got-gotten
    They**'ve** already **gotten** them.
    They **got** them yesterday.

sing-sang-sung
He's already **sung** it.
He **sang** it a few minutes ago.

eat-ate-eaten
I've already **eaten** there.
I **ate** there at lunchtime.

write-wrote-written
He's already **written** it.
He **wrote** it an hour ago.

3. **Time Expressions**

He went there **this morning.**
this afternoon.
today.
yesterday.
yesterday afternoon.
last night.
last week.
the other day.
a few minutes ago.
an hour ago.
a little while ago.

FUNCTIONS

Asking for and Reporting Information

Has *Bob gone to the bank* yet?
Yes, he has.
He's already *gone there*.
He *went there this morning.*

Has *Barbara spoken to her supervisor* yet?
Yes, she has.
She's already *spoken to her.*
She *spoke to her this afternoon.*

Have you *seen the top secret report* yet?
Yes, we have.
We've already *seen it.*
We *saw it a few minutes ago.*

Have *the employees worn their new
uniforms* yet?
Yes, they have.
They've already *worn them.*
They *wore them today.*

VOCABULARY

Job Procedures

do *the dishes*
drive *a van*
give a presentation
go to *the bank*
meet *a new supervisor*
read *a contract*
see *a report*
speak to *a supervisor*
take inventory
wear *a uniform*
write *a letter*

People on the Job

bank manager
employee
stock clerk
supervisor

Additional Employment Vocabulary

bonus
cafeteria
contract
letter of resignation
presentation
promotion
report
uniform
vault

COMMENTARY

In line 3, Speaker A reacts positively to the information by saying, "Oh, good."

GETTING READY

1. Introduce the present perfect tense with different pronouns.

a. Write the following on the board:

I have	I've
we have	we've
they have	they've
he has	he's
she has	she's

b. Model the following and have students repeat:

A. Have you done your homework yet?
B. Yes, I have. I've already done it.

A. Have you and Sally done your homework yet?
B. Yes, we have. We've already done it.

A. Have Tom and Tim done their homework yet?
B. Yes, they have. They've already done it.

c. Point out the contraction of *have* to *'ve*.

d. Continue with the third person. Have students repeat:

A. Has Bob done his homework yet?
B. Yes, he has. He's already done it.

A. Has Betty done her homework yet?
B. Yes, she has. She's already done it.

e. Point out the contraction of *has* to *'s*.

2. Introduce past participles.

a. Write the following verbs on the board:

do	did	done
drive	drove	driven
eat	ate	eaten
get	got	gotten
give	gave	given
go	went	gone
see	saw	seen
sing	sang	sung
speak	spoke	spoken
take	took	taken
wear	wore	worn
write	wrote	written

b. Remind students that many past participles are irregular, such as those on the board.

c. Model the following and have students practice it with each of the verbs on the board:

I do	I did	I've already done
I drive	I drove	I've already driven
I eat	I ate	I've already eaten
I get	I got	I've already gotten

d. Remind students that other times the past participle is the same form as the past tense.

e. Write the following verbs on the board and have students practice saying them:

make	made	made
meet	met	met
read	read	read
work	worked	worked

f. Model the following and have students practice it with each of the verbs on the board:

I make	I made	I've already made
I meet	I met	I've already met

THE MODEL CONVERSATIONS

There are four model conversations. Introduce and practice each model before going to the next one. For each model:

1. **Set the Scene:**

   Model 1: "A manager is talking to a supervisor."
   Model 2: "Two co-workers are talking."
   Model 3: "Two spies are talking."
   Model 4: "A restaurant manager is talking to a supervisor."

2. **Listen to the Model.**

3. **Class Practice.**

4. **Read.**

5. **Pair Practice.**

THE EXERCISES

Examples

1. A. Has Bruno done the dishes yet?
   B. Yes, he has. He's already done them.
   A. Oh, good. When?
   B. He did them a little while ago.

2. A. Has Sarah given the presentation yet?
   B. Yes, she has. She's already given it.
   A. Oh, good. When?
   B. She gave it yesterday afternoon.

Before doing each exercise, check students' understanding of the vocabulary and introduce any unfamiliar words or phrases. For student reference, leave on the board the list of verbs from the *Getting Ready* activities.

Exercise Practice (optional). Have pairs of students simultaneously practice all the exercises.

Exercise Presentations. Call on pairs of students to present the exercises.

ORIGINAL STUDENT CONVERSATIONS

Have pairs of students create and present original conversations based on the models. (You may want students to prepare their original conversations as homework, then practice them the next day with another student and present them to the class.)

EXPANSION

1. Janet's Busy Day

a. Put the following schedule on the board:

```
Friday, June 15
    9:00    go to library
   10:00    do my homework
   11:00    meet with my teacher
   12:00    eat lunch with Cindy
    1:00    get groceries
    2:00    go to the bank
    3:00    write a report for English class
    7:00    see movie with Paul
```

b. Tell students that this is Janet's schedule for Friday, June 15th. She has a lot of things to do today.

c. Write on the board:

```
A.  It's _____ o'clock. Has she
    _____ yet?
B.  Yes, she has. She _____
    at _____ o'clock.
```

d. Model the following and have students repeat:

A. It's 10:00. Has she gone to the library yet?
B. Yes, she has. She went to the library at 9:00.

e. Have pairs of students create similar conversations, using Janet's schedule and the conversational framework on the board.

2. Accomplishments of the Day!

a. Brainstorm with students a list of daily chores and activities. Write their ideas on the board. For example:

```
make my bed
clean my room
feed the cat
clean the house
take a shower
take the garbage out
read the newspaper
do the dishes
```

b. Have students make a list of all the things they've already done today.

c. Have students read their list of *accomplishments* to the class.

3. Information Gap: David's Busy Day

a. Divide the class into pairs.

b. Tell them that each has different information about someone named David and his schedule for the day. Give one member of each pair *Schedule A* and the other member of the pair *Schedule B*.

Schedule A:

```
Saturday, March 7
    9:00    go to the gym
   10:00
   11:00    pick up flowers
   12:00    eat lunch with Anne
    1:00
    2:00
    3:00    get a haircut
    4:00
    5:00

Notes for the Day:

pick up my dry cleaning
drop off my library books
pay my bills
get a birthday present for Frank
```

Schedule B:

```
Saturday, March 7
    9:00
   10:00    drop off my library books
   11:00
   12:00
    1:00
    2:00    pay my bills
    3:00
    4:00    get a birthday present for
            Frank
    5:00    pick up my dry cleaning

Notes for the Day:

get a haircut
eat lunch with Anne
pick up flowers
go to the gym
```

c. Tell them that it is now 6:00 in the evening. They need to ask each other questions in order to find out when David did each of the activities on his list. Write the following framework on the board for them to use as they ask each other questions:

A. Has David _____ yet?

B. Yes, he has. He _____ at _____ o'clock.

For example:

Student A: Has David picked up his dry cleaning yet?

Student B: Yes, he has. He picked it up at 5:00.

Student A: Okay. [*writes the information in Schedule A*] Has he dropped off his library books?

etc.

d. The pairs continue until each has a filled calendar.

e. Have the pairs then check each other's schedules to make sure they heard the information correctly.

Constructions Ahead!

1. Have students look at the grammar chart at the top of the page.

   a. Model sentences with the present perfect tense, and have students repeat. For example:

      I have eaten
      I've eaten

      We have eaten
      We've eaten

      He has eaten
      He's eaten

   b. Model yes/no questions and short answers, and have students repeat. For example:

      A. Have you eaten?
      B. Yes, I have.

      A. Have they eaten?
      B. Yes, they have.

      A. Has he eaten?
      B. Yes, he has.

2. Call students' attention to the *Construction Note*. Tell them that unless you or the textbook tells them otherwise, the past participle is the same as the past tense.

Have students do the activity individually, in pairs, or as a class. You may want to assign this exercise as homework.

1.	b	8.	a
2.	b	9.	b
3.	b	10.	b
4.	a	11.	b
5.	b	12.	b
6.	a	13.	b
7.	b	14.	a

CrossTalk

1. Point out the grammar chart at the top of the page. Note the use of *for* with a period of time *(for many years/for five years/for the past few years)* and the use of *since* with a specific point in time *(since 1994/since last year/since I retired)*.

2. Call on individual students to read the quotes from the six people on student text page 81 who are telling about themselves.

3. Have pairs of students talk about skills or personal experiences they're especially proud of. Then have the pairs report back to the class.

Your Turn

Have students discuss the activity as a class, in pairs, or in small groups. Then have students write their responses at home, share their written work with other students, and discuss in class.

FOCUS

TOPICS

Employment/Getting a Job: Stating Skills and Qualifications
Personal Information: Work Experience

GRAMMAR

1. **Present Perfect Tense**

   Have you ever **flown** a 747?
   > No, I **haven't**, but I**'ve flown** a DC-10.

2. **Able to**

   I'm confident I'd **be able to** learn to fly a 747 very easily.

3. **Could**

   I'm confident I **could** sell computers very easily.

FUNCTIONS

1. **Asking for and Reporting Information**

   Have you ever *flown a 747?*
   > No, I haven't, but I've *flown a DC-10.*

2. **Certainty/Uncertainty**

   Inquiring about . . .

   Are you sure about that?
   Are you positive about that?
   Are you certain about that?
   Do you really think so?

   Expressing Certainty

   I'm positive.
   I'm sure.
   I'm certain.
   I'm a hundred percent sure.

3. **Ability/Inability**

   Expressing Ability

   I'm confident I'd be able to *learn.*
   I'm confident I could *learn.*

VOCABULARY

Job Procedures and Skills

fly *a 747*
give *ballet lessons*
make *pastries*
ride *a horse*
sell *computers*
sing

COMMENTARY

1. This conversation is the part of a job interview in which the interviewer is asking about the applicant's previous experience.

2. The applicant admits a lack of experience but expresses confidence in his ability to learn the job.

3. "Oh, yes" (line 6) is a strong, positive answer.

GETTING READY

Ask each student to tell the class about something he or she has done in school or in a job. For example:

> I've studied two languages — Chinese and English.
> I've fixed cars.
> I've made clothing.
> I've taken care of people in the hospital.
> I've picked fruit and vegetables.
> I've worked in a factory/store/office/ restaurant/gas station.
> I've used a typewriter/computer.
> I've taught dance/art.

THE MODEL CONVERSATION

1. **Set the Scene.** "An interviewer is interviewing someone who is applying for a job as an airplane pilot."

2. **Listen to the Model.**

3. **Class Practice.**

4. **Reading.**

5. **Pair Practice.**

6. **Alternative Expressions.**

THE EXERCISES

Examples

1. A. Have you ever given ballet lessons?
   B. No, I haven't, but I've given tap dance lessons, and I'm confident I'd be able to learn to give ballet lessons very easily.
   A. Are you sure about that?
   B. Oh, yes. I'm positive.

2. A. Have you ever sold computers?
   B. No, I haven't, but I've sold stereo equipment, and I'm confident I could learn to sell computers very easily.
   A. Are you positive about that?
   B. Oh, yes. I'm sure.

Before doing each exercise, check students' understanding of the vocabulary and introduce any unfamiliar words or phrases. Have students use the footnoted expressions or any of their alternatives as they do the exercises.

Exercise Practice (optional). Have pairs of students simultaneously practice all the exercises.

Exercise Presentations. Call on pairs of students to present the exercises.

ORIGINAL STUDENT CONVERSATIONS

Have pairs of students create and present original conversations based on the model. (You may want students to prepare their original conversations as homework, then practice them the next day with another student and present them to the class.)

EXPANSION

1. Expressing Confidence

Have students practice gaining confidence through talking about themselves and their abilities.

a. Ask your students to think of jobs, tasks, or activities that they are good at. Have volunteers tell the class. For example:

> "I can drive very well."
> "I can fix machines."
> "I can cook extremely well."

b. Ask students to think of activities or jobs they haven't done but would like to try. Write the model below on the board, and have students complete the sentence as many ways as they wish:

> I've never _____ before, but I'm confident I'd be able to learn to _____ very easily.

2. Find Someone Who . . .

a. Collect some information about students' work experience and skills.

b. Put this information in the following form:

> Find a classmate who has done the following:
>
> 1. fly an airplane
>   Have you _____ before?
>   Name: _____
>
> 2. give dance lessons
>   Have you _____ before?
>   Name: _____
>
> 3. make pastries
>   Have you _____ before?
>   Name: _____
>
> 4. sing in a play
>   Have you _____ before?
>   Name: _____
>
> 5. give a presentation
>   Have you _____ before?
>   Name: _____

c. Have students write out the correct questions and then circulate around the room asking each other the questions to identify the above people.

d. The first student to identify all the people correctly wins.

3. Information Gap: A Job Interview

a. Write the following lists on separate papers and duplicate.

List A:

> Employer's Requirements
>
> We need someone who . . .
>
> has used a word processor
> types 200 words per minute
> has written letters and memos
> has finished high school
> has given professional presentations
> can answer telephones professionally
> knows how to use a photocopy machine
>
> Notes:

List B:

> Applicant's Experience
>
> You . . .
>
> have used a typewriter for ten years
> can type 180 words a minute
> can write memos
> have finished college
> have given class presentations
> have answered the telephone at home
> have used a photocopy machine
>
> Notes:

b. Divide the class into pairs. Give each partner a different list. One person is the *interviewer* and the other the *job applicant.*

c. Have students role-play an interview in which they ask and answer questions about the applicant's experience. Encourage them to take notes during the interview.

d. Have the pairs present their interviews to the class, and have each interviewer tell whether he or she would hire that person for the job.

e. Have the class discuss the outcomes of each interview.

Constructions Ahead!

Have students do the activity individually, in pairs, or as a class. You may want to assign this exercise as homework.

1. driven, I haven't
2. written, he hasn't
3. gone, they have
4. done, she has
5. spoken, I have
6. been, we haven't
7. flown, it hasn't
8. asked, you have

InterView

Have students circulate around the room to conduct their interviews, or have students interview people outside the class. Students should then report back to the class about their interviews.

FOCUS

TOPIC

Employment/On the Job: Making and Fulfilling Requests

GRAMMAR

1. **Present Perfect Tense**

   Have you **given** out the paychecks yet?
   Have you **written** your monthly report yet?
      No, I **haven't**.

2. **Past Continuous to Express Future Intention**

   I **was planning** to give them out this afternoon.
   I **was planning** to oil it a little later.

FUNCTIONS

1. **Intention**

   Expressing . . .

   I was planning to *set them in a little while*.
   I was going to *write it at the end of the week*.

   I'll *do it* right away.

2. **Requests**

   Direct, Polite

   Please *do it as soon as possible*.
   Can you please *do it as soon as possible*?
   Will you please *do it as soon as possible*?
   Would you please *do it as soon as possible*?
   I'd like you to *do it as soon as possible*.

3. **Obligation**

   Expressing . . .

   The paychecks are supposed to *be given out before lunch hour*.
   The tables are supposed to *be set an hour before we open*.

4. **Apologizing**

   I'm sorry. I didn't know that.
   I'm sorry. I didn't realize that.
   I'm sorry. I wasn't aware of that.

VOCABULARY

Job Procedures and Skills

give out *the paychecks*
oil *the conveyor belt*
polish *the tables*
set *the tables*
write *your monthly report*

Additional Employment Vocabulary

break (n.)
lunch hour
paycheck
shift (n.)

Objects on the Job

conveyor belt
monthly report
paycheck
table

Places on the Job

lobby

COMMENTARY

1. "The paychecks are supposed to be given out before lunch hour" (line 5). This passive statement is more polite than a direct statement, such as "You're supposed to give the paychecks out before lunch hour."

2. "I'm sorry. I didn't know that" (line 7). It is appropriate to apologize and explain after making a mistake.

THE MODEL CONVERSATION

1. **Set the Scene.** "This man is very busy working at his desk. His boss comes over to speak to him."

2. **Listen to the Model.**

3. **Class Practice.**

4. **Read.**

5. **Pair Practice.**

6. **Alternative Expressions.**

THE EXERCISES

Examples

> 1. A. Have you set the tables yet?
>   B. No, I haven't. I was planning to set them in a little while.
>   A. Please do it as soon as possible. The tables are supposed to be set an hour before we open.
>   B. I'm sorry. I didn't know that. I'll do it right away.

> 2. A. Have you written your monthly report yet?
>   B. No, I haven't. I was going to write it at the end of the week.
>   A. Can you please do it as soon as possible? The monthly reports are supposed to be written by the last day of the month.
>   B. I'm sorry. I didn't realize that. I'll do it right away.

Before doing each exercise, check students' understanding of the vocabulary and introduce any unfamiliar words or phrases. Have students use the footnoted expressions or any of their alternatives as they do the exercises.

Exercise Practice (optional). Have pairs of students simultaneously practice all the exercises.

Exercise Presentations. Call on pairs of students to present the exercises.

Language Note

Exercise 5: "10 o'clock sharp" means "exactly 10 o'clock."

Culture Note

Exercise 4: A "break" is a rest time. Many employers in the United States give their employees a certain number of breaks during the work day. These breaks are usually about fifteen minutes long.

146 EXIT FIVE

ORIGINAL STUDENT CONVERSATIONS

Have pairs of students create and present original conversations based on the model. (You may want students to prepare their original conversations as homework, then practice them the next day with another student and present them to the class.)

EXPANSION

1. Information Gap: I'm Just Checking

a. Divide the class into pairs. Have one student in each pair be the *boss* and the other an *employee.*

b. Give each boss a list of tasks that the employee should have completed. For example:

In an Office

type the letters
have the letters signed
make copies of the letters
mail the letters
file the copies
get the mail from the mailroom
open the mail
clean the typewriter
clean the copying machine
fill out your time sheet

In a Restaurant

vacuum the floor
set up the tables
wipe off the chairs
put chairs around the tables
set the tables
put the glasses on the tables
arrange the flowers
pour water in the glasses

---

c. Tell the boss: "You have a new employee. Check to see what jobs have been completed."

d. Give the employee a list of the tasks that he or she has completed. The list should include some, but not all, of the tasks on the boss's list.

In an Office

type the letters
have the letters signed
make copies of the letters
get the mail from the mailroom
clean the copying machine

In a Restaurant

set up the tables
put chairs around the tables
set the tables
put the glasses on the tables

---

e. Tell the employee: "You're at work and have finished these tasks. Your boss is coming to check your work. If you haven't finished some of the work he or she asks about, be sure to find out when it is supposed to be done."

f. Have the pairs role-play the situations. Encourage students to practice different expressions for making requests and apologizing.

2. Mystery Conversations

a. Divide the class into pairs.

b. Have the pairs write a conversation between a manager and an employee, using the present perfect tense as much as possible. In their conversations, they shouldn't mention what the employee's job is.

c. Have students take turns presenting their conversations. The class must listen and guess what the employee's job is.

    A. Have you washed the floors yet?
    B. No, I haven't, but I've polished all the tables in the lobby and I've made all the beds.
    A. How about the windows? Have you have washed them yet?
    B. Yes, I have. And I've also vacuumed the rugs.
    A. Good job!

    [*The employee is a housekeeper in a hotel.*]

Listen

Listen and put a check next to the task that each employee has already done and an X next to the task that the employee hasn't done yet.

1. A. Howard, have you typed those letters yet?
   B. Yes, I have, Mrs. Johnson. I typed them this afternoon.
   A. That's good. And have you also made copies of them?
   B. No, I haven't made the copies yet. I'll do that in a few minutes.
   A. Oh, and one more thing, Howard. Have you gotten the mail from the mailroom yet?
   B. Not yet, Mrs. Johnson. I'll get the mail right after I make the copies of the letters.
   A. That's fine. Oh, and before I forget, Howard. You need to speak to Mr. Chen in Personnel about changing your work schedule for next month.
   B. I've already spoken with him, and everything has been arranged.

2. A. Stella, have you fixed the copy machine yet? It's been broken for over a week.
   B. I've already fixed it, Mr. Leonard. I fixed it early this morning.
   A. That's great. And have you cleaned the supply room yet?
   B. Not yet. I'll do that later this morning, after I go to the post office.
   A. Oh, by the way, Stella. I noticed that you haven't filled out your time sheet for this week.
   B. I'm sorry, Mr. Leonard. I'll do it right away.

3. A. Mrs. Giannini, I've already set the tables, I've put the glasses out, and I've arranged all the flowers.
   B. That's wonderful, Richard. I guess we're all ready for tonight. By the way, have you vacuumed the floor yet? It really needs to be done.
   A. Sorry, Mrs. Giannini. I'll vacuum it right away.
   B. Thanks, Richard.

4. A. I'm sorry I haven't written that report yet, Mr. Davis. I'll write it over the weekend.
   B. No problem, Richard.
   A. And I'm also sorry I haven't given out the paychecks yet, Mr. Davis. I'll give them out right away.

   B. Please do that, Richard. The paychecks are supposed to be given out right after lunch.
   A. Oh, that reminds me, Mr. Davis. I haven't had lunch yet.
   B. Richard. Have you met with your supervisor recently?
   A. You mean Mr. Cooper? No, I haven't. I haven't met with him in a long time.
   B. Richard, I think there are a few things you need to talk to Mr. Cooper about . . . as soon as possible!
   A. Of course, Mr. Davis, I'll speak to him right away . . . after I eat lunch.

5. A. Shirley, the animals seem to be very hungry today. Have you fed them yet?
   B. Yes, I have. I fed them a few minutes ago. And I also cleaned all the cages.
   A. You did? That's great. By the way, Shirley, you were going to repair the van. It really needs to be fixed.
   B. No, problem, Mr. Miller. I'll repair it in a little while.
   A. One last thing, Shirley. Have you walked Mrs. Carter's dog? Remember, you're supposed to walk him a few times a day.
   B. I've already walked him twice today, Mr. Miller, but I'll walk him again if you want me to.
   A. No, that's fine. Twice is enough.

6. A. Mrs. Hernandez, I've made all the beds and I've polished the tables in the lobby.
   B. That's wonderful, Emily. Now you need to wash the uniforms.
   A. I've already washed them, Mrs. Hernandez.
   B. You have? That's great.
   A. Yes, I washed them all this morning.
   B. By the way, Emily. Do you know that we have several new rules and regulations for employees here at the Royal Plaza Hotel?
   A. Yes, I know, Mrs. Hernandez. I've already read them all.

Answers

1. __✔__ type the letters
   __X__ make copies
   __X__ get the mail
   __✔__ speak to Mr. Chen

2. __✔__ fix the copy machine
   __X__ clean the supply room
   __X__ go to the post office
   __X__ fill out my time sheet

3. __✔__ set the tables
   __✔__ put the glasses out
   __✔__ arrange the flowers
   __✗__ vacuum the floor

4. __✗__ write the report
   __✗__ give out the paychecks
   __✗__ eat lunch
   __✗__ meet with Mr. Cooper

5. __✔__ feed the animals
   __✔__ clean the cages
   __✗__ repair the van
   __✔__ walk the dog

6. __✔__ make the beds
   __✔__ polish the tables
   __✔__ wash the uniforms
   __✔__ read the new rules and regulations

CrossTalk

Have students first work in pairs and then share with the class what they talked about.

FOCUS

TOPICS

Employment/Getting a Job: Stating Skills and Qualifications
Personal Information: Work Experience

GRAMMAR

1. **Present Perfect Continuous Tense**

   I**'ve been using** word processors for a long time.
   I**'ve been repairing** gas heaters for ten years.

2. **Since/For**

   I've been using the Internet **for** the past five years.
   I've been operating forklifts **since** 1985.

3. **Can**

   Can you play Broadway show tunes?

4. **Able to**

   Are you **able to** prepare pancakes and omelettes?

FUNCTIONS

1. **Ability/Inability**

   Inquiring about . . .
   Do you know how to ⎫
   Can you　　　　　　⎬ *use a word processor?*
   Are you able to 　 ⎭

   Expressing Ability

   I've been *using word processors* ⎱ for *a long time.*
   　　　　　　　　　　　　　　　 ⎰ since *1990.*

2. **Hesitating**

   Well, let me see . . .

3. **Checking and Indicating Understanding**

   Checking One's Own Understanding
   Since 1990?

4. **Agreement/Disagreement**

   Expressing Agreement
   I guess I do.

VOCABULARY

Job Procedures and Skills

operate *a forklift*
play *show tunes*
prepare *pancakes*
repair *a gas heater*
use *a word processor*

Objects on the Job

forklift
word processor

Occupations

cook (n.)

COMMENTARY

1. "Well, let me see . . ." (line 5) is an expression used to hesitate while thinking.

2. In line 9, Speaker A is complimenting Speaker B when he says, "Well, you certainly have a lot of experience."

3. "I guess I do" (line 10) is a polite and modest response to a compliment.

GETTING READY

Introduce the present perfect continuous tense by presenting examples and having students talk about where they live and how long they have been living there.

   a. Write the underlined verbs on the board and read the examples.

      (1) Martha <u>lives</u> in Minneapolis. <u>She's (She has) been living</u> in Minneapolis since 1985. She thinks Minneapolis is the nicest city in the world.

      (2) Mr. Parker is driving to work. Right now, <u>he's waiting</u> in a long line of cars. <u>He's (He has) been waiting</u> for twenty minutes because there was an accident.

      (3) Kenji <u>is studying</u> English in school. <u>He's (He has) been studying</u> English for nine years. Of course his English is excellent!

   b. Ask students, "Where do you live?" and "How long have you been living there?" Have students answer, "I live in _____." "I've been living there for _____ months/years."

   c. Have students ask and answer: "How long have you been studying English?" "I've been studying English for _____ weeks/months/years."

THE MODEL CONVERSATION

1. **Set the Scene.** "An interviewer is asking a job applicant about his skills and work experience."

2. **Listen to the Model.**

3. **Class Practice.**

4. **Reading.**

   Language Note

   A "word processor" (line 1) is a computerized typewriter.

5. **Pair Practice.**

6. **Alternative Expressions.**

THE EXERCISES

Examples

1. A. Do you know how to operate a forklift?
   B. Yes. I've been operating forklifts for a long time.
   A. How long?
   B. Well, let me see . . . I've been operating forklifts since 1985.
   A. Since 1985?
   B. Yes, that's right.
   A. Well, you certainly have a lot of experience.
   B. I guess so.

2. A. Can you repair a gas heater?
   B. Yes. I've been repairing gas heaters for a long time.
   A. How long?
   B. Well, let me see . . . I've been repairing gas heaters for ten years.
   A. For ten years?
   B. Yes, that's right.
   A. Well, you certainly have a lot of experience.
   B. I guess I do.

Before doing each exercise, check students' understanding of the vocabulary and introduce any unfamiliar words or phrases. Have students use the footnoted expression or any of its alternatives as they do the exercises.

Exercise Practice (optional). Have pairs of students simultaneously practice all the exercises.

Exercise Presentations. Call on pairs of students to present the exercises.

Culture Notes

Exercise 4: The "Internet" is an international computer network.

Exercise 5: "Broadway show tunes" are songs from popular musical plays from the theater district of New York City known as "Broadway."

ORIGINAL STUDENT CONVERSATIONS

Have pairs of students create and present original conversations based on the model. (You may want students to prepare their original conversations as homework, then practice them the next day with another student and present them to the class.)

EXPANSION

1. Practice Using For *and* Since

a. Review the time expressions in the exercises on student text page 86:

> since 1985
> for ten years
> since my days as a cook in the army
> for the past five years
> since I was a teenager

Have students analyze when the words *for* and *since* are used. Point out that *for* is usually followed by a reference to a specific length of time (*for five years*). *Since* is usually followed by a reference to a point in time (*since last year, since I was a teenager*).

b. Say the following time expressions, and have students add *for* or *since* as they repeat each expression:

> Teacher: ten years
> Student: for ten years
>
> Teacher: 1986
> Student: since 1986
>
> Teacher: the past three years
> Student: for the past three years

> Teacher: 5 o'clock
> Student: since 5 o'clock
>
> Teacher: yesterday afternoon
> Student: since yesterday afternoon
>
> Teacher: thirty minutes
> Student: for thirty minutes
>
> Teacher: a very long time
> Student: for a very long time
>
> Teacher: last week
> Student: since last week
>
> Teacher: a year ago
> Student: since a year ago
>
> Teacher: two years
> Student: for two years

2. Class Survey: Machines We Know and Love

a. Have students brainstorm names of machines they have seen or used in their everyday lives or work. Have a student take notes on the board.

b. Have each person select a machine and survey all the students to find out how many people know how to use the machine and how long they have been using it. For example, a student might ask classmates: "Do you know how to cook with a microwave oven?" "How long have you been cooking with a microwave oven?"

c. Ask students to report back to the class. What are the most commonly used machines? Were there machines that no one knows how to use? Which machines would students like to learn how to use?

3. Find Someone Who . . .

a. Collect some information about students in the class. For example:

> where they live and how long they've been living there
> where they work and how long they've been living there
> how long they've been in this country
> what their hobbies are and how long they've been doing them

b. Put this information in the following form:

Find someone who . . .

1. has been living in the
   U.S. for ten years. _____

2. has been working at
   Jane's Place for two weeks. _____

3. has been living in Oakland
   for three years. _____

4. is studying pharmacology. _____

5. has been playing the piano
   for fifteen years. _____

c. Have students circulate around the room asking each other questions to identify the above people.

d. The first student to identify all the people correctly wins.

4. Reading Resumes

a. Bring to class several examples of resumes, and distribute them to students.

b. Ask students questions about the information in the resumes. For example:

> How long has this person been working at Apex Corporation?
> How long as he/she been inspecting widgets?
> How many jobs has he/she had in the past ten years?

Variation: Make statements about the information in the resumes. Some statements should be true and others false. Have students decide whether each statement is true or false and correct the false ones.

5. Writing Resumes

a. Bring to class several examples of resumes and distribute them to students.

b. Have students chose a style that fits their field and then use it as a guide for writing their own resumes.

c. Divide the class into pairs, and have students read each other's resume and help check for errors or ambiguities.

d. Have students hand in a final copy of their resumes for your review.

6. Class Discussion: Retooling for the Job Market

The rapidly changing workplace forces many workers to develop new tools and skills or to retool their past expertise. This activity can help students think about their employment histories and future plans.

a. In pairs or small groups, have students discuss the following questions:

> What occupation would you like to have ten years from now?
> What skills does that occupation require?
> What skills have you already developed?
> Where did you learn these skills?
> How long have you been using these skills?
> How can you learn the other required skills?

b. Have the pairs report back to the class.

7. Who's Telling the Truth?

In this activity several students give the same information, but only one is telling the truth. The class has to find out who.

a. Divide the class into groups of three.

b. Have the students in each group share information with each other about their hobbies or work experiences. Then have each group choose one person who they will *pretend to be.* They need to learn everything they can about that person's hobbies and work experience.

c. Have the groups take turns sitting as a panel in the front of the class and answering people's questions. The class tries to figure out which one of the three people is telling the truth.

d. Any group that succeeds in *tricking* the class wins.

Constructions Ahead!

Have students do the activity individually, in pairs, or as a class. You may want to assign this exercise as homework.

1. I've been typing
2. She's been taking
3. They've been doing
4. He's been selling
5. It's been snowing
6. We've been singing and dancing

CrossTalk

Have students first work in pairs and then share with the class what they talked about.

FOCUS

TOPIC

**Employment/Getting a Job: Inquiring about
Job Responsibilities**

GRAMMAR

1. **Present Perfect Continuous Tense**

   I**'ve been overseeing** the company's finances for several years.

2. **Present Perfect vs. Past Tense**

   While I **haven't done** the payroll in my current position,
   I **did** the payroll in the job I had before that.

FUNCTIONS

1. **Asking for and Reporting Additional Information**

   Can you tell me a little more
   Can you tell me anything more } (about *the position*)?
   Can you tell me anything else

2. **Asking for and Reporting Information**

   What would you like to know?

   What exactly are the *bookkeeper's* responsibilities?

3. **Ability/Inability**

   Inquiring about . . .
   Do you think you'd be able to }
   Do you think you could   } *handle those responsibilities*?

4. **Certainty/Uncertainty**

   Expressing Certainty
   Absolutely!
   Definitely!
   Positively!

5. **Checking and Indicating Understanding**

   Indicating Understanding
   I see.

VOCABULARY

Getting a Job

position
responsibilities

Job Procedures and Skills

do *the payroll*
oversee *the finances*

Occupations

bookkeeper

Additional Employment Vocabulary

company
finances
job
payroll

COMMENTARY

1. The model dialog represents a portion of a job interview. At this point in the interview, the applicant, Speaker A, is asking the interviewer for more information about the job opening. It is important and appropriate for an applicant to ask any questions he or she may have about the job.

2. "What exactly are the bookkeeper's responsibilities?" (line 3) is a request for clarification. Speaker A has a general idea what the responsibilities are, but she would like more detailed information.

3. In lines 6–7, Speaker B asks, "Do you think you'd be able to handle those responsibilities?" In this context, "to handle" means "to manage or do the necessary tasks."

4. "Yes, absolutely" is a very strong, positive answer. Speaker A is expressing confidence in her ability to handle the job.

GETTING READY

Introduce the topic of job responsibilities by discussing a bookkeeper's job.

a. Ask students, "What does a bookkeeper do?" "What are a bookkeeper's job responsibilities?" Discuss their answers as well as the responsibilities mentioned in the model conversation: *to oversee the company's finances* and *to do the payroll.*

b. Call on pairs of students to ask for and give information about the job of bookkeeper. For example:

   A. What does a bookkeeper do?
   B. A bookkeeper oversees the company's finances and does the payroll.

c. Practice other tenses. Tell the class, "Mrs. Williams is a bookkeeper." Ask a variety of questions such as those below, and have students answer in complete sentences.

   A. What has Mrs. Williams been doing in her job?
   B. She's been overseeing the company's finances and doing the payroll.

   A. Has she done the payroll?
   B. Yes. She's done the payroll.

   A. What does she do every day?
   B. She oversees the company's finances and does the payroll.

d. Practice other pronouns and negative answers. Ask students questions such as those following, and have them answer in complete sentences.

   A. Are you a bookkeeper?
   B. No, I'm not.

   A. Is *Mr.* Williams a bookkeeper?
   B. No, he isn't.

A. Have you done the payroll?
B. No. I haven't done the payroll.

A. Has Mr. Williams done the payroll?
B. No. He hasn't done the payroll.

A. Have you been overseeing the company's finances?
B. No. I haven't been overseeing the company's finances.

A. Has Mr. Williams been overseeing the company's finances?
B. No. He hasn't been overseeing the company's finances.

THE MODEL CONVERSATION

1. **Set the Scene:** "A job interview is almost finished. The applicant has just a few more questions."
2. **Listen to the Model.**
3. **Read.**
4. **Pair Practice.**
5. **Alternative Expressions.**

Now have pairs of students create and present original conversations, using the model dialog as a guide. Encourage students to be inventive and to use new vocabulary. (You may want to assign this as homework, having students prepare their conversations, practice them the next day with another student, and then present them to the class.) Students should present their conversations without referring to the written text, but they should also not memorize them. Rather, they should feel free to adapt and expand them any way they wish.

Fill It In!

Have students do the activity individually, in pairs, or as a class. You may want to assign this exercise as homework.

1. a   5. b
2. b   6. b
3. b   7. a
4. a   8. a

Listen

Listen and choose the correct answer.

1. Roger took violin lessons for five years.
2. My daughter has been studying Spanish for two years.
3. Mark was an architect.
4. My children have known how to ski for a long time.
5. Elena has been a computer programmer since college.

6. I've been working in the Accounting Department for a long time.
7. Irene was a receptionist until the office shut down.
8. The truth is, I haven't been happy in my job for a long time.

Answers

1. b   5. b
2. a   6. a
3. b   7. b
4. a   8. a

InterView

Have students circulate around the room to conduct their interviews. Students should then report back to the class about their interviews.

Reading: *The Job Interview*

Preview: Have students discuss the following questions:

Have you ever had a job interview?
What questions did the employer ask you?
What questions did you ask the employer?
How did you prepare for the interview?

Then have students read the passage silently, or have them listen to the passage and take notes as you read it or play the audiotape.

True or False?

Have students do the activity individually, in pairs, or as a class. You may want to assign this exercise as homework.

1. False
2. True
3. False
4. True
5. False

What's the Answer?

Have students do the activity individually, in pairs, or as a class. You may want to assign this exercise as homework.

1. b
2. a
3. c
4. b
5. c

Figure It Out!

1. Have pairs make a list of DOS and DON'TS for a job interview.
2. Have the pairs read their list to the class, and have the class decide if each item on the list is a *do* or a *don't*.
3. Create a master list on the board of students' suggestions.

InterActions

Have pairs of students practice role-playing the activity and then present their role plays to the class. Have the class discuss why each interview was successful or unsuccessful.

Looking Back

Have students look at the list of expressions. Encourage them to ask you any questions about the meaning or pronunciation of any of the words. If students ask for the pronunciation, repeat after the student until the student is satisfied with his or her pronunciation of the word.

Review Activities

To review the language introduced in the unit, do the following activities.

1. Association Game

a. Divide the class into several teams.

b. Call out a topic category from the *Looking Back* section on student text page 92.

c. Have students in each group work together to see how many phrases they can associate with that category. For example:

Asking about Certainty:

Are you sure about that?
Are you positive about that?
Are you certain about that?
Do you really think so?

d. The team with the most items wins.

2. Create a Conversation!

a. Divide the class into pairs of students.

b. Tell each pair they have three minutes to make up a conversation using one item from each category from the *Looking Back* section on page 92 of the student text.

c. Have students present their conversations to the class.

EXIT 6

OVERVIEW
Student Text
Pages 93–114

Topics	Functions	Grammar

P. 94 I Want to Report an Emergency!

Emergencies: Reporting a Home Emergency Personal Information: Name, Address, Telephone Number	Identifying Asking for and Reporting Information Asking for Repetition	Present Perfect Tense

P. 96 I Want to Report an Accident!

Emergencies: Reporting an Accident or Incident	Identifying Asking for and Reporting Information Directions–Location Checking and Indicating Understanding Correcting	Present Perfect Tense Prepositions of Location

P. 98 Can You Recommend Something for a Stuffy Nose?

Drug Store: Over-the-Counter Drugs, Locating Items Health: Ailments and Symptoms	Advice–Suggestions Checking and Indicating Understanding Hesitating Directions–Location	Prepositions of Location

P. 100 I'm Not Feeling Very Well

Health: Ailments and Symptoms, Making an Appointment	Asking for and Reporting Information Checking and Indicating Understanding Want–Desire	Present Perfect Tense Present Perfect Continuous Tense Since/For

Topics	Functions	Grammar

P. 102   Do You Have Any Allergies?

Health: Giving a Medical History	Asking for and Reporting Additional Information Asking for and Reporting Information	Present Perfect Tense Question Formation Short Answers

P. 104   I Strongly Advise You to Change Your Diet

Health: Medical Advice	Fear–Worry–Anxiety Checking and Indicating Understanding Advice–Suggestions Obligation	Must Should Might Could

P. 106   Be Sure to Follow the Directions on the Label

Drug Store: Prescriptions	Instructing Obligation Checking and Indicating Understanding Asking for and Reporting Additional Information Possibility/Impossibility Fear–Worry–Anxiety	Supposed to Have to/Have Got to Need to Must Might May Could

P. 110   Can I Offer a Suggestion?

Health: Medical Advice	Asking for and Reporting Information Advice–Suggestions	Should Ought to Could Might

LOOKING AHEAD

Grammar This Exit

Present Perfect Tense

A tour bus **has overturned.**
Someone **has** just **broken into** my house.
A man **has been run over** by a car.

Have you ever **been** hospitalized?
  No, I **haven't.**

How long **have** you **had** a migraine headache?
How long **hasn't** he **been** able to move his neck?

break-broke-broken
Someone **broke into** Henry Wilson's house last night.
Someone **has** just **broken into** my house.

fall-fell-fallen
His mother **fell** down a flight of stairs yesterday.
My mother **has** just **fallen** down a flight of stairs.

have-had-had
Her husband **had** a heart attack yesterday evening.
My husband **has** just **had** a heart attack.

Since/For

How long have you had a bad toothache?
  Since Sunday morning.

How long have you had a migraine headache?
  For two days.

Present Perfect Continuous Tense

How long **have** you **been** feel**ing** dizzy?
How long **has** your right ear **been** ring**ing**?

Prepositions of Location

At the corner of Maple and B Street.
At the intersection of Harrison Road and 30th Street.
Across the street from Charlie's Café.
On the north side of Crystal Pond.
In front of the Save-Rite Store **on** Fifth Street.
Near Exit 17.

It's **in** Aisle 3, **on** the right.
It's **in** Aisle 2, **halfway down on** the left.
It's **on** the top shelf, **next to** the toothpaste.
It's **in** the last aisle, **on** the bottom shelf.
It's **in** the Cold Medicine Section.
It's **in the front of** the store, **near** the checkout counter.

Question Formation

Do you have any allergies**?**
Are you on a special diet of any kind**?**
Have you ever been hospitalized**?**

Short Answers

No, I don't.
No, I'm not.
No, I haven't.

Must

You **must** take one tablet.

Have to/Have Got to

You **have to** take one tablet.
You**'ve got to** take one tablet.

Need to

You **need to** take one tablet.

Supposed to

You're **supposed to** take one tablet.

Should

You **should** eat less salty food.

Ought to

You **ought to** blow into a paper bag.

Might

You **might** look for a cookbook that has low-fat recipes.

It **might** be a good idea.
You **might** feel tired.

Could

You **could** join a health club.

You **could** possibly feel tired.

May

You **may** feel tired.

Asking for and Reporting Information

What's your name?
And the address?
(What's your) telephone number?

What's the matter?
What's wrong?
What's the problem?

What seems to be the problem?

Where did *the accident* happen?

How long have you *had a migraine headache*?

Do you have *any allergies*?

Have you ever *been hospitalized*?

Is *9:00 tomorrow morning* convenient?

Tell me, _____?

I want to report an emergency/an accident!

I'm not feeling very well.

Asking for and Reporting Additional Information

Just one or two more questions, if that's okay.

And one more thing.

Correcting

Giving Correction
No. "B" Street.

Want–Desire

Inquiring about . . .
Would you like to _____?

Advice–Suggestions

Asking for . . .
Can you recommend _____?
Can you suggest _____?

Do you have any suggestions *(that might help)?*

Any other suggestions?

Offering . . .
I strongly advise you to _____.
I strongly recommend that you _____.
I urge you to _____.

You should _____.
You ought to _____.

I recommend _____.
I'd recommend _____.
I suggest _____.
I'd suggest _____.
Try _____.

You might _____.
You could _____.
It might be a good idea to _____.
Why don't you _____?

Can I offer a suggestion?

Obligation

Expressing . . .
You must _____.
You have to _____.
You've got to _____.
You need to _____.
You're supposed to _____.

It's absolutely essential.

Possibility/Impossibility

Expressing Possibility
You might _____.
You may _____.
You could possibly _____.
It's possible you'll _____.

Directions–Location

Inquiring about Location
Where can I find it?
Where is it located?

Giving Location
At the corner of *Maple and B Street.*
At the intersection of *Harrison Road* and *30th Street.*
On the *north* side of *Crystal Pond.*
In front of *the Save-Rite Store* on *Fifth Street.*
Near *Exit 17.*
Across the street from *Charlie's Café* on *M Street.*

It's in Aisle *3*, on the *right.*
It's in Aisle *2*, halfway down on the *left.*
It's in Aisle *1*, on the *top* shelf next to the *toothpaste.*
It's in the *last* aisle, on the *bottom* shelf.
It's in the *Cold Medicine* section, next to the *aspirin.*
It's in the front of *the store,* near the *checkout counter.*

Fear–Worry–Anxiety

Expressing . . .
I'm concerned about _____.

Responding to . . .
Don't worry.

Instructing

Be sure to *follow the directions.*

Take *1 tablet 2 or 3 times a day.*

Identifying

Police.
Fire Department.

Checking and Indicating Understanding

Checking One's Own Understanding
Did you say _____?
Was that _____?

A stuffy nose?
My blood pressure?

Indicating Understanding

I see.
I understand.

That's right.

Hesitating

Let's see . . .

Asking for Repetition

What was that?
What's that?
Excuse me?
What did you say?

PREVIEWING EXIT 6: CHAPTER-OPENING PHOTOS

Have students talk about the people and the situations and, as a class or in pairs, predict what the characters might be saying to each other. Students in pairs or small groups may enjoy practicing role plays based on these scenes and then presenting them to the class.

Text Page 94: I Want to Report an Emergency!

FOCUS

TOPICS

Emergencies: Reporting a Home Emergency
Personal Information: Name
                 Address
                 Telephone Number

GRAMMAR

Present Perfect Tense

Someone **has** just **broken into** my house.
My husband **has** just **had** a heart attack.

FUNCTIONS

1. **Identifying**

   Police.
   Fire Department.

2. **Asking for and Reporting Information**

   I want to report an emergency!

   What's your name?
   And the address?
   (What's your) telephone number?

3. **Asking for Repetition**

   What was that?
   What's that?
   Excuse me?
   What did you say?

VOCABULARY

Emergencies	Housing
ambulance	basement
ambulance service	chimney
break into	flight of stairs
emergency	hot water heater
emergency medical team	stairs
engine unit	
fall down	
fire (n.)	
fire department	
flood	
heart attack	
police	
police emergency unit	
repairperson	
report (v.)	
squad car	

COMMENTARY

1. With "Yes. Go ahead" (line 3), Speaker A acknowledges the information received and signals that the caller should tell what the emergency is.

2. By saying "Okay" (line 5), Speaker A acknowledges the information he has been given.

GETTING READY

1. Discuss home emergency situations with students and ask them to give examples of emergency situations at home. You might ask, "What do you do in an emergency?" "Who do you call for a fire/for a serious injury or heart attack/for a break-in?" "Do you know the telephone number(s)?" "How can you get the telephone numbers?"

2. Have students practice *dialing* telephone numbers.

   a. Create a picture of a push-button telephone dial, such as the one shown on the right, and make a copy for every student.

1	2 ABC	3 DEF
4 GHI	5 JKL	6 MNO
7 PRS	8 TUV	9 WXY
*	0 OPER	#

   b. Dictate the following numbers and have students *dial* them on their telephone dials. Then have students take turns dictating numbers for the class to dial.

752-1168	236-5775
429-3361	925-8138
832-7071	267-4004
984-7732	775-4671
369-0021	237-1277
285-3786	862-1098

THE MODEL CONVERSATION

1. **Set the Scene.** "A man is calling the police for help."

2. **Listen to the Model.**

3. **Class Practice.**

4. **Read.**

   Language Note

   A "squad car" (line 13) is a police car.

5. **Pair Practice.**

6. **Alternative Expressions.**

THE EXERCISES

Examples

---

1. A. Fire Department.
   B. I want to report an emergency!
   A. Yes. Go ahead.
   B. A fire has just broken out in my basement.
   A. Okay. What's your name?
   B. Linda Wu.
   A. And the address?
   B. 94 Pine Street.
   A. Telephone number?
   B. What was that?
   A. What's your telephone number?
   B. 236-5775.
   A. All right. We'll send an engine unit right away.
   B. Thank you.

2. A. Ajax Ambulance Service.
   B. I want to report an emergency!
   A. Yes. Go ahead.
   B. My mother has just fallen down a flight of stairs.
   A. Okay. What's your name?
   B. Alexander Franklin.
   A. And the address?
   B. 1471 Bedford Boulevard.
   A. Telephone number?
   B. What's that?
   A. What's your telephone number?
   B. 429-3361.
   A. All right. We'll send an ambulance right away.
   B. Thank you.

Before doing each exercise, check students' understanding of the vocabulary and introduce any unfamiliar words or phrases. Have students use the footnoted expression or its alternative as they do the exercise.

Exercise Practice (optional). Have pairs of students simultaneously practice all the exercises.

Exercise Presentations. Call on pairs of students to present the exercises.

ORIGINAL STUDENT CONVERSATIONS

Have pairs of students create and present original conversations based on the model. (You may want students to prepare their original conversations as homework, then practice them the next day with another student and present them to the class.)

EXPANSION

1. First-Aid Situations

a. On cue cards, write such situations as the following:

You just spilled hot coffee on your hand, and it hurts! Ask a friend, "What should I do?"

Last night you went dancing, and today you have blisters on your feet. What will help? What should you do? Ask a friend for advice.

You were playing in the park with your children, and you scraped your leg on an old nail. Should you see a doctor? Ask a friend for advice.

Last weekend you played soccer with some friends. Since that day, your back has been hurting. What can you do for your back? Ask a friend for advice.

You've had an awful headache ever since you got up this morning. Tell your friend about it. Maybe your friend can suggest something.

Your friend's 5-year-old daughter cut her knee at the playground. What should your friend do? Talk to your friend about it.

You have a toothache. You've had the toothache since yesterday. Talk to a friend about it. Should you see a dentist?

Your neighbor's little girl has just burned her hand on an iron. What should you put on the burn?

You got stung by a bee a few minutes ago. Now the sting is starting to swell. What should you do? Ask a friend.

b. Divide the class into pairs or small groups and give out the cue cards. Have students role-play the situations.

c. Have students present their role plays to the class. Encourage everyone to express their opinion about each situation and give additional advice.

2. Listen Carefully!

a. Tell students a short story about an emergency situation.

b. Make several statements about the story. Some statements should be true and others false.

c. Have students listen to the statements and decide if each is true or false. If a statement is false, have them correct it. For example:

> Teacher: The father was in the kitchen when the fire started.
> Student: False. He was in the dining room.

Variation: This activity can be done as a game with two competing teams. The teams take turns deciding whether each statement is true or false.

3. Guest Speaker

If possible, invite an emergency response worker (firefighter, police officer, emergency medical team specialist) to come to your class to talk about safety and emergency procedures. In advance, have students prepare questions to ask the guest. Have every student ask one prepared question.

4. Investigation

a. Divide the class into teams.

b. Assign each team one of the following topics:

> Fire Department
> Emergency Medical Team
> Police Department
> Animal Patrol
> Poison Control

c. Have students contact the agency and find out about the following:

> prevention measures
> steps to take in an emergency
> steps not to take in an emergency

d. Have the teams present their findings to the class.

What's the Word?

Have students do the activity individually, in pairs, or as a class. You may want to assign this exercise as homework.

1. a repairperson
2. an animal removal specialist
3. a squad car
4. an engine unit
5. an ambulance

Listen

Listen and choose the correct conclusion.

1. Could you please send an engine unit right away?
2. I think there's a robber in my neighbor's house!
3. Call the animal removal specialist right away!
4. The kitchen floor has flooded!
5. Please send an ambulance right away!
6. Can you send a squad car?

Answers

1. a
2. a
3. b
4. a
5. b
6. a

Community Connections

Have pairs of students make a list of emergency telephone numbers and then share their list with the rest of the class. Create a master list of emergency phone numbers based on students' suggestions.

FOCUS

TOPIC

Emergencies: Reporting an Accident or Incident

GRAMMAR

1. **Present Perfect Tense**

   A man **has been run over** by a car.
   A young boy **has fallen** through the ice.

2. **Prepositions of Location**

   At the corner of Maple and B Street.
   At the intersection of Harrison Road and 30th Street.
   On the expressway **near** Exit 17.
   Across the street from Charlie's Café **on** M Street.
   On the north side of Crystal Pond.
   In front of the Save-Rite Store **on** Fifth Street.

FUNCTIONS

1. **Identifying**

   Police.

2. **Asking for and Reporting Information**

   What's your name?

   Where did *the accident* happen?

   I want to report an accident!

3. **Directions–Location**

   Giving Location
   At the corner of *Maple and B Street.*
   At the intersection of *Harrison Road* and *30th Street.*
   On the *north* side of *Crystal Pond.*
   In front of *the Save-Rite Store* on *Fifth Street.*
   Near *Exit 17.*
   Across the street from *Charlie's Café* on *M Street.*

4. **Checking and Indicating Understanding**

   Checking One's Own Understanding
   Did you say ⎫
   Was that ⎭ *P Street?*

5. **Correcting**

   No. *"B" Street.*

VOCABULARY

Emergencies

accident
fall through the ice
highway patrol
mug
mugging
overturn
rob
robbery
run over

GETTING READY

Prepare a list of street addresses, such as those in the lesson in the student text on page 94 (*47 Locust Lane, 94 Pine Street, 112 Bay Avenue*). Bring a tape recorder and a blank tape to class.

a. Have students record their voices as they dictate a few of the addresses on the list. Have students read each address two times.

b. Play back the tape and have the class write the addresses as they listen.

c. Have students compare their answers with the list. Ask students, "Which street names were difficult?" "Why?" "Which numbers were difficult?" "Why?"

THE MODEL CONVERSATION

1. **Set the Scene:** "A woman has just seen an accident, and she's calling the police."

2. **Listen to the Model.**

3. **Class Practice.**

4. **Read.**

5. **Pair Practice.**

6. **Alternative Expressions.**

THE EXERCISES

Examples

1. A. Police.
   B. I want to report a robbery!
   A. Yes. Go ahead.
   B. A grocery store has been robbed.
   A. What's your name?
   B. Howard Stone.
   A. Where did the robbery happen?

B. At the intersection of Harrison Road and 30th Street.
   A. Did you say 13th Street?
   B. No. "30th" Street.
   A. All right. We'll be there right away.

2. A. Police.
   B. I'm calling to report an accident.
   A. Yes. Go ahead.
   B. A young boy has fallen through the ice.
   A. What's your name?
   B. Helen Lee.
   A. Where did the accident happen?
   B. On the north side of Crystal Pond.
   A. Was that the south side?
   B. No. The north side.
   A. All right. We'll be there right away.

Before doing each exercise, check students' understanding of the vocabulary and introduce any unfamiliar words or phrases. Have students use the footnoted expression or its alternative as they do the exercises.

Exercise Practice (optional). Have pairs of students simultaneously practice all the exercises.

Exercise Presentations. Call on pairs of students to present the exercises.

Language Notes

Exercise 4: A "highway patrol" is a division of a state police department.

Exercise 5: "U.F.O." refers to an Unidentified Flying Object.

ORIGINAL STUDENT CONVERSATIONS

Have pairs of students create and present original conversations based on the model. (You may want students to prepare their original conversations as homework, then practice them the next day with another student and present them to the class.)

EXPANSION

1. Reading Maps

a. Prepare a map-reading assignment using copies of a map of your city or town. Ask students to locate streets, highways, parks, and geographical landmarks. Also ask questions that require interpretation of the map. For example:

> What street goes around (*Fort Pond*)?
> What highway crosses the (*Madison*) River?
> What highway(s) go all the way around the city?
> What's the most direct route from (*Central Park*) to (*the harbor*)?
> How many bodies of water are there in the city?

b. Bring several copies of the map to class. Divide students into small groups, and give each group a map and the assignment. As students work, offer to assist the groups in finding and using the street indexes and locating other references on the map.

c. Have the groups compare their answers.

2. Location! Location!

a. Have students choose a building or agency in the community. For example:

> a fire station
> a police station
> a hospital
> a clinic

b. Have them write two or three sentences describing the location of the building. For example:

> It's on the north side of the city, near the baseball stadium.
> It's on Central Avenue, across from the university.
> It's at the corner of Arlington Street and Bay Boulevard.

c. Have students read their sentences aloud as the class listens and tries to guess the building.

Variation: This activity can be done in pairs or in small groups.

3. Make a Map

a. Divide the class into pairs or small groups.

b. Have each pair or group draw a map of the school's neighborhood, indicating the location of any important emergency agencies, such as a police station, hospital, clinic, or fire station.

c. Have students compare their maps.

4. Listen Carefully!

a. Tell students a short story about an emergency situation.

b. Make several statements about the story. Some statements should be true and others false.

c. Have students listen to the statements and decide if each is true or false. If a statement is false, have them correct it. For example:

> Teacher: The accident happened on the bridge.
> Student: False. It happened on the expressway.

Variation: This activity can be done as a game with two competing teams. The teams take turns deciding whether each statement is true or false.

5. What Really Happened?

a. Find two articles from two different newspapers about an accident or emergency situation that is reported.

b. Make copies of the articles and distribute them to the class.

c. Divide the class into pairs.

d. Have students read the two articles and compare the information in each. For example:

> "In the *Evening Gazette*, it says the man didn't see the robber."
> "In the *Daily Times*, it says he identified the robber."

e. Have students report their findings to the class.

6. Tell a Story!

a. Have students sit in a circle.

b. Begin the story by saying, "There was a terrible accident on Interstate 99 this morning."

c. The first student continues the story with one or two sentences. For example:

> "A bus filled with commuters overturned."

d. Continue around the room in this fashion, with each student adding a new sentence to the story.

172 EXIT SIX

Fill It In!

Have students do the activity individually, in pairs, or as a class. You may want to assign this exercise as homework.

1. a   5. a
2. a   6. a
3. b   7. a
4. b   8. b

Listen

Listen to the conversation and then answer true or false.

A. Police.
B. I want to report an accident.
A. Okay.
B. An airplane has landed on the expressway.
A. What's your name?
B. Rick Walters.
A. Where did this occur?
B. About two miles south of the airport, near Exit 4.
A. Okay. We'll be there right away.

1. There was an accident at the airport.
2. Rick Walters called to report the accident.

Now listen to the next conversation.

A. Police.
B. I want to report a robbery.
A. Okay. Go ahead.
B. A drug store has just been robbed at Milford Shopping Mall.
A. What's your name?
B. Helen Nichols.

3. Helen Milford called to report a robbery.
4. Someone robbed a drug store.

Now listen to the next conversation.

A. Sergeant Garner.
B. I'd like to report a mugging.
A. Yes. Go on.
B. A man just mugged two women in front of my apartment building. The address is forty-two fifty-three Harrison Street.

5. Two women just mugged someone.
6. Sergeant Garner called to report the mugging.

Now listen to the next conversation.

A. Police Department.
B. There's been an accident on Highway 85. A patrol car has been hit by a bus.

7. An accident has just occurred on Highway 85.
8. A police car and a bus were in an accident.

Answers

1. b   5. b
2. a   6. b
3. b   7. a
4. a   8. a

CrossTalk

Have students first work in pairs and then share with the class what they talked about.

InterActions

Have pairs of students practice role-playing the activity and then present their role plays to the class.

FOCUS

TOPICS

Drug Store: Over-the-Counter Drugs
Locating Items
Health: Ailments and Symptoms

GRAMMAR

Prepositions of Location

It's **in** Aisle 3, **on** the right.
It's **in** Aisle 2, **halfway down on** the left.
It's **on** the top shelf, **next to** the toothpaste.
It's **in** the last aisle, **on** the bottom shelf.
It's **in** the Cold Medicine section.
It's **in the front** of the store, **near** the checkout
  counter.

FUNCTIONS

1. **Advice–Suggestions**

    Asking for . . .

    Can you recommend ⎫
    Can you suggest ⎬ *something for a stuffy nose?*

    Offering . . .

    I recommend   ⎫
    I'd recommend ⎪
    I suggest   ⎬ *Sinus-Aid Decongestant Spray.*
    I'd suggest   ⎪
    Try   ⎭

2. **Checking and Indicating Understanding**

    Checking One's Own Understanding

    A stuffy nose?

3. **Hesitating**

    Let's see . . .

4. **Directions–Location**

    Inquiring about Location

    Where can I find it?

    Giving Location

    It's in Aisle *3*, on the *right*.
    It's in Aisle *2*, halfway down on the *left*.

    It's in Aisle *1*, on the *top* shelf next to the
      toothpaste.
    It's in the *last* aisle, on the *bottom* shelf.
    It's in the *Cold Medicine* section, next to
      the *aspirin*.
    It's in the front of the *store*, near the
      checkout counter.

VOCABULARY

Health	Medicine	Weather
cough (n.)	aspirin	cold weather
dry skin	cough medicine	dry weather
eyes	decongestant spray	freezing weather
frizzy hair	eye drops	heat wave
hair	lotion	humidity
headache	tablet	smog
itchy		
skin		
stuffy nose		
water eyes		

COMMENTARY

1. "Excuse me" (line 1) is commonly used to attract the attention of a clerk or salesperson in a store.

2. "Getting to me" (lines 4–5) means "bothering me" or "annoying me."

3. "I know what you mean" (line 6) expresses sympathy and understanding.

GETTING READY

Discuss students' weather preferences.

a. Check students' knowledge of basic weather vocabulary (for example: *hot/cold/warm/ cool, sunny, rain/rainy/raining, snow/snowy/ snowing, windy/cloudy, dry/humid*).

b. Write on the board:

> I like/enjoy _____ weather
>   because _____.
>
> I don't like/don't enjoy _____
>   weather because _____.

c. Ask the class what kind of weather they like and dislike. If they wish, students can use one of the models on the board to answer. For example, "I enjoy warm, sunny weather because I can take my children to the playground." "I don't like the snow because it's too cold and it's hard to walk on the sidewalk."

THE MODEL CONVERSATION

1. **Set the Scene:** "A woman is talking to a pharmacist in a drug store."

2. **Listen to the Model.**

3. **Class Practice.**

4. **Read.**

   Language Note
   "A stuffy nose" (line 2) is a congested nose. This person is having difficulty breathing easily.

5. **Pair Practice.**

6. **Alternative Expressions.**

THE EXERCISES

Examples

> 1. A. Excuse me. Can you recommend something for a bad cough?
>   B. A bad cough?
>   A. Yes. This dry weather is really getting to me.
>   B. I know what you mean. Let's see . . . a bad cough. I recommend Hacker's Cough Medicine.
>   A. Where can I find it?
>   B. It's in Aisle 2, halfway down on the left.
>   A. Thanks.
>
> 2. A. Excuse me. Can you suggest something for itchy, watery eyes?
>   B. Itchy, watery eyes?
>   A. Yes. This smog is really getting to me.
>   B. I know what you mean. Let's see . . . itchy, watery eyes. I'd recommend Optimal Eyedrops.
>   A. Where can I find them?
>   B. They're in Aisle 1, on the top shelf next to the toothpaste.
>   A. Thanks.

Before doing each exercise check students' understanding of the vocabulary and introduce any unfamiliar words or phrases. Have students use the footnoted expressions or any of their alternatives as they do the exercises.

Exercise Practice (optional). Have pairs of students simultaneously practice all the exercises.

Exercise Presentations. Call on pairs of students to present the exercises.

Language Notes

Exercise 4: A "heat wave" refers to a period of very hot weather.

Exercise 5: The "checkout counter" is the place where customers pay the cashier.

ORIGINAL STUDENT CONVERSATIONS

Have pairs of students create and present original conversations based on the model. (You may want students to prepare their original conversations as homework, then practice them the next day with another student and present them to the class.)

EXPANSION

1. Association Game

a. Divide the class into teams.

b. Call out different types of weather, such as:

> freezing cold
> dry heat
> heat wave
> rainy and humid
> smoggy

c. Have the students in each team work together to see how many health problems they can associate with that type of weather. For example:

> heat wave: dizzy/headaches/irritability

d. The team with the most items wins.

2. Guess What's Wrong!

a. Have each student choose an ailment and write recommendations for medicines to cure or relieve that ailment. Students should not mention the name of the ailment. For example:

> "I recommend aspirin, a cup of coffee, rest, and a cold washcloth on the head."

b. Have students taken turns reading their recommendations aloud. The class must listen and guess the name of the ailment.

[*a headache*]

3. Which Aisle?

a. Brainstorm with students the names of different aisles that might be found in a drug store, or pharmacy. For example:

> Cold and Cough
> First Aid
> Skin Care
> Hair Care

b. Call out the names of various over-the-counter medicines and health products, and have students identify the aisle name for each.

Fill It In!

Have students do the activity individually, in pairs, or as a class. You may want to assign this exercise as homework.

1. a
2. a
3. b
4. a
5. a
6. a
7. b
8. a

Listen

Listen and decide what each person's problem is.

1. Can you suggest a good lotion?
2. I recommend this new decongestant spray.
3. I need a couple of aspirin.
4. It gets frizzy in this humidity.
5. Try these eyedrops.
6. I didn't sleep well last night.

Answers

1. b
2. a
3. a
4. b
5. b
6. a

InterView

Have students circulate around the room to conduct their interviews, or have students interview people outside the class. Students should then report to the class about the results of their interviews.

FOCUS

TOPICS

Health: Ailments and Symptoms
Making an Appointment

GRAMMAR

1. **Present Perfect Tense**

   How long **have** you **had** a migraine headache?
   How long **hasn't** he **been** able to move his neck?

2. **Present Perfect Continuous Tense**

   How long **have** you **been** feel**ing** dizzy and nauseous?
   How long **has** your right ear **been** ring**ing**?

3. **Since/For**

   Since Sunday morning.
   Since he got tackled in last Saturday's football game.

   For two days.
   For over a week.

FUNCTIONS

1. **Asking for and Reporting Information**

   What seems to be the problem?

   How long have you *had a migraine headache*?

   Is *9:00 tomorrow morning* convenient?

2. **Checking and Indicating Understanding**

   Indicating Understanding
   I see.

3. **Want–Desire**

   Inquiring about . . .
   Would you like to *make an appointment*?

VOCABULARY

Health

dizzy
ear
migraine headache
nauseous
neck
ringing (ear)
toothache

GETTING READY

Review *since/for* and question formation with the present perfect tense.

a. Write the following on the board:

> A. You don't look very well. What's the matter?
> B. _____ .
> A. That's too bad. How long _____?
> B. For/Since _____ .

b. Model the following conversation, and have students repeat after you:

> A. You don't look very well. What's the matter?
> B. I have a headache.
> A. That's too bad. How long have you had a headache?
> B. For two days.

c. Call on a pair of students to present the conversation.

d. Give *illness cue cards* to several students. For example:

stomachache three days	sore throat a week
earache last week	backache yesterday morning

e. Have pairs of students create conversations based on the illnesses on their cue cards and the model on the board.

THE MODEL CONVERSATION

1. **Set the Scene:** "Someone is calling a doctor's office to make an appointment."
2. **Listen to the Model.**
3. **Class Practice.**
4. **Read.**
5. **Pair Practice.**

THE EXERCISES

Examples

> 1. A. Dentist's office.
>   B. Hello. This is Peter Johnson calling.
>   A. Yes, Mr. Johnson. What can I do for you?
>   B. I'm not feeling very well.
>   A. What seems to be the problem?
>   B. I have a bad toothache.
>   A. I see. Tell me, how long have you had a bad toothache?
>   B. Since Sunday morning.
>   A. Would you like to make an appointment?
>   B. Yes, please.
>   A. Is 2:00 today convenient?
>   B. Yes. That's fine. Thank you very much.
>
> 2. A. Riverside Clinic.
>   B. Hello. This is Thelma Walters calling.
>   A. Yes, Ms. Walters. What can I do for you?
>   B. I'm not feeling too well.
>   A. What seems to be the problem?
>   B. I'm feeling dizzy and nauseous.
>   A. I see. Tell me, how long have you been feeling dizzy and nauseous?

B. For the past three days.
A. Would you like to make an appointment?
B. Yes, please.
A. Is 3:30 tomorrow afternoon convenient?
B. Yes. That's fine. Thank you very much.

Before doing each exercise, check students' understanding of the vocabulary and introduce any unfamiliar words or phrases.

Exercise Practice (optional). Have pairs of students simultaneously practice all the exercises.

Exercise Presentations. Call on pairs of students to present the exercises.

Culture Note

Exercise 2: A "clinic" is a health center. There are both public and private clinics in the United States. Patients visiting a clinic might not be able to choose their doctors. Some clinics see patients on a "walk-in" basis (without appointments). Clinics that receive government funds have much lower rates than private doctors.

ORIGINAL STUDENT CONVERSATIONS

Have pairs of students create and present original conversations based on the model. (You may want students to prepare their original conversations as homework, then practice them the next day with another student and present them to the class.)

EXPANSION

1. Information Gap: How about the 25th at 3:30?

a. Find or make a calendar of five weekdays with room for you to write in information about morning and afternoon activities. Make a copy for each student. For example:

	MONDAY	TUESDAY	WEDNESDAY	THURSDAY	FRIDAY
A.M.					
P.M.					

b. Have each student fill in the calendar with his or her actual weekly schedule.

c. Have pairs of students role-play calling a doctor's office or clinic to make an appointment. One student plays the assistant at the doctor's office or clinic and suggests possible times for the appointment. The other uses his or her own calendar to choose a realistic time for the appointment. Have students take turns playing both roles. For example:

A. Hello. Riverside Medical Associates.
B. Hello. This is Gregory Martinez calling. I'd like to make an appointment for a checkup with Dr. Tabor.
A. Okay, Mr. Martinez. Have you seen Dr. Tabor before?
B. Yes, I have.
A. All right. Let's see . . . How about Tuesday the 25th at 3:30?
B. Sorry, but I'll be at work then. Do you have any openings in the morning?
A. Not on that day. Let me see. Is Friday at 8:00 in the morning okay?
B. That's fine.
A. Okay, Mr. Martinez. We'll see you on Friday the 28th at 8:00 A.M.
B. Thank you very much.
A. You're welcome. Good-bye.

2. What's the Question?

a. Dictate the following answers to the class:

For two hours.
Since last week.
For a few years.
Since I came here.
Since I met her.
Since I was a child.
For five minutes.

b. Have students write questions for which these answers would be correct. For example:

(*For two hours*.) How long have you been in class?
(*Since last week.*) How long have you been feeling dizzy?

c. Have students share their questions with each other.

What's the Answer?

Have students do the activity individually, in pairs, or as a class. You may want to assign this exercise as homework.

1. been able to, since
2. has been, for
3. hasn't, for
4. been able to, since
5. had, since
6. has been, for

InterActions

Arrange the desks and chairs in your classroom to look like a clinic. Assign students the following roles:

> doctors
> nurses
> receptionist
> patients and their families

Let students freely engage in this simulation. You may even want to join in as a character!

FOCUS

TOPIC

Health: Giving a Medical History

GRAMMAR

1. **Present Perfect Tense**

   Have you ever **been** hospitalized?
       No, I **haven't.**

2. **Question Formation**

   Do you have any allergies**?**
   Are you on a special diet of any kind**?**
   Have you ever had back trouble before**?**

3. **Short Answers**

   No, I don't.
   No, I'm not.
   No, I haven't.

FUNCTIONS

1. **Asking for and Reporting Additional Information**

   Just one or two more questions, if that's okay.

2. **Asking for and Reporting Information**

   Do you have *any allergies*?

   Have you ever *been hospitalized*?

VOCABULARY

Health

acupuncture	hospitalized
allergic	medical history
allergies	penicillin
anesthesia	reaction
back trouble	smoke (v.)
diet	surgery
heart disease	

COMMENTARY

1. It is common for doctors' offices and clinics in the United States to request information concerning a patient's medical history during a patient's first appointment.

2. "Please take a seat. The doctor will be with you in a few minutes" (lines 10–11) is typical *doctor's office talk*. Patients usually wait in a waiting room where there are chairs and magazines.

GETTING READY

Review question formation, as well as affirmative and negative short answers.

a. Write the following cues relating to health on the board:

> (have) any allergies
> (be) on a special diet
> (be) allergic to penicillin
> (smoke)
> (have) a history of heart disease

b. Introduce *Mr. and Mrs. Lane* by drawing their faces on the board:

c. Call on students to use the cues on the board to form questions about the Lanes. Have other students provide *yes* answers to the questions about Mr. Lane, and *no* answers to the questions about Mrs. Lane. For example:

A. Does Mr. Lane have any allergies?
B. Yes, he does.
A. Does Mrs. Lane have any allergies?
B. No, she doesn't.

A. Is Mr. Lane on a special diet?
B. Yes, he is.
A. Is Mrs. Lane on a special diet?
B. No, she isn't.

THE MODEL CONVERSATION

1. **Set the Scene:** "A nurse is talking to a patient at the doctor's office."
2. **Listen to the Model.**
3. **Class Practice.**
4. **Read.**
5. **Pair Practice.**

THE EXERCISES

Examples

---

1. A. Well, Ms. Penfield, I think you've given me almost all the information I need for your medical history. Just one or two more questions, if that's okay.
   B. Certainly.
   A. Are you on any kind of special diet?
   B. No, I'm not.
   A. And have you ever had back trouble before?
   B. No, I haven't.
   A. All right, Ms. Penfield. Please take a seat. The doctor will be with you in a few minutes.

2. A. Well, Mr. Park, I think you've given me almost all the information I need for your medical history. Just one or two more questions, if that's okay.
   B. Certainly.
   A. Are you allergic to penicillin?
   B. No, I'm not.
   A. And have you ever had surgery?
   B. No, I haven't.
   A. All right, Mr. Park. Please take a seat. The doctor will be with you in a few minutes.

Before doing each exercise, check students' understanding of the vocabulary and introduce any unfamiliar words or phrases.

Exercise Practice (optional). Have pairs of students simultaneously practice all the exercises.

Exercise Presentations. Call on pairs of students to present the exercises.

ORIGINAL STUDENT CONVERSATIONS

Have pairs of students create and present original conversations based on the model. (You may want students to prepare their original conversations as homework, then practice them the next day with another student and present them to the class.)

EXPANSION

1. Vocabulary Enrichment

Have the class work together to create a reference list of medical specialists.

a. Ask students what kinds of doctors they know of. For example: What do you call an eye doctor? (*an optometrist*) A tooth doctor? (*a dentist*) A children's doctor? (*a pediatrician*) A bone doctor? (*an orthopedist*) A women's doctor? (*a gynecologist*) A specialist in childbirth? (*an obstetrician*) A heart specialist? (*a cardiologist*) Encourage students to use dictionaries.

b. Based on your students' ideas, prepare a list and make copies for the class.

2. Conversations About Allergies

Have students create conversations about their own or other people's allergies.

a. Write the following conversational model on the board:

A. You know, (I'm/my friend _____)
   is allergic to _____.
B. Really? I guess that means _____
   _____.
A. That's right.

---

b. Have students present their conversations to the class. For example:

A. You know, I'm allergic to milk products.
B. Really? I guess that means you can't eat ice cream.
A. That's right.

A. You know, my friend Peter is allergic to grass pollen.
B. Really? I guess that means he has to take allergy medicine.
A. That's right.

3. Medical History Interviews

a. Write on the board various issues that may be covered in a medical history. For example:

> past surgery
> allergies
> special diet
> family history of disease
> special medical conditions
> current medication

b. In pairs, have students role-play a medical history interview. One student is the patient and the other is the interviewer. They may refer to the issues on the board as a guide to the interview.

4. Class Survey

Have students brainstorm health history questions and then conduct a survey of their classmates. Have them report their findings to the class.

5. Filling Out Medical Histories

Get copies of a medical history sheet at your doctor's office or a local clinic. Have students complete the form individually for their own reference.

6. Presentation Project

a. Divide the class into teams. Have each team research one of the following topics:

> common allergies
> special diets
> acupuncture
> alternative medical practices
> heart disease
> back trouble
> antibiotics and current resistances

b. Have each team write a report of their research and then deliver a short presentation to the class.

What's the Question?

Have students do the activity individually, in pairs, or as a class. You may want to assign this exercise as homework.

1. Is your son allergic to any medicine?
2. Have you ever had acupuncture before?
3. Has your daughter ever had anesthesia before?
4. Do I have to go on a special diet?
5. Does my mother have to have surgery?

Fill It In!

Have students do the activity individually, in pairs, or as a class. You may want to assign this exercise as homework.

1. a
2. b
3. a
4. b
5. b
6. b

Cultural Intersections

Have students discuss the questions in pairs, in small groups, or as a class.

FOCUS

TOPIC

Health: Medical Advice

GRAMMAR

1. **Must**

   You really **must** (change your diet).

2. **Should**

   You **should** eat less salty food.

3. **Might**

   You **might** look for a cookbook that has
   low-fat recipes.

4. **Could**

   You **could** join a health club.

FUNCTIONS

1. **Fear–Worry–Anxiety**

   Expressing . . .
   I'm concerned about *your blood pressure*.

2. **Checking and Indicating Understanding**

   Checking One's Own Understanding
   My blood pressure?

   Indicating Understanding
   I understand.

3. **Advice–Suggestions**

   Offering . . .
   I strongly advise you to
   I strongly recommend that you } *change your diet.*
   I urge you to

   You should *eat less salty food.*

   You might
   You could } *join a health club.*
   It might be a good idea to

VOCABULARY

Health

blood pressure	low-fat
exercise routine	lungs
hearing (n.)	salty food
lifestyle	weight

COMMENTARY

1. "Hmm. That won't be easy" (line 4). Speaker B hesitates after hearing the doctor's strong advice and then expresses concern.

2. "You really must. It's absolutely essential" (lines 5–6). The doctor is strongly advising the patient to do as she says.

GETTING READY

Practice expressions for giving advice and suggestions.

a. Introduce a character named George by drawing a tired-looking face on the board. Tell the class that George is very tired because he doesn't sleep well at night.

b. Write the following expressions on the board for giving advice and suggestions:

> He should _____.
> He could _____.
> He might _____.
> It might be a good idea to _____.

c. Have students in the class offer advice and suggestions. For example:

> "He should drink a glass of milk before bed."
> "He could take a walk before bedtime."
> "It might be a good idea to take a hot shower before bed."

THE MODEL CONVERSATION

1. **Set the Scene:** "A doctor has finished examining a patient and is giving him some medical advice."

2. **Listen to the Model.**

3. **Class Practice.**

4. **Read.**

5. **Pair Practice.**

6. **Alternative Expressions.**

THE EXERCISES

Examples

1. A. I'm concerned about your weight.
   B. My weight?
   A. Yes. I strongly advise you to lose several pounds.
   B. Hmm. That won't be easy.
   A. I know, but you really must. It's absolutely essential.
   B. I understand. Do you have any suggestions that might help?
   A. Yes. You should start jogging. And you might join a health club.
   B. Thank you. Those are good suggestions.

2. A. I'm concerned about your back.
   B. My back?
   A. Yes. I strongly recommend that you begin a daily exercise routine.
   B. Hmm. That won't be easy.
   A. I know, but you really must. It's absolutely essential.
   B. I understand. Do you have any suggestions that might help?
   A. Yes. You should do sit-ups three times a day. And you could take up swimming or join a yoga class.
   B. Thank you. Those are good suggestions.

Before doing each exercise, check students' understanding of the vocabulary and introduce any unfamiliar words or phrases. Have students use the footnoted expressions or any of their alternatives as they do the exercises.

Exercise Practice (optional). Have pairs of students simultaneously practice all the exercises.

Exercise Presentations. Call on pairs of students to present the exercises.

Language Notes

Exercise 2: "Sit-ups" are exercises that strengthen the stomach muscles. A person lies down with the back flat on the floor and then pulls up to a sitting position without using the arms or legs for support.

Exercise 4: To "kick the habit" is to break or stop a bad habit.

ORIGINAL STUDENT CONVERSATIONS

Have pairs of students create and present original conversations based on the model. (You may want students to prepare their original conversations as homework, then practice them the next day with another student and present them to the class.)

EXPANSION

1. Information Gap: Some Friendly Advice

a. Write the following information on index cards, and make enough copies for the class.

b. Divide the class into pairs. Give Role A to one member of the pair and Role B to the other.

c. Have students role-play the situations.

1.

Role A:

You haven't had a medical checkup for a long time. You feel fine and healthy, and you don't think it's necessary. Discuss this with your friend.

Role B:

You believe that everybody should have a medical checkup once a year. You're worried because your friend never gets checkups. Give your friend some advice about going to see a doctor.

2.

Role A:

You sometimes have problems with your back. When you ride in a car for a long time, your back hurts. Right now you're working as a taxi driver, so you drive all day long. Ask your friend for advice.

Role B:

Your friend wants to talk to you about a medical problem. Listen carefully and try to give your friend some good advice.

3.

Role A:

You've been getting a lot of headaches lately, and your eyes get tired very easily. Tell your friend about it. Maybe your friend can give you some advice.

Role B:

Your friend wants to tell you about a problem. You have a problem, too. You want to get more exercise, but you don't have much free time. Ask your friend for advice.

4.

Role A:

You're a new parent. Your 9-month-old baby refuses to eat vegetables. He just throws them on the floor. You've tried giving him cooked carrots, peas, and beans, but he won't eat them. Ask a friend for advice.

Role B:

Your children are now teenagers. You've had a lot of experience as a parent. One of your friends is a new parent and needs your advice.

5.

Role A:

You like your friend very much, but this friend worries about everything. Your friend always tells you about a problem he or she is having. You always listen, but usually say, "Don't worry so much! It's not serious."

Role B:

You've been feeling very tired since last week. You have a little cold, and your nose is stuffy. You also think you might have a fever. Your head is a little warm. You don't know what to do. Talk to your friend about it.

2. Suggestion Game

a. Divide the class into several teams.

b. Pretend that you are a patient with a lot of medical problems. Tell the class about different types of medical problems you have, such as:

> high blood pressure
> back pain
> stress and exhaustion
> ringing ears
> insomnia
> dizziness
> migraine headaches

c. Have the students in each team work together to see how many appropriate health suggestions they can make for each of your medical problems. For example:

> Teacher: My doctor says that I have high blood pressure.
> Team 1: You should go on a low-fat diet. You should stop eating salty foods. We strongly recommend that you exercise daily.

d. The team with the most suggestions wins.

3. Class Survey: Health Habits

a. Have students work in pairs to develop a questionnaire about health habits. Each pair may focus on a different theme. For example:

> diet
> exercise

> medicines and vitamins
> sleep
> stress reduction
> skin care
> ear and eye care

b. Have each team conduct a survey of their classmates, compile the results, and report their findings to class.

Variation: You may want students to do a school-wide survey. They could then *publish* their findings in a bulletin or post them in a hallway exhibit.

4. Find Someone Who . . .

a. Collect some information about students' health habits.

b. Put this information in the following form:

> Find someone who . . .
>
> 1. jogs two miles a day. _____
> 2. does fifty sit-ups every morning. _____
> 3. is a vegetarian. _____
> 4. drinks eight glasses of water a day. _____
> 5. sleeps eight hours every night. _____

c. Have students ask each other questions to identify the above people.

d. The first student to identify all the people correctly wins.

5. Advice! Advice!

a. Divide the class into pairs.

b. Have students write a conversation of *giving and receiving advice* between any of the following people:

> doctor/patient
> mother/daughter
> father/son
> big brother/little sister
> teacher/student
> friend/friend

c. Have students take turns acting out their conversations, *without telling who the characters are*. The class must listen and guess the role of the speakers.

What's the Meaning?

Have students do the activity individually, in pairs, or as a class. You may want to assign this exercise as homework.

1. c
2. b
3. c
4. c
5. c
6. a

Your Turn

Have students develop their presentations on their own and then share them with the class. Before students make their presentation, review some aspects of good presentation delivery. For example:

Practice at home.
Don't speak directly from the index cards.
Look at your audience.
Project your voice.
Use props or other visual aids.

FOCUS

TOPIC

Drug Store: Prescriptions

GRAMMAR

1. **Supposed to**

   You're **supposed to** take one tablet three times a day.

2. **Have to/Have Got to**

   You **have to** take two tablets four times a day.
   You**'ve got to** take one capsule after each meal.

3. **Need to**

   You **need to** take two pills one half-hour before eating.

4. **Must**

   You **must** take two teaspoons as needed.

5. **Might**

   You **might** feel tired after taking this medication.

6. **May**

   You **may** have a slight headache after taking this medication.

7. **Could**

   You **could** possibly feel dizzy after taking this medication.

FUNCTIONS

1. **Instructing**

   Be sure to *follow the directions on the label.*

2. **Obligation**

   Expressing . . .

   You're supposed to ⎫
   You have to   ⎪
   You've got to   ⎬ *take one tablet three times a day.*
   You need to   ⎪
   You must   ⎭

3. Checking and Indicating Understanding

Indicating Understanding
I see.
I understand.

4. Asking for and Reporting Additional Information

And one more thing.

5. Possibility/Impossibility

Expressing Possibility
You might
You may
You could possibly } *feel tired.*
It's possible you'll

6. Fear–Worry–Anxiety

Responding to . . .
Don't worry.

VOCABULARY

Health	Medicine	
appetite	capsule	prescription
lightheaded	label (n.)	side effect
sleepy	medication	tablet
tired	pill	teaspoon

COMMENTARY

1. The pharmacist says "Okay" (line 1) to attract the customer's attention.

2. "Now be sure to" (line 3) is a friendly way of prefacing advice.

3. "And one more thing" (line 8) is an expression used to introduce additional instructions.

4. "Oh?" (line 11) indicates that Speaker B is hesitating. Her question intonation expresses concern and possibly a wish for more information.

5. In lines 12–13, Speaker A responds by reassuring her, "Yes, but don't worry. That's a common side effect."

6. A "side effect" (line 13) is a symptom or problem caused by a medication.

GETTING READY

Practice giving directions for taking medicine.

a. Write the following on the board:

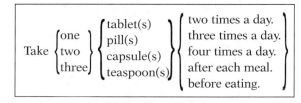

b. Check students' understanding of the words *tablet, pill, capsule,* and *teaspoon.*

c. Practice giving directions chorally and individually. Point to different words in each column to create different directions.

THE MODEL CONVERSATION

1. **Set the Scene:** "A pharmacist is handing a woman her medicine. He's checking to make sure that she understands the directions."
2. **Listen to the Model.**
3. **Class Practice.**
4. **Read.**
5. **Pair Practice.**
6. **Alternative Expressions.**

THE EXERCISES

Examples

---

1. A. Okay. Here's your prescription.
   B. Thank you.
   A. Now be sure to follow the directions on the label. You're supposed to take two tablets four times a day.
   B. I understand. Two tablets four times a day.
   A. That's right. And one more thing. You might have a slight headache after taking this medication.
   B. Oh?
   A. Yes, but don't worry. That's a common side effect.
   B. I see. Well, thanks very much.

2. A. Okay. Here's your prescription.
   B. Thank you.
   A. Now be sure to follow the directions on the label. You have to take one capsule after each meal.
   B. I understand. One capsule after each meal.
   A. That's right. And one more thing. You may feel dizzy after taking this medication.
   B. Oh?
   A. Yes, but don't worry. That's a common side effect.
   B. I see. Well, thanks very much.

Before doing each exercise, check students' understanding of the vocabulary and introduce any unfamiliar words or phrases. Have students use the footnoted expressions or any of their alternatives as they do the exercises.

Exercise Practice (optional). Have pairs of students simultaneously practice all the exercises.

Exercise Presentations. Call on pairs of students to present the exercises.

Language Note

Exercise 4: "Lightheaded" means dizzy.

ORIGINAL STUDENT CONVERSATIONS

Have pairs of students create and present original conversations based on the model. (You may want students to prepare their original conversations as homework, then practice them the next day with another student and present them to the class.)

EXPANSION

1. Survival Skills: Read the Label Carefully!

a. Collect a wide variety of prescription and nonprescription medicine labels (or copy the text from a variety of labels).

b. Create a reading activity in which students read the labels and answer questions about them. For example:

> How often do you take this medicine?
> How much do you take at one time?
> Do you have to keep it in the refrigerator?
> Can you refill this prescription?
> What are the possible side effects of this medicine?
> Can children take this medicine?
> Can pregnant women or nursing mothers take this medicine?
> What is the expiration date?
> How much can you take in one day (24 hours)?

2. Writing a List: What Do We Need in the Medicine Cabinet?

This activity provides vocabulary enrichment and an opportunity to discuss cultural differences in treating common health and beauty problems.

a. Have students imagine that they are moving to a new apartment and need to buy supplies for the medicine cabinet.

b. Divide the class into pairs or small groups, and have them create lists of first-aid supplies, medicine, and health and beauty products they want to have in their medicine cabinets. Encourage students to use dictionaries. For example:

aspirin	decongestant
acetaminophen	toothpaste
adhesive bandages	mouthwash
alcohol	dental floss
burn ointment	hand lotion
antiseptic cream	hair spray

bandages and tape shaving lotion
ipecac (for young children) razors
thermometer cotton balls
cough medicine antacid tablets

3. Telephone

a. Divide the class into large groups. Have each group sit in a circle.

b. Whisper a set of directions for taking medication to one student. For example:

"Take two tablets every four hours with food. Do not take more than eight tablets a day. Finish all the medication."

c. The first student whispers the directions to the second student, and so forth around the circle. The student listening may repeat for clarification by saying, "I understand. Two tablets every four hours."

d. When the message gets to the last student, that person says it aloud. Is it the same set of directions you started with? The group with the most accurate message wins.

4. Research Project

There are many different systems for paying the high costs of medicine. In some countries, governments support the cost of medicine. In others, insurance companies do.

a. Divide the class into teams.

b. Have each team research some of the health care systems available today around the world. When students do their research, they should consider the following questions:

What are the advantages of this system?
What are the disadvantages of this system?
Why is medicine so expensive?
Who pays the cost of research?
Are pharmaceutical companies allowed to advertise to the general public?
Are there different brands of the same kind of medicine?
How does a doctor decide which brand to prescribe?

c. Have the teams present their findings to the class.

Constructions Ahead!

Have students do the activity individually, in pairs, or as a class. You may want to assign this exercise as homework.

1. You're supposed to take
2. They're supposed to call
3. She's supposed to have
4. He's supposed to meet us
5. It's supposed to land
6. We're supposed to arrive
7. I'm supposed to return their call

What's the Word?

Have students do the activity individually, in pairs, or as a class. You may want to assign this exercise as homework.

1. You're, your
2. You've
3. you'll
4. You
5. You've, you'll
6. You, you
7. You've, your, you're

Reading: *It Might Work for You*

Preview: Have students look at the illustrations and discuss the following questions:

> What remedies do you think these people are using?
> Do you use any special home remedies? If so, what are they?

Then have students read the passage silently, or have them listen to the passage and take notes as you read it or play the audiotape.

True or False?

Have students do the activity individually, in pairs, or as a class. You may want to assign this exercise as homework.

1. False
2. True
3. False
4. True
5. True
6. False

Do You Remember?

Have students do the activity individually, in pairs, or as a class. You may want to assign this exercise as homework.

1. b
2. c
3. b
4. a
5. c

Reflections

Have students discuss the questions in pairs or small groups and then share their ideas with the class.

Your Turn

Have students write their responses at home and then share their written work with other students and discuss in class.

FOCUS

TOPIC

Health: Medical Advice

GRAMMAR

1. **Should**

   You **should** blow into a paper bag.

2. **Ought to**

   You **ought to** blow into a paper bag.

3. **Could**

   You **could** hold your breath and count to twenty.

4. **Might**

   You **might** hold your breath and count to twenty.

FUNCTIONS

1. **Asking for and Reporting Information**

   What's the matter?
   What's wrong?
   What's the problem?

2. **Advice–Suggestions**

   Asking for . . .
   Any other suggestions?

   Offering . . .
   You should
   You ought to } *blow into a paper bag.*

   You might *hold your breath.*
   You could *hold your breath.*
   It might be a good idea to *hold your breath.*
   Why don't you *hold your breath?*

   Can I offer a suggestion?

VOCABULARY

Health

bloody nose
breath
hiccups
leg
muscle cramp
stomach
upset stomach

COMMENTARY

1. "Oh no!" (line 1) expresses dismay.
2. "I'll give it a try" (line 12) is an informal way of saying "I'll try it."

GETTING READY

Introduce the word *hiccups* and the expression *(have) the hiccups*. Point out that the word *hiccup* sounds like what it names — the hiccup. Ask your students what the word for *hiccup* is in other languages.

THE MODEL CONVERSATION

1. **Set the Scene:** "Someone at an office has the hiccups. His co-worker is giving him some advice."
2. **Listen to the Model.**
3. **Class Practice.**
4. **Read.**
5. **Pair Practice.**
6. **Alternative Expressions.**

Now have pairs of students create and present original conversations using the model dialog as a guide. Encourage students to be inventive and to use new vocabulary. (You may want to assign this exercise as homework, having students prepare their original conversations, practice them the next day with another student, and then present them to the class.) Students should present their conversations without referring to the written text, but they also should not memorize them. Rather, they should feel free to adapt and expand them any way they wish.

Matching Lines

Have students do the activity individually, in pairs, or as a class. You may want to assign this exercise as homework.

1. e
2. h
3. i
4. b
5. g
6. d
7. c
8. f
9. a

Read the Label

Have students do the activity individually, in pairs, or as a class. You may want to assign this exercise as homework.

1. b
2. c
3. a
4. c

Looking Back

Have students look at the list of expressions. Encourage them to ask you any questions about the meaning or pronunciation of any of the words. If students ask for the pronunciation, repeat after the student until the student is satisfied with his or her pronunciation of the word.

Review Activities

To review the language introduced in the unit, do the following activities.

1. Association Game

a. Divide the class into several teams.

b. Call out a topic category from the *Looking Back* section on student text page 112.

c. Have students in each group work together to see how many phrases they can associate with that category. For example:

Giving Advice: You should
You ought to
I recommend
I suggest
You might
You could

d. The team with the most phrases wins.

2. Create a Conversation!

a. Divide the class into pairs of students.

b. Tell each pair they have three minutes to make up a conversation using one item from each category from the *Looking Back* section on page 112 of the student text.

c. Have students share their conversations with the class.

Have students talk about the people and the situations and then present role plays based on the scenes. Students may refer to previous lessons as a resource, but they should not simply reuse specific conversations. (You may want to assign these exercises as written homework, having students prepare their conversations, practice them the next day with another student, and then present them to the class.)

1. **FOCUS: Housing: Obtaining Housing**

   A family is looking for an apartment. They're talking with a real estate agent.

2. **FOCUS: Supermarket: Locating Items**

   A young man is shopping in the supermarket, and he can't find some of the things on his shopping list.

3. **FOCUS: Employment/Getting a Job: Stating Skills and Qualifications; Inquiring about Job Responsibilities; Describing Personal Background; Inquiring about Wages, Hours, and Benefits**
   Personal Information: Work Experience

   Someone is at a job interview.

4. **FOCUS: Employment/On the Job: Making and Fulfilling Requests**

   A supervisor is talking to an employee who hasn't done something he was supposed to do.

5. **FOCUS: Emergencies: Reporting a Home Emergency, Reporting an Accident or Incident**
   Personal Information: Name, Address, Telephone Number

   There has been an emergency, and someone is calling the police.

6. **FOCUS: Drug Store: Over-the-Counter Drugs, Locating Items**
   Health: Ailments and Symptoms

   A clerk at a drug store is helping someone with a terrible sunburn.

7. **FOCUS: Health: Ailments and Symptoms, Making an Appointment**

   Someone is calling the doctor's office.

8. **FOCUS: Health: Medical Advice**

   A patient is talking to the doctor after a medical examination.

EXIT 7

OVERVIEW
Student Text
Pages 115–132

Topics	Functions	Grammar

P. 116 Where Can I Find Washing Machines?

Department Store: Locating Items	Attracting Attention Directions–Location Checking and Indicating Understanding	Prepositions of Location

P. 118 I'd Like to Buy a Sony Color TV

Department Store: Purchasing an Item	Offering to Help Want–Desire Identifying	One/Ones

P. 120 I'm Looking for a Leather Belt for My Husband

Department Store: Purchasing an Item Clothing: Describing Clothing, Selecting Clothing	Attracting Attention Requests Offering to Help Want–Desire Certainty/Uncertainty Checking and Indicating Understanding	Adjectives

P. 122 I'd Like to Return This Coat

Department Store: Returning an item Clothing: Describing Clothing	Want–Desire Asking for and Reporting Information Satisfaction/ Dissatisfaction	Adjectives Too Comparatives One/Ones

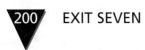

Topics	Functions	Grammar

P. 126 I'd Like to Purchase a Money Order, Please

Post Office: Using
  Postal Services

Want–Desire
Apologizing
Checking and Indicating
  Understanding

Passives
Singular/Plural

P. 128 I'd Like to Mail This Package to Minneapolis

Post Office: Mailing
  Packages

Want–Desire
Hesitating
Checking and Indicating
  Understanding
Agreement/Disagreement
Asking for and Reporting
  Information

Future: Will

Pp. 130–131 I'm Interested in This Car

Automobiles: Buying a
  Car

Offering to Help
Asking for and Reporting
  Information
Focusing Attention
Hesitating

Passives

LOOKING AHEAD

Grammar This Exit

Prepositions of Location

They're **in** the Household Appliances Department
  in the basement.
They're **on** the second floor.
You'll see Children's Clothing **on** the left.
You'll see Furniture **on** the right **in** the corner.
They're **at the rear of** the store.
There's an elevator **near** the main entrance.
Walk **up** this staircase.
Walk **down** this aisle **past** Women's Clothing.
Take the escalator over there **down** one floor.

Adjectives

I'm looking for a **leather** belt.
I think he's a **size 36**.
A **size 36 dark brown leather** belt.
It's too **lightweight**.
They're too **long**.

Too

It's **too** lightweight.
They're **too** long.

Comparatives

Would you like to exchange them for some
    shorter   ones?
    heavier
    bigger
    larger
    more difficult

One/Ones

Which **one** are you interested in?
  I'd like the **one** with the 25-inch screen.
Would you like to exchange it for a heavier **one**?

Would you like to exchange them for some
  shorter **ones**?

Passives

Money orders can **be purchased** at Window
  Number 3.
The controls on the dashboard **are**
  computerized.

Future: Will

How long **will** it take?
How much **will** it cost?
That**'ll** cost five ninety-four.
I'll send it parcel post.

Singular/Plural

I'd like to purchase a money order.
Money order**s** can be purchased at Window
  Number 3.

Functions This Exit

Want–Desire

Inquiring about . . .

Would you like to _____?
Do you want to _____?
[*more formal*]
Would you care to _____?

Which one are you interested in?

What *color* would you like?

How would you like to *send it*?

Expressing . . .

I'd like to _____.
I want to _____.

I'd like (to buy) _____.
I want to buy _____.
I'd like to purchase _____.
I'm looking for _____.

Asking for and Reporting Information

May I ask _____?
Can I ask _____?
Could I ask _____?

Tell me, _____?

How long will that take?

How much will it cost?
  That'll cost _____.

Offering to Help

Making an Offer

May I help you?
Can I help you?

What can I do for you?

Would you like me to _____?

Identifying

The one with *the 25-inch screen*.
The one that *makes 12 cups*.

Directions–Location

Asking for Directions

Could you tell me how to get there?
Can you tell me how to get there?

Giving Directions

Take the *escalator* (over there) down *one* floor.
Walk up (this staircase) *one* flight and you'll be on "3."
Walk down this aisle (past *Women's Clothing*) and you'll see *Furniture* on the *right* in the corner.
You can walk *down* the steps (over there) *two* flights.
Walk down that way until you come to *the snack bar*.

Inquiring about Location

Where can I find _____?
Where are _____?
Where are _____located?

Giving Location

They're in *the Household Appliances Department*
{ in the *basement*.
  on the *second* floor.
  at the *rear* of the *store*.
  on the *ground level*.
  near the *side entrance*.

Satisfaction/Dissatisfaction

Expressing Dissatisfaction

It's too _____.
They're too _____.

Attracting Attention

Excuse me.

Requests

Direct, More Polite

Could you help me?
Can you help me?

Responding to Requests

Certainly.
Of course.
I'd be happy to.
I'd be glad to.

Certainty/Uncertainty

Expressing Certainty

I'm sure _____.

Apologizing

I'm sorry.
Sorry.

Agreement/Disagreement

Expressing Agreement

I suppose it is.
I guess it is.

Checking and Indicating Understanding

Checking One's Own Understanding

Washing machines?
In the basement?
Window Number 3?

Let's see . . . *a size 36 dark brown leather belt.*

Did you say _____?
Was that _____?

Indicating Understanding

I see.

Hesitating

Let's see.
Let me see.
Let's see now.

Uh . . .

Focusing Attention

Let me point out . . .
Notice (that) . . .
I should (also) point out (that) . . .
Let me mention that . . .

PREVIEWING EXIT 7: CHAPTER-OPENING PHOTOS

Have students talk about the people and the situations and, as a class or in pairs, predict what the characters might be saying to each other. Students in pairs or small groups may enjoy practicing role plays based on these scenes and then presenting them to the class.

Text Page 116: Where Can I Find Washing Machines?

FOCUS

TOPIC

Department Store: Locating Items

GRAMMAR

Prepositions of Location

They're **in** the Household Appliances
   Department **in** the basement.
They're **on** the second floor.
You'll see Children's Clothing **on** the left.
You'll see Furniture **on** the right **in** the corner.
They're **at the rear of** the store.
There's an elevator **near** the main entrance.
Walk **up** this staircase.
Walk **down** this aisle **past** Women's Clothing.
Take the escalator over there **down** one floor.

FUNCTIONS

1. **Attracting Attention**

   Excuse me.

2. **Directions–Location**

   Asking for Directions

   Could you tell me how to get there?
   Can you tell me how to get there?

   Giving Directions

   Take the *escalator* over there down *one*
      floor.
   Walk up this staircase *one* flight and you'll
      be on "3."

   Inquiring about Location

   Where can I find *washing machines*?
   Where are *washing machines*?
   Where are *washing machines* located?

   Giving Location

   They're in *the Household Appliances
   Department* in the *basement*.

3. **Checking and Indicating Understanding**

   Checking One's Own Understanding

   Washing machines?

   Indicating Understanding

   I see.

VOCABULARY

Clothing	Department Store	
jeans	aisle	Children's Clothing Department
designer jeans	basement	Furniture Department
necktie	elevator	Home Entertainment Department
	escalator	Household Appliances
	ground level	Department
	main entrance	Housewares Department
	side entrance	Men's Clothing Department
	snack bar	Women's Clothing Department
	staircase	
	steps	bedroom set
		pots and pans
		videocassette recorder
		washing machine

GETTING READY

1. Tell students that the class is going to talk about department stores.

   a. Ask if they know the names of some departments in a store. Write their suggestions on the board. Be sure to include: *Children's Clothing Department, Furniture Department, Home Entertainment Department, Household Appliances Department, Housewares Department, Men's Clothing Department, Women's Clothing Department, Shoe Department, Stationery Department, Toy Department*.

   b. Name an item and have students tell in which department they would find it. For example:

a dress	(Women's Clothing Department)
a sofa	(Furniture Department)
a refrigerator	(Household Appliances Department)
a CD player	(Home Entertainment Department)
dishes	(Housewares Department)

   c. Call on students to think of items, and have other students name the departments.

2. Bring in a department store map, or draw a simple floor plan on the board or on a handout. Have students locate various departments and practice describing their locations using prepositions of location. For example:

   "Where's the Housewares Department?" ("It's near the main entrance." "It's on the right." "It's in the basement.")

THE MODEL CONVERSATION

1. **Set the Scene:** "A customer in a department store wants to buy a washing machine. He's asking a salesperson where they are."

2. **Listen to the Model.**

3. **Class Practice.**

4. **Read.**

5. **Pair Practice.**

6. **Alternative Expressions.**

THE EXERCISES

Examples

1. A. Excuse me. Where can I find neckties?
   B. Neckties? They're in the Men's Clothing Department on the 2nd floor.
   A. On the 2nd floor? I see. Could you tell me how to get there?
   B. Sure. There's an elevator near the main entrance to the store.
   A. Thanks very much.

2. A. Excuse me. Where are pots and pans?
   B. Pots and pans? They're in the Housewares Department on the 3rd floor.
   A. On the 3rd floor? I see. Can you tell me how to get there?
   B. Sure. Walk up this staircase one flight and you'll be on "3."
   A. Thanks very much.

Before doing each exercise, check students' understanding of the vocabulary and introduce any unfamiliar words or phrases. Have students use the footnoted expressions or any of their alternatives as they do the exercises.

Exercise Practice (optional). Have pairs of students simultaneously practice all the exercises.

Exercise Presentations. Call on pairs of students to present the exercises.

Language Notes

Exercise 2: "On '3'" means "on the third floor."

Exercise 4: "The ground level" is the lowest floor in the building.

Culture Notes

Exercise 5: "Designer jeans" refers to jeans that carry the "signature" or emblem of the designer, usually on the back pocket.

Exercise 5: "Snack bar." Many large department stores in the United States have snack bars, coffee shops, or restaurants, where shoppers can sit down and eat.

ORIGINAL STUDENT CONVERSATIONS

Have pairs of students create and present original conversations based on the model. (You may want students to prepare their original conversations as homework, then practice them the next day with another student and present them to the class.)

EXPANSION

1. Information Gap: Asking for Directions in a Store

a. Divide the class into pairs. Have one person in each pair be a *salesperson* and the other a *customer* in a department store.

b. Give all the salespeople in each pair a *store directory* or map. This page could be a copy of a real store directory, or it could be a page you have created.

c. Give all the customers in each pair a cue card with three items that can be found in different departments. For example:

```
stove
woman's coat
cassette tape
```

Tell that student: "You need to find these items in the store, and you don't know where the departments are. Ask the salesperson to give you directions."

d. Have the pairs role-play the situation. Encourage students to practice checking and indicating understanding while they are talking.

2. Class Discussion: The Best Stores in Town

a. Have students talk about stores where they like to shop. Possible questions are:

In your opinion, what's the best department store in town?
Where is it located?
Why do you think it's the best store?

b. Name an item, and ask students the best place to buy it. For example:

In your opinion, where's the best place to buy a refrigerator? a winter coat? a CD player?

3. Draw, Write, and Read

a. Have students think of a store they visited recently and draw a floor plan. Then have them write a description to accompany the picture.

b. In pairs, have students describe the floor plans as they show their pictures. As students describe their plans, they may wish to add more details, which they should also add to their diagrams.

4. Picture This!

Describe the layout of a department store and have students draw what you describe. For example:

"There are five floors in this store. The escalators are in the middle of the store, and the staircase is in the back near the elevators. The Jewelry Department and the Shoe Department are on the first floor. The Women's Clothing Department is on the second floor. (etc.)"

ExpressWays

Have students do the activity individually, in pairs, or as a class. You may want to assign this exercise as homework. You may wish to point out to students that *B* is an abbreviation for *Basement*.

1. Furniture, first
2. Household Appliances, sixth
3. Home Entertainment, third
4. Housewares, basement
5. Children's Clothing, second
6. Women's Clothing, fifth
7. Men's Clothing, fourth
8. Customer Service, seventh

Listen

Listen and complete the sentence.

1. I parked the car near . . .
2. Take the elevator to . . .
3. Household appliances? They're on . . .
4. We left it at the front of the . . .
5. Did they put the boxes in . . . ?
6. The staircase is on the . . .

Answers

1. a
2. a
3. b
4. b
5. a
6. b

Figure It Out!

Do the activity as a class, in pairs, or in small groups. You may want to do the activity as a game with competing teams.

FOCUS

TOPIC

Department Store: Purchasing an Item

GRAMMAR

One/Ones

Which **one** are you interested in?
I'd like the **one** with the 25-inch screen and remote control.
I'd like the **one** that's also a calculator.

FUNCTIONS

1. **Offering to Help**

    Making an Offer
    May I help you?
    Can I help you?

2. **Want–Desire**

    Inquiring about . . .
    Which one are you interested in?

    Expressing . . .
    I'd like to buy *a Sony color TV.*
    I'd like *the one with the 25-inch screen.*

3. **Identifying**

    The one with *the 25-inch screen.*
    The one that *makes 12 cups.*

VOCABULARY

Department Store

automatic ice maker	self-cleaning oven
calculator	TV
coffeemaker	color TV
gas range	model
in stock	remote control
personal computer	screen
refrigerator	watch (n.)

COMMENTARY

1. "Hmm" (line 3). Speaker A, the salesperson, hesitates in order to think about the customer's request and to consider what additional information she needs.

2. "In stock" (line 8). It is common for stores selling large appliances to have display models for customers to choose from. The salesperson will tell the customer if those items are actually available ("in stock") at the moment.

GETTING READY

1. Talk about products and brand names.

   a. Review the names of household appliances. Ask students to tell you the names of appliances. If possible, bring in pictures of various appliances and have students identify them.

   b. Write on the board some popular brand names of appliances. See if students can give you examples of the appliances each company sells. For example:

Sony	(*TV, radios, stereos*)
General Electric	(*stoves, refrigerators, TVs*)
Westinghouse	(*refrigerators, stoves*)
IBM	(*computers, typewriters*)
Casio	(*watches, calculators*)
Norelco	(*coffeemakers, razors, hair dryers*)

   c. Ask students to tell you other brand names they know. Write them on the board.

2. Introduce *the one with* . . .

   a. Put on the board:

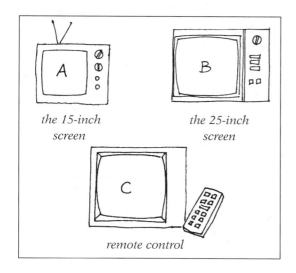

   the 15-inch screen

   the 25-inch screen

   remote control

   b. Tell students: "These are all TVs." Point to the first and say, "Which TV is this? The one with the 15-inch screen." Ask students again and have them answer.

   c. Ask students about the other TVs. Pointing to B, ask, "Which TV is this?" (*"The one with the 25-inch screen."*) Pointing to C, ask, "Which TV is this?" (*"The one with remote control."*)

3. Introduce *the one that* . . .

   a. Put on the board:

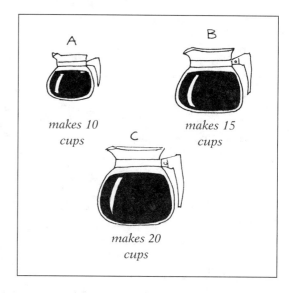

   makes 10 cups

   makes 15 cups

   makes 20 cups

   b. Tell students: "These are all coffeemakers." Point to the first and say: "Which coffeemaker is this? The one that makes 10 cups." Ask students again and have them answer.

   c. Continue with coffeemakers B and C as above.

THE MODEL CONVERSATION

1. **Set the Scene:** "A customer is looking for a TV in a department store. He knows exactly what kind of TV he wants to buy."

2. **Listen to the Model.**

3. **Class Practice.**

4. **Read.**

5. **Pair Practice.**

6. **Alternative Expressions.**

THE EXERCISES

Examples

> 1. A. May I help you?
>   B. Yes. I'd like to buy a General Electric gas range.
>   A. Hmm. We carry General Electric gas ranges in several different models. Which one are you interested in?
>   B. I'd like the one with the self-cleaning oven.
>   A. All right. Let me see if that's in stock. I'll be right back.
>
> 2. A. Can I help you?
>   B. Yes. I want to buy the Westinghouse refrigerator.
>   A. Hmm. We carry Westinghouse refrigerators in several different models. Which one are you interested in?
>   B. I'd like the one with an automatic ice maker.
>   A. All right. Let me see if that's in stock. I'll be right back.

Before doing each exercise, check students' understanding of the vocabulary and introduce any unfamiliar words or phrases. Have students use the footnoted expressions or their alternatives as they do the exercises.

Exercise Practice (optional). Have pairs of students simultaneously practice all the exercises.

Exercise Presentations. Call on pairs of students to present the exercises.

Language Note

Exercise 5: "16 megabytes" is a technical term for the memory capacity of a computer.

ORIGINAL STUDENT CONVERSATIONS

Have pairs of students create and present original conversations based on the model. (You may want students to prepare their original conversations as homework, then practice them the next day with another student and present them to the class.)

EXPANSION

1. Concentration/Matching Game: Appliances and Features

a. Divide the class into pairs or two teams that will compete with each other.

b. Give each pair or group two sets of cards. On one set of cards, write the names of appliances. On the other set, write a feature. For example:

On one card write:

TV

On another card write:

a 25-inch screen

c. Tell students that they need to match an appliance and an appropriate feature. Mix the cards in each set and turn them face-down. Students take turns choosing two cards (one from each set), reading them, and asking for the appliance and feature — for example: "I'd like a TV with a 25-inch screen." If the cards match, the second student or other team member says: "Yes, we have one." If the cards don't match (for example, "I need a TV with an ice maker"), the second student or team member says: "No, we don't have one."

d. Pairs or teams take turns choosing until all their cards are matched. The pair or team that matches all the cards first wins. Possible cards:

Appliance Cards

TV	toaster oven	refrigerator
food processor	stove	telephone
cassette player	sewing machine	iron
washine machine	dryer	CD player

Feature Cards

remote control	can record	an answering system	a self-cleaning oven	a timer	three temperatures
a 25-inch screen	two speakers	is cordless	a clock	twelve speeds	six washing cycles
a freezer on the side	shuts off automatically	sews buttonholes	a microwave oven	kneads dough	shuts off automatically
an ice maker	broils and bakes	a sewing cabinet	a microphone	a 3-quart bowl	headphones

2. Role Play: Let Me See If That's in Stock

a. Divide the class into pairs. Have one person in each pair be a customer and the other a salesperson in a department store.

b. Give all the salespeople a list of items that the store carries. For example (see below):

c. Give each customer a cue card with the product he or she wants to buy. For example:

toaster oven Proctor-Silex broils and bakes	stove General Elactric a microwave

Some of the cards should contain items that the store doesn't carry. For example:

TV Sony 13-inch screen	personal computer IBM 16 megabytes of memory

d. Have the pairs practice conversations based on the salesperson's stock list and the customer's cue card.

ITEM	BRAND	FEATURES	NUMBER IN STOCK
TV	Sony	25-inch screen	5
TV	Sony	19-inch screen and remote control	12
TV	RCA	25-inch screen and remote control	0
stove	Westinghouse	a self-cleaning oven	2
stove	General Electric	a microwave	0
food processor	Sunbeam	twelve speeds	9
food processor	Oster	kneads dough	1
iron	Black & Decker	shuts off automatically	3
toaster oven	Panasonic	a timer	8
toaster oven	Proctor-Silex	broils and bakes	11
sewing machine	Kenmore	sews buttonholes	6
sewing machine	Singer	a sewing cabinet	4

3. Reading Advertisements: True or False?

a. Bring in printed advertisements of appliances. Make true and false statements about the products featured in the ads.

b. Have students say whether each of your statements is true or false. If a statement is false, have students correct it. For example:

> Teacher: This IBM model has a 9-inch screen.
> Student: False. It has a 13-inch screen.

Variation: This activity can be done as a game with two competing teams.

4. Twenty Questions

a. Bring to class several copies of an appliance store sale flier, and distribute them to groups of three or four students.

b. Have a student in each group choose a product in the flier.

c. The other students in the group then try to guess the product by asking *yes/no* questions. For example:

> Student 1: I'm think of a product in this flier.
> Student 2: Is it a stereo system?
> Student 1: No.
> Student 3: It is a TV?
> Student 1: Yes.
> Student 4: Is it the one with a 13-inch screen?
> Student 1: No.
> Student 2: Is it the one with a 19-inch screen?
> Student 1: Yes.
> Student 3: Is it the one with close captioning?
> Student 1: No.
> Student 4: Is it the Gold Star 125X?
> Student 1: Yes.

5. Consumer Research Project

a. Divide the class into teams. Have each team do some research on a type of appliance. In their research, have teams answer the following questions:

> What are the five best models on the market today?
> What are some of the most interesting features now offered?
> Which models are the most reliable?
> Which models perform the best?
> Which models have the most convenient features?
> Which models have the best value?
> What changes in technology will affect future models?
> Where did you find this information?

b. Have the teams write a report of their research and make a presentation to the class.

What's the Word?

Have students do the activity individually, in pairs, or as a class. You may want to assign this exercise as homework.

1. refrigerator
2. coffeemaker
3. TV
4. computer
5. watch
6. gas range

Listen

Listen to the conversation. What are these people talking about?

1. A. Which one are you interested in?
   B. The one with the 18-inch screen.

2. A. Which one would you like?
   B. The one that beeps every hour.

3. A. Which one would you like to buy?
   B. The one with two doors.

4. A. Which one would you like to try?
   B. The one with a manual transmission.

5. A. Which one should we buy?
   B. The one that's on sale.

6. A. Which one do you want?
   B. The one with the largest memory.

7. A. Which one should we buy?
   B. The one with remote control.

8. A. Which one did you get?
   B. The self-cleaning one.

Answers

1. a
2. a
3. b
4. a
5. a
6. b
7. a
8. a

CrossTalk

Have students first work in pairs and then share with the class what they talked about.

FOCUS

TOPICS

Department Store: Purchasing an Item
Clothing: Describing Clothing, Selecting Clothing

GRAMMAR

Adjectives

A **size 36 dark brown leather** belt.
A **medium bright red sleeveless** blouse.

FUNCTIONS

1. **Attracting Attention**

   Excuse me.

2. **Requests**

   Direct, More Polite
   Could you help me?
   Can you help me?

   Responding to Requests
   Certainly.
   Of course.
   I'd be happy to.
   I'd be glad to.

3. **Offering to Help**

   Making an Offer
   What can I do for you?

4. **Want–Desire**

   Inquiring about . . .
   What *color* would you like?

   Expressing . . .
   I'm looking for *a leather belt*.

5. **Certainty/Uncertainty**

   Expressing Certainty
   I'm sure *he will*.

6. **Checking and Indicating Understanding**

   Checking One's Own Understanding
   Let's see . . . *a size 36 dark brown leather belt*.

VOCABULARY

Clothing	Describing	Colors	Finances
belt	large	beige	cash (n.)
blouse	medium	blue	charge (n.)
jogging suit	small	brown	credit card
shirt		red	personal check
dress shirt		white	
permanent press			
sneakers			
sweater			

214   EXIT SEVEN

COMMENTARY

1. "I'm looking for . . ." (line 3) is an expression that shoppers use to tell salespeople what they are interested in buying.

2. The salesperson says "Let's see" (line 8) as he begins to look for the right belt.

3. "I'll take it" (line 11) means "I'll buy it."

4. "Will this be cash or charge?" (line 12) means "Will you be paying cash, or will you be charging your purchase with a charge card?" Stores in the United States have different policies on how customers can pay. In addition to cash, many stores allow customers to pay with charge cards (also called *credit cards*), such as MasterCard, Visa, or American Express. Some large stores have their own credit services and credit cards ("our own store credit card" in lines 14–15) and may or may not allow the use of other cards. Many stores allow customers to pay with a personal check if they have appropriate identification — usually a driver's license and a major credit card.

5. "Oh. In that case, I'll pay cash" (line 16). Speaker A had wanted to use her MasterCard to pay for the belt. When she is told that the store doesn't accept MasterCard, she says "Oh" to acknowledge this information and express slight surprise. The phrase "In that case" introduces her new decision or alternate plan: "I'll pay cash."

GETTING READY

1. Review clothing.

   a. Point to articles of clothing in the room, and have students identify them. You can also bring in your own visuals or use *ExpressWays* Picture Cards 99–128.

   b. Review colors, sizes, and types of materials by pointing to articles of clothing or objects in the room and having students describe them.

   c. Introduce descriptive phrases for styles of clothing (*sleeveless, long-sleeved, V-neck, pullover*, and so on) by using your own visuals or using articles of clothing in the room.

   d. Practice phrases with adjectives. Show a visual of a car, house, or other object, and ask students for some descriptive words. On the board, write the phrases. For example:

large	white		car
small	green	wooden	house
dark	brown	leather	belt

   e. Show other visuals and continue writing the adjectives students suggest in lists: *size + color + material/style + object*.

2. Introduce the terms *credit card* and *charge*. If possible, bring in some examples of credit cards. Ask students if they have any credit cards or have friends who do.

THE MODEL CONVERSATION

1. **Set the Scene:** "A customer in a department store wants to buy a belt for her husband. She's asking the salesperson to help her."

2. **Listen to the Model.**

3. **Class Practice.**

4. **Read.**

5. **Pair Practice.**

6. **Alternative Expressions.**

THE EXERCISES

Examples

1. A. Excuse me. Could you help me?
   B. Certainly. What can I do for you?
   A. I'm looking for a V-neck sweater for my sister.
   B. What size does she wear?
   A. Small . . . I think.
   B. What color would you like?
   A. Beige, if you have it.
   B. Okay. Let's see . . . a small beige V-neck sweater. Do you think your sister will like this one?
   A. Yes. I'm sure she will. I'll take it.
   B. Will this be cash or charge?
   A. Do you take Visa?
   B. No, I'm afraid not. We only accept our own store credit card.
   A. Oh. In that case, I'll pay cash.

2. A. Excuse me. Can you help me?
   B. Of course. What can I do for you?
   A. I'm looking for a permanent press dress shirt for my son.
   B. What size does he wear?
   A. Size 15 . . . I think.
   B. What color would you like?

A. Light blue, if you have it.
B. Okay. Let's see . . . a size 15 light blue permanent press dress shirt. Do you think your son will like this one?
A. Yes. I'm sure he will. I'll take it.
B. Will this be cash or charge?
A. Do you take the Diner's Club card?
B. No, I'm afraid not. We only accept our own store credit card.
A. Oh. In that case, I'll pay cash.

Before doing each exercise, check students understanding of the vocabulary and introduce any unfamiliar words or phrases. Have students use the footnoted expressions or any of their alternatives as they do the exercises.

Exercise Practice (optional). Have pairs of students simultaneously practice all the exercises.

Exercise Presentations. Call on pairs of students to present the exercises.

Language Notes

Exercise 2: "Permanent press" refers to a fabric made of cotton and polyester that needs little or no ironing.

Exercise 5: A "jogging suit" is an exercise outfit.

ORIGINAL STUDENT CONVERSATIONS

Have pairs of students create and present original conversations based on the model. (You may want students to prepare their original conversations as homework, then practice them the next day with another student and present them to the class.)

EXPANSION

1. Guessing Game: Describing Clothing

Have a student describe another student's clothing by answering questions from the class. The class tries to guess which student is being described by asking *yes/no* questions about the clothing. Students can be divided into teams or do the activity as a class.

a. Choose one student to be *it.* He or she decides on another student to be described.

b. The class or the teams ask *yes/no* questions to determine which student he or she has selected. For example:

"Is the person wearing a sweater?"
"Does the person have a blue sweater?"
"Is it a blue V-neck sweater?"

c. After the person has been named, another student becomes *it,* and the game starts again.

2. What's My Partner Wearing?

Have pairs of students sit back-to-back and describe what each other is wearing.

Note: To make this activity more fun, don't tell students beforehand what they're going to do so that they don't have a chance to look carefully at their partner's clothing.

3. What's the Size?

Have students investigate sizes for different types of clothing and different ages. For example:

women's shoes	men's shoes
dresses	men's suits
women's shirts	jeans
men's shirts	children's shoes

a. Have students find out how each type of size is measured (for example, men's shirt sizes are determined by neck size, while jeans are determined by waist measurement and length of leg) and how sizes differ (for example, men's size 9 shoe vs. women's size 9 shoe).

b. Have students share their findings with the class.

4. Which Picture Is It?

a. Bring in magazine pictures of people wearing different kinds of clothing.

b. Have each student choose one picture and write a detailed description of what the person is wearing.

c. Have students take turns reading their descriptions aloud, without identifying the picture. The class must look at the pictures while they listen and identify which picture is being described.

5. Memory Game

a. Bring to class several pictures of people wearing different kinds of clothing.

b. Show a picture to the class for ten seconds. Then give the students three minutes to write down as detailed a description as possible of the clothing they saw.

c. Allow students to look at the picture again. Discuss the details they missed.

6. True or False Memory Game

a. Bring to class several pictures of people wearing different kinds of clothing.

b. Display one picture to students for ten seconds.

c. Put the picture away and make several statements about the clothing in the picture. Some statements should be true and others false.

d. Have students say if each of the statements is true or false. If a statement is false, have students correct it. For example:

> Teacher: The man was wearing a blue tuxedo.
> Student: False. He was wearing a black tuxedo.

e. Then have students look at the picture to see if they were right.

Variation: Do the activity as a game with two competing teams.

Constructions Ahead!

Have students do the activity individually, in pairs, or as a class. You may want to assign this exercise as homework.

1. b
2. c
3. b
4. c
5. a
6. b

Listen

Listen to the conversation. What word do you hear?

1. A. I'm looking for a brown leather belt.
   B. What size?
   A. 34.

2. A. Do you know what size you are?
   B. Yes. I'm a 15 neck and a 33 sleeve.
   A. All right. One moment, please.

3. A. Which one do you like?
   B. The blue one.

4. A. I'd like this skirt in a medium.
   B. Yes. Here you are.

5. A. I usually wear a size 7.
   B. Here. Try this in a small.

6. A. Which one will you take?
   B. I'll take the red and white one.

7. A. I'll take this brown one.
   B. Okay. Will this be cash or charge?

8. A. I'd like to buy a blue permanent press blouse.
   B. What size?
   A. Twelve, I think.

9. A. Do you think your brother will like this coat?
   B. Yes. Definitely. I'll take it.

10. A. I want to buy a beige belt . . . size 32.
    B. All right. Let's look on that rack over there.

11. A. Do you have this shirt in a permanent press?
    B. Yes, we do.

12. A. Will this be cash?
    B. No. I'll pay with my MasterCard.

Answers

1.	a	7.	a
2.	a	8.	b
3.	a	9.	b
4.	b	10.	a
5.	a	11.	b
6.	a	12.	b

CrossTalk

Have students first work in pairs and then share with the class what they talked about.

FOCUS

TOPICS

Department Store: Returning an Item
Clothing: Describing Clothing

GRAMMAR

1. **Adjectives**

   It's too **lightweight**.
   They're too **long**.

2. **Too**

   It's **too** fancy.
   They're **too** big.

3. **Comparatives**

   Would you like to exchange it for a **heavier** one?
   Would you like to exchange it for a **more powerful** one?

4. **One/Ones**

   Would you like to exchange it for a more conservative **one**?
   Would you like to exchange them for some shorter **ones**?

FUNCTIONS

1. **Want–Desire**

   Inquiring about . . .
   Would you like to ⎫
   Do you want to ⎪
   [*more formal*] ⎬ *exchange it?*
   Would you care to ⎭

   Expressing . . .
   I'd like to *return this coat.*
   I want to *return these pajamas.*

2. **Asking for and Reporting Information**

   May I ask ⎫
   Can I ask ⎬ *why you're returning it?*
   Could I ask ⎭

3. **Satisfaction/Dissatisfaction**

   Expressing Dissatisfaction
   It's too *lightweight.*
   They're too *long.*

VOCABULARY

Clothing	Department Store	Describing
coat	exchange (v.)	big
earrings	receipt	conservative
jeans	refund (n.)	difficult
necktie		fancy
pajamas	jigsaw puzzle	heavy
	walkie-talkie set	large
		lightweight
		long
		powerful
		short
		simple
		small
		tight
		weak

COMMENTARY

In the United States, it is common to return an unsatisfactory item you have purchased or received as a gift. Items are often returned because they don't fit or work properly or because the customer has changed his or her mind. Many large stores have a "Return Counter" where the customer can bring the receipt and the unused item. A store usually gives a refund (returns your money) or allows the customer to exchange the item. Some stores don't give refunds or exchanges. These stores have signs stating this policy. It is against the law for some items, such as pierced earrings and bathing suits, to be returned.

GETTING READY

1. Review articles of clothing, pronouns, and demonstrative adjectives.

   a. Point to an article, model the following conversation, and have students repeat after you:

      A. Do you like this coat?
      B. Yes. I like it very much.

      A. Do you like these shoes?
      B. Yes. I like them very much.

   b. Call on pairs of students to continue the practice, using their own articles of clothing or visuals that you provide.

2. Review comparative adjectives.

   a. Ask students for descriptive words about their hometown. Write their suggestions on the board. For example: *big, busy, beautiful, noisy, dangerous, safe, expensive, pretty, ugly, dirty, clean, interesting, exciting.*

   b. Have students compare their hometown with another city or town they know. For example, "Chicago is busier than Hartford." "New York is older than Denver." "Mexico City is more crowded than Acapulco."

THE MODEL CONVERSATIONS

There are two model conversations. Introduce and practice the first before going to the second. For each model:

1. **Set the Scene:**

   Model 1: "Someone is returning a coat to a department store."
   Model 2: "Someone is returning pajamas to a department store."

2. **Listen to the Model.**

3. **Class Practice.**

4. **Read.**

5. **Pair Practice.**

6. **Alternative Expressions.**

THE EXERCISES

Examples

---

1. A. I'd like to return this necktie.
   B. All right. Do you have the receipt?
   A. Yes. Here you are.
   B. May I ask why you're returning it?
   A. Yes. It's too fancy.
   B. Would you like to exchange it for a more conservative one?
   A. No, I don't think so. I'd just like a refund, please.
   B. Certainly.

2. A. I want to return these earrings.
   B. All right. Do you have the receipt?
   A. Yes. Here you are.
   B. Can I ask why you're returning them?
   A. Yes. They're too big.
   B. Do you want to exchange them for some smaller ones?
   A. No, I don't think so. I'd just like a refund, please.
   B. Certainly.

Before doing each exercise, check students' understanding of the vocabulary and introduce any unfamiliar words or phrases. Have students use the footnoted expressions or any of their alternatives as they do the exercises.

Exercise Practice (optional). Have pairs of students simultaneously practice all the exercises.

Exercise Presentations. Call on pairs of students to present the exercises.

Language Note

Exercise 5: A "walkie-talkie set" is a toy two-way radio receiver.

ORIGINAL STUDENT CONVERSATIONS

Have pairs of students create and present original conversations based on the models. (You may want students to prepare their original conversations as homework, then practice them the next day with another student and present them to the class.)

EXPANSION

1. What's the Opposite?

   a. Divide the class into teams.

   b. Call out any of the following adjectives:

big	comfortable	conservative
cute	dark	difficult
fancy	heavy	large
light	lightweight	long
powerful	short	simple
small	tight	ugly
uncomfortable	weak	

   c. Have the teams take turns calling out opposite adjectives.

   d. The team with the greatest number of accurate responses wins.

2. Simulation Activity: Purchasing and Returning Items

   a. In the classroom, set up several department store areas: a *Return Counter,* a *Cashier Counter,* and a *Sales Area.*

   b. Assign some students to work in each of the areas. Other students will be customers in the store who are either buying or returning items. The Return Counter should have refund slips; the Cashier Counter should have real or play money; and the Sales Area should have receipts.

   c. Give customers the name of an item they want to buy for a friend or relative. The customers will go to the Sales Area to purchase it. Encourage the customers to practice describing items while they are talking to the salespeople.

   d. Other people are in the store to return items. They go to the Return Counter and then to the Cashier Counter to get their money back. Give these customers a cue card with the items to be returned. They can decide the reasons they're returning them. Give sales receipts to some of the customers, but not to others. Those customers without receipts may have difficulty returning their items.

3. Opinions About Products

   a. Have students bring in newspaper or magazine advertisements or store catalogs. If this is not possible, bring in pictures of various articles of clothing or products bought in department stores.

   b. Have pairs of students look through the advertisements and point out items they like or dislike. Have them explain why they like or don't like items. For example:

   > "I like these pajamas. They're very fancy."
   > "I don't like this skirt. I think it's ugly."
   > "I don't like this radio. It's too large."

4. *Investigating Store Return Policies*

a. Brainstorm with students the names of popular stores in your area. Write the store names on the board.

b. Assign each student a different store. Have students call or visit their assigned store to find out its return policy. Have students learn the answers to the following questions:

> Where does a customer go in the store to return an item?
> What is the time limit for a return?
> Does a customer get cash back or store credit?
> Does the item need to be in the original box and have the original price tags?
> What if a customer finds a defect or stain on the item after purchasing it?
> What if the item falls apart within a week of purchasing it?
> Are there items that are not returnable?

c. Have students report their findings to the class.

What's the Answer?

Have students to the activity individually, in pairs, or as a class. You may want to assign this exercise as homework.

1. bigger
2. easy
3. lightweight
4. shorter
5. more powerful
6. conservative

Listen

Listen and choose the best answer.

1. Could you carry this box for me?
2. This recipe is very simple.
3. You know, we need a larger rug.
4. These earrings are too tight!
5. This tie is too conservative!
6. It's too short!
7. Hmm. This brown belt is too dark!
8. I had trouble with this exercise!

Answers

1. a
2. b
3. b
4. a
5. b
6. b
7. b
8. b

InterActions

Have pairs of students practice role-playing the activity and then present their role plays to the class.

Reading: *Catalog Stores*

Preview: Have students look at the illustrations and discuss the following questions:

What is this man doing?
What is different about this kind of shopping?

Then have students read the passage silently, or have them listen to the passage and take notes as you read it or play the audiotape.

True or False?

Have students do the activity individually, in pairs, or as a class. You may want to assign this exercise as homework.

1. True
2. False
3. True
4. False
5. False

What's the Answer?

Have students do the activity individually, in pairs, or as a class. You may want to assign this exercise as homework.

1. b
2. a
3. c
4. c
5. a

Cultural Intersections

Have students do the activity as a class, in pairs, or in small groups.

Survey

Have students develop their own survey questions and then conduct their surveys by circulating around the room asking and answering each other's questions. If they wish, they can also ask friends, family members, or other people in the community. Then have students report their findings to the class, compile them, and publish a *Community Shopping Guide.*

EXIT SEVEN   223

FOCUS

TOPIC

Post Office: Using Postal Services

GRAMMAR

1. **Passives**

   Money orders can **be purchased** at Window Number 3.
   Registered letters can **be sent** at the next window.

2. **Singular/Plural**

   I'd like to purchase **a money order**.
   I'd like to buy **some stamps**.

FUNCTIONS

1. **Want–Desire**

   Expressing . . .
   I'd like to *purchase a money order.*

2. **Apologizing**

   I'm sorry.
   Sorry.

3. **Checking and Indicating Understanding**

   Checking One's Own Understanding
   Did you say *Window Number 3?*
   Was that *Window Number 3?*

VOCABULARY

Post Office

change of address form
mail
money order
package
post office box
registered letter
stamps
window

COMMENTARY

"I'm sorry. You've got the wrong window" (line 2). The post office worker is apologizing because he cannot help the customer. She has come to the wrong desk. Work stations at banks and post offices are often referred to as *windows*.

GETTING READY

1. Introduce the vocabulary related to the post office. If possible, bring in examples of a change of address form, a money order, and a registered letter.

2. Introduce the passive voice.

   a. Write on the board:

   > You can purchase money orders here.
   > Money orders can be purchased here.

   b. Explain that there is a change in emphasis in the two sentences. In the second sentence, the focus is on the subject *(money orders)*.

   c. Have students practice changing other sentences from active to passive. Possible sentences include:

   > You can write the address here.
   > (The address can be written here.)

   > You can send the letter tomorrow.
   > (The letter can be sent tomorrow.)

   > You can buy stamps over there.
   > (Stamps can be bought over there.)

   > You can pick up the forms at the table.
   > (The forms can be picked up at the table.)

   > You can mail packages at Window Number 2.
   > (Packages can be mailed at Window Number 2.)

THE MODEL CONVERSATION

1. **Set the Scene:** "Someone is at the post office."

2. **Listen to the Model.**

3. **Class Practice.**

4. **Read.**

   Language Note

   A "money order" is a guaranteed check you can buy at a post office.

5. **Pair Practice.**

6. **Alternative Expressions.**

THE EXERCISES

Examples

> 1. A. I'd like to buy some stamps, please.
>   B. I'm sorry. You've got the wrong window. Stamps can be bought at Window Number 1.
>   A. Did you say Window Number 1?
>   B. Yes, that's right.
>   A. Thanks very much.
>
> 2. A. I'd like to send a registered letter, please.
>   B. Sorry. You've got the wrong window. Registered letters can be sent at the next window.
>   A. Was that the next window?
>   B. Yes, that's right.
>   A. Thanks very much.

Before doing each exercise, check students' understanding of the vocabulary and introduce any unfamiliar words or phrases. Have students use the footnoted expressions or their alternatives as they do the exercises.

Exercise Practice (optional). Have pairs of students simultaneously practice all the exercises.

Exercise Presentations. Call on pairs of students to present the exercises.

Culture Notes

Exercise 2: "Registered letter." Important or valuable documents are usually sent by "registered mail." When a person receives a registered letter, he or she must sign for it.

Exercise 3: A "change of address form" allows the post office to deliver all of a person's mail to his or her new address, including mail that has an old or incorrect address on it.

ORIGINAL STUDENT CONVERSATIONS

Have pairs of students create and present original conversations based on the model. (You may want students to prepare their original conversations as homework, then practice them the next day with another student and present them to the class.)

EXPANSION

1. What's the Object?

a. Call out one of the following verbs:

apply for
file
mail
purchase
send

b. Have students add direct objects related to postal services. For example:

apply for: a passport/a post office box

Variation: Do the activity as a game with two competing teams.

2. Put It in the Passive!

a. Divide the class into teams.

b. Call out any of the following post office services:

I can buy stamps.
I can file a change of address form.
I can send packages.
I can mail letters.
I can apply for a post office box.
I can apply for a passport.
I can purchase a money order.
I can ship books.
I can pick up my mail from the post office box.
I can buy shipping boxes at the post office.
I can pick up registered mail at the post office.

c. Have the teams take turns switching the phrase into the passive voice. For example:

Teacher: I can buy stamps at the post office.
Student: Stamps can be bought at the post office.

3. Simulation Activity: I'd Like to Purchase a Money Order, Please

a. Set up the classroom as a post office. Have three *windows* with one student behind each as a post office worker. Give each post office worker a list of items and services available at his or her window. For example:

Window 1	Window 2	Window 3
stamps	registered	money orders
aerogrammes	certified	post office
packages	change of	boxes
	address	
	forms	

b. The other students will wait in line and ask for the items they need. If they're at the correct window, they can purchase the items. (Encourage students to ask for the price and other related questions.) If they're at the wrong window, the post office worker should direct them to the correct window. The students should then go to the correct window and complete their business.

c. Encourage students to practice checking their understanding while they are talking.

Constructions Ahead!

Have students do the activity individually, in pairs, or as a class. You may want to assign this exercise as homework.

1. can be sent
2. can be bought
3. can be returned
4. can be seen
5. can be picked up
6. can be taken

Fill It In!

Have students do the activity individually, in pairs, or as a class. You may want to assign this exercise as homework.

1. b
2. c
3. a
4. c
5. b
6. a

Community Connections

Have students do the activity individually, in pairs, or in small groups and then report back to the class.

FOCUS

TOPIC

Post Office: Mailing Packages

GRAMMAR

Future: Will

How much **will** it cost?
That**'ll** cost five ninety-four.

FUNCTIONS

1. **Want–Desire**

   Expressing . . .
   I'd like to *mail this package.*

2. **Hesitating**

   Let's see.
   Let me see.
   Let's see now.

3. **Checking and Indicating Understanding**

   Checking One's Own Understanding
   Ten eight-one?

4. **Agreement/Disagreement**

   Expressing Agreement
   I guess it is.
   I suppose it is.

5. **Asking for and Reporting Information**

   How long will that take?
   How much will it cost?
       That'll cost *five ninety-four.*

VOCABULARY

Post Office	Family Members	Education
first class	daughter	graduate school
mail (v.)	niece	military academy
package	son	roommate
parcel post	uncle	unabridged
send		dictionary

COMMENTARY

1. "lb." and "lbs." are the abbreviations for "pound" and "pounds."

2. "First class." Most letters and many small packages in the United States are sent by first class mail and arrive within one to three days. Heavier packages are normally sent by *parcel post*.

3. In line 4, Speaker A says "Let's see" while he is weighing the package.

4. When Speaker A replies "I guess it is" (line 9), he is expressing reluctant agreement.

GETTING READY

1. Discuss with students how to send packages. Have students talk about their experiences in sending packages: How did they send them? Where did they send them? How much did it cost? How long did they take to get there? and so on. Introduce the terms *first class* and *parcel post*.

2. Using a map of the United States, have students locate the cities and states mentioned in the exercises:

> Minneapolis, Minnesota
> San Francisco, California
> Birmingham, Alabama
> West Point, New York
> Salt Lake City, Utah
> Trenton, New Jersey

THE MODEL CONVERSATION

1. **Set the Scene:** "Someone is mailing a package at the post office."

2. **Listen to the Model.**

3. **Class Practice.**

4. **Read.**

   Culture Note

   Minneapolis is a city in the state of Minnesota. The speaker doesn't give the name of the state because he assumes the postal worker knows it.

5. **Pair Practice.**

6. **Alternative Expressions.**

THE EXERCISES

Examples

1. A. I'd like to mail this package to San Francisco.
   B. How would you like to send it?
   A. First class, please.
   B. Okay. Let's see. It's thirteen pounds, so that'll be fifteen dollars and seventy-three cents.
   A. Fifteen seventy-three?
   B. Yes. That's a pretty heavy package you've got there.
   A. Hmm. I guess it is. It's a wedding gift I'm sending to my college roommate.
   B. Well, it can be sent parcel post, if you want.
   A. How long will that take?
   B. Around fourteen days.
   A. And how much will it cost?
   B. Let's see. Thirteen pounds . . . to San Francisco. That'll cost twelve seventy-eight.
   A. Okay. I'll send it parcel post.

2. A. I'd like to mail this package to Birmingham, Alabama.
   B. How would you like to send it?
   A. First class, please.
   B. Okay. Let me see. It's fifteen pounds, so that'll be twelve dollars and eighty-six cents.
   A. Twelve eighty-six?
   B. Yes. That's a pretty heavy package you've got there.
   A. Hmm. I suppose it is. It's an electric train set I'm sending to my niece and nephew.
   B. Well, it can be sent parcel post, if you want.
   A. How long will that take?
   B. About a week.
   A. And how much will it cost?
   B. Let's see now. Fifteen pounds . . . to Birmingham, Alabama. That'll cost six fifty-four.
   A. Okay. I'll send it parcel post.

Before doing each exercise, check students' understanding of the vocabulary and introduce any unfamiliar words or phrases. Have students use the footnoted expressions or any of their alternatives as they do the exercises.

Exercise Practice (optional). Have pairs of students simultaneously practice all the exercises.

Exercise Presentations. Call on pairs of students to present the exercises.

Language Notes

Exercise 1: "Around 14 days" means "approximately 14 days."

Exercise 2: "About a week" is another way of saying "approximately a week."

ORIGINAL STUDENT CONVERSATIONS

Have pairs of students create and present original conversations based on the model. (You may want students to prepare their original conversations as homework, then practice them the next day with another student and present them to the class.)

EXPANSION

1. Mailing Packages

a. Have each student choose a city where he or she might want to send a package.

b. Have students either go to the post office, call the post office, or ask people they know for the following information:

What's the cheapest way to send a
  (1-lb./5-lb.) package to _____?
How much does that cost?
How long will it take?

What's the most expensive way to send a
  (1-lb./5-lb.) package to _____?
How much does that cost?
How long will it take?

c. Have students report their findings to the class, and make a chart on the board based on that information.

2. Cost Comparisons

a. Brainstorm with students the names of some of the different package delivery companies available.

b. Divide the class into teams and assign each team a different company to investigate. Have them find answers to the following questions:

What different delivery services do they
  provide?
What is their fastest service? Using that
  service, how long does it take to deliver
  a package?

What is their slowest service? Using that
  service, how long does it take to deliver
  a package?
What happens if a package gets lost?
Can a package be traced if it is lost?

c. Have students compare their finding and then publish a *mail service recommendation chart,* explaining which services are the best and why.

3. Class Discussion: Comparing Postal Systems

Have students talk about the postal systems in their countries. Have them discuss the following questions:

How much does it cost to send a letter in
  that country?
How much does it cost to send a letter
  overseas?
Is it expensive to mail packages?
When you mail packages, do you have to use
  special boxes?
Where can you buy stamps?
What other kinds of services does the post
  office provide?

4. Postal Problems!

a. Write out the following postal problem cards:

> I've just moved, and no mail is being delivered to my new address.

> I haven't received a package that was mailed locally over four months ago.

> I received a package in the mail, but the contents were damaged.

> I'd like to buy some stamps, but I work during post office hours.

> I'm receiving a lot of "junk mail" that I don't want.

```
┌─────────────────────────────────────┐
│                                       │
│   I'm receiving someone else's mail.  │
│                                       │
└─────────────────────────────────────┘
```

```
┌─────────────────────────────────────┐
│                                       │
│  I'm leaving on vacation, and I won't │
│   be able to pick up my mail for      │
│          three weeks.                 │
│                                       │
└─────────────────────────────────────┘
```

```
┌─────────────────────────────────────┐
│                                       │
│  No one in my building has received   │
│       any mail for three days.        │
│                                       │
└─────────────────────────────────────┘
```

b. Give each student one card.

c. Have students go to their local post office and find out the answers to their *problem situations.*

d. Have students report their findings to the class.

5. *Postal Knowledge Contest*

a. Prepare questions about the postal system, including its prices and services. For example:

> How much does it cost to send a letter?
> How much does it cost to send a postcard?
> What do you need in order to pick up a piece of registered mail?
> Can you get money orders from the post office?
> How many classes of mail are there?
> Which is cheaper — parcel post or first class?

b. Divide the class into groups and have the groups take turns answering your questions. The group that gives the most correct answers wins.

Variation: Have students write the questions for the game.

Crossed Lines

Have students do the activity individually, in pairs, or as a class. You may want to assign this exercise as homework.

__9__   Will it take longer to get there?

__6__   Yes. That's what it'll cost to send it first class.

__4__   Let me see. It's fifteen pounds, so that'll be sixteen ninety-five.

__8__   Oh, yes. Parcel post . . . to Pittsburgh. That would be nine eighty.

__1__   I'd like to mail this package to Pittsburgh.

__11__   A week? Hmm. I think I'd better send it first class. It's a birthday gift for my Cousin Charlie, and his birthday is this Thursday.

__2__   How would you like to send it?

__10__   Yes. It'll take about a week.

__12__   If you send it first class, I'm sure your Cousin Charlie will get his birthday gift by this Thursday.

__5__   Sixteen ninety-five?

__7__   Would it be cheaper to send it parcel post?

__3__   First class, please.

Listen

Listen and choose the correct number.

1. A. How long will it take?
   B. It'll take about ten days.
2. A. How much will it cost?
   B. It'll be twelve dollars and ninety-six cents.
3. A. How much does it weigh?
   B. It's eleven pounds.
4. A. What's the cost?
   B. Fourteen sixty-eight.
5. A. When will it get there?
   B. It'll get there in about nine days.
6. A. How heavy is it?
   B. Four pounds.
7. A. How much will that be?
   B. It'll be thirteen seventy-eight.
8. A. How much do I owe you?
   B. Twelve sixty-four.

Answers

1. a
2. b
3. b
4. a
5. b
6. a
7. a
8. b

Your Turn

Have students discuss the activity as a class, in pairs, or in small groups. Then have students write their responses at home, share their written work with other students, and discuss in class.

FOCUS

TOPIC

Automobiles: Buying a Car

GRAMMAR

Passives

The controls **are computerized.**

FUNCTIONS

1. **Offering to Help**

   Making an Offer

   Can I help you?

   Would you like me to *write up an order slip*?

2. **Asking for and Reporting Information**

   Can I ask *how much it costs?*

3. **Focusing Attention**

   Let me point out *some of its special features.*
   Notice (that) *the controls are all computerized.*
   I should (also) point out (that) *an AM-FM stereo radio is included.*
   Let me mention that *we offer a very good installment plan.*

4. **Hesitating**

   Uh . . .

VOCABULARY

Driving	Finances
controls (n.)	installment plan
dashboard	payments
passenger	
trip (n.)	

COMMENTARY

1. This conversation has many examples of *sales talk* and the cultural conventions used by salespeople in the United States. Salespeople often try to present a product as the best of its kind. They often use a formal, polite style of speaking.

2. "You have very good taste" (line 3). The car salesman is flattering the customer to attract the customer's interest and impress him.

3. "AM-FM stereo radio" (line 12). Radio programs in the United States are broadcast on either *AM* or *FM* radio frequencies. Most radios in the United States provide both frequencies.

4. In line 14, the salesman says, "This particular car costs $20,000." United States car dealers set their own prices for automobiles. Prices for the same car vary from dealer to dealer. Automobile salespeople are known for offering *deals* (special prices) as a way of attracting and convincing customers to buy from their company.

5. An *installment plan* (line 15) is a loan program similar to those offered by banks in which the customer makes an initial down payment and then makes monthly payments of principal and interest until the loan is paid off.

6. "Would you like me to write up an order slip for you?" (line 17). Here the salesman is trying to *close* the sale; he wants the customer to decide to buy the car. An order slip is a purchase agreement. The dealer may have the car in stock, or the car may have to be ordered.

7. "Uh . . . not right now, thanks. I want to shop around a little more" (line 18). The customer hesitates, saying "Uh . . ." in order to think. Because he is not ready to make a decision yet, he says ". . . not right now, thanks." This response is an appropriate refusal because in the United States customers are expected to look for the best buy. This also lets the salesperson know that the customer is aware of the competitors' prices.

GETTING READY

1. Brainstorm with students about attractive features to look for when buying a car. Write their ideas on the board.

2. Have students brainstorm phrases a salesperson uses when trying to sell an item. Write their ideas on the board.

THE MODEL CONVERSATION

1. **Set the Scene:** "A customer is looking at a car in an auto showroom. A salesperson comes over and talks with him."

2. **Listen to the Model.**

3. **Class Practice.**

4. **Read.**

5. **Pair Practice.**

Now have pairs of students create and present original conversations using the model dialog as a guide. Encourage students to be inventive and to use new vocabulary. (You may want to assign this exercise as homework, having students prepare their original conversations, practice them the next day with another student, and then present them to the class.) Students should present their conversations without referring to the written text, but they also should not memorize them. Rather, they should feel free to adapt and expand them any way they wish.

Your Turn

Have students discuss the activity as a class, in pairs, or in small groups. Then have students write their responses at home, share their written work with other students, and discuss in class.

Looking Back

Have students look at the list of expressions. Encourage them to ask you any questions about the meaning or pronunciation of any of the words. If students ask for the pronunciation, repeat after the student until the student is satisfied with his or her pronunciation of the word.

Review Activities

To review the language introduced in the unit, do the following activities.

1. Association Game

a. Divide the class into several teams.

b. Call out a topic category from the *Looking Back* section on student text page 132.

c. Have students in each group work together to see how many phrases they can associate with that category. For example:

Asking for Information:

Could you tell me . . . ?
Can you tell me . . . ?
May I ask . . . ?
Can I ask . . . ?
Could I ask . . . ?

d. The team with the most items wins.

2. Create a Conversation!

a. Divide the class into pairs of students.

b. Tell each pair they have three minutes to make up a conversation using one item from each category from the *Looking Back* section on page 132 of the student text.

c. Have students share their conversations with the class.

EXIT 8

OVERVIEW
Student Text
Pages 133–154

Topics	Functions	Grammar

P. 134 What Do You Want to Do Today?

Recreation: Recreational and Entertainment Activities

Want–Desire
Advice–Suggestions

Gerunds
Infinitives
Present Perfect Tense

P. 136 What Would You Prefer to Do?

Recreation: Recreational and Entertainment Activities

Advice–Suggestions
Want–Desire
Indifference
Preference

Gerunds
Infinitives

P. 138 Would You Like to Go Skiing Tomorrow?

Social Communication: Invitations
Recreation: Recreational and Entertainment Activities
Weather: Weather Conditions, Weather Forecasts

Invitations
Asking for and Reporting Information
Possibility/Impossibility
Certainty/Uncertainty
Agreement/Disagreement

Infinitives
Gerunds
Present Perfect Tense
Supposed to

P. 140 Maybe Some Other Time

Social Communication: Invitations
Recreation: Recreational and Entertainment Activities

Invitations
Checking and Indicating Understanding
Ability/Inability
Obligation
Disappointment

Gerunds
Infinitives
Can
Able to
Have to/Have Got to
Supposed to

P. 142 I Hadn't Seen a Play in Ages!

Social Communication:
   Making Conversation
Recreation: Recreational
   and Entertainment
   Activities

Asking for and Reporting
   Information
Likes–Dislikes

Past Tense
Past Perfect Tense
Gerunds
Infinitives

P. 144 They Had Been Looking Forward to It for a Long Time

Social Communication:
   Making Conversation
Recreation: Recreational
   and Entertainment
   Activities

Initiating a Topic
Asking for and Reporting
   Information
Sympathy
Agreement/Disagreement

Past Tense
Past Perfect Continuous
   Tense
Possessive Adjectives

P. 146 Would You Like to See a Movie Tonight?

Recreation: Listings and
   Schedules

Want–Desire
Advice–Suggestions
Asking for and Reporting
   Information
Hesitating
Preference

Pp. 148–149 What Do You Want to Watch?

Recreation: Listings and
   Schedules

Want–Desire
Asking for and Reporting
   Information
Preference
Advice–Suggestions
Checking and Indicating
   Understanding
Indifference

LOOKING AHEAD

Grammar This Exit

Gerunds/Infinitives

I don't feel like **seeing** a movie.
I'm not really in the mood **to see** a movie.

Would you be interested in **going** skiing?
Would you like **to go** skiing?

Going skiing wouldn't be a very good idea.
Going dancing sounds like a lot more fun than **working** overtime.

I prefer **to go** to the town pool.

Past Tense

What **did** you **do** over the weekend?
　I **saw** a play.
　I **went** sailing.

They **were** really disappointed.
The weather **was** miserable.

Present Perfect Tense

I **haven't gone** skiing in a long time.
We **haven't seen** a movie in a long time.

Past Perfect Tense

I **had gone** sailing the weekend before THAT, too!
I **had driven** to the mountains the weekend before THAT, too!

I **hadn't seen** a play in ages!
I **hadn't worked** in my garden in ages!

Past Perfect Continuous Tense

They **had been looking** forward to their vacation.
They **had been talking** about it for weeks!

Possessive Adjectives

They had been looking forward to **their** vacation.
She had been looking forward to **her** dinner.
He had been looking forward to **his** ski vacation.
You had been looking forward to **your** flight.

Supposed to

Isn't it **supposed to** be very warm tomorrow?
I'm **supposed to** work overtime.

Can

I'm afraid I **can't.**

Able to

I'm afraid I won't be **able to.**

Have to/Have Got to

I **have to** work overtime.

I**'ve got to** work overtime.

Functions This Exit

Want–Desire

Inquiring about . . .

What do you want to *do today*?

What would you like to *see*?

Where do you want to *go*?

Would you like to *see a movie tonight*?

Are you interested?

Expressing . . .

I don't really feel like *going to the ballgame.*
I'm not really in the mood to *go to the ballgame.*

Advice–Suggestions

Asking for . . .

Do you have any suggestions?

Any other ideas?

How about *The Missing Jewels*?
What about *The Missing Jewels*?

Offering . . .

How about *going jogging*?
What about *playing tennis*?

We could always *swim at the lake.*

Responding to . . .

Good idea!
Good suggestion!

Asking for and Reporting Information

What did you do *over the weekend*?
  I *saw a play*.

Didn't you *go sailing the weekend before*?
  Yes, I did.

How about you?

How did *your parents enjoy their vacation in Florida*?

What's it about?
Who's in it?
What time is it *showing*?
What's on?

Is there anything else to *watch*?

I heard it *on the radio*.
I read it *in the paper*.
I saw *the forecast on TV*.
They said so *on the morning news*.
The cashier at the drug store told me.

Possibility/Impossibility

Inquiring about . . .

Isn't it supposed to *be very warm tomorrow*?

Agreement/Disagreement

Expressing Agreement

I guess you're right.

Certainty/Uncertainty

Expressing Certainty

I'm pretty sure *it's supposed to be very warm*.

Likes/Dislikes

Inquiring about . . .

Did you enjoy it?

Expressing Likes

You really enjoy *going sailing*!

I like to *go sailing* whenever I can.

Agreement/Disagreement

Expressing Agreement

I know.

I guess you're right.

Sympathizing

That's a shame!
That's too bad!
What a shame!
What a pity!

Indifference

It doesn't make any difference to me.
It doesn't matter to me.
I don't care.

Whatever *you'd like to watch* is fine with me.

Preference

Inquiring about . . .

What would you prefer to do?
What would you rather do?

Expressing . . .

I think I'd prefer to *go to the town pool*.
I think I'd rather *go to the rink*.

I'd rather not *watch Dr. Goodbody*.

Invitations

Extending . . .

Would you like to *go skiing tomorrow*?
How would you like to *go on a picnic tomorrow*?
Do you want to *go to the beach tomorrow*?
Would you be interested in *taking a ride in the country tomorrow*?
Would you by any chance be interested in *going dancing tomorrow night*?

Accepting . . .

That sounds great.

That sounds like fun.
I'd love to.
I'd like to.

Declining . . .

I'm afraid I can't.
I'm afraid I won't be able to.

Ability/Inability

Expressing Inability

I'm afraid I can't.
I'm afraid I won't be able to.

Obligation

Expressing . . .

I have to *work overtime*.
I've got to *finish a term paper*.
I'm supposed to *attend a business meeting*.

Disappointment

That's too bad.

Hesitating

Hmm.
Let's see.
Let me see.

Checking and Indicating Understanding

Checking One's Own Understanding

Tomorrow night?
This weekend?
This Saturday afternoon?

Initiating a Topic

Tell me, _____?

PREVIEWING EXIT 8: CHAPTER-OPENING PHOTOS

Have students talk about the people and the situations and, as a class or in pairs, predict what the characters might be saying to each other. Students in pairs or small groups may enjoy practicing role plays based on these scenes and then presenting them to the class.

----- Text Page 134: What Do You Want to Do Today? -----

FOCUS

TOPIC

Recreation: Recreational and Entertainment Activities

GRAMMAR

1. **Gerunds**

   How about **going** to the ballgame?
   Well, what about **seeing** a movie?
   I don't really feel like **going** to the ballgame.

2. **Infinitive**

   I'm not really in the mood **to see** a movie.

3. **Present Perfect Tense**

   We **haven't seen** a movie in a long time.
   We **haven't driven** to the mountains in a long time.

FUNCTIONS

1. **Want–Desire**

   Inquiring about . . .
   What do you want to *do today*?

   Expressing . . .
   I don't really feel like *going to the ballgame*.
   I'm not really in the mood to *play basketball*.

2. **Advice–Suggestions**

   Asking for . . .
   Do you have any suggestions?

   Any other ideas?

   Offering . . .
   How about *playing tennis*?
   What about *going jogging*?

   Responding to . . .
   Good idea!
   Good suggestion!

VOCABULARY

Recreation and Entertainment	Community
ballgame	shopping mall
beach	
fishing	**Sports**
hang out (v.)	
mountains	basketball
movie	bowling
picnic	fishing
tennis	jogging
zoo	swimming
	tennis

COMMENTARY

It is common in conversation to use shortened sentences, such as "Any other ideas?" (line 6) and "Good idea" (line 8).

GETTING READY

1. Review leisure activities, such as: *swimming, skiing, skating, jogging, fishing, bowling, playing tennis/baseball/basketball/football/soccer/golf, having a picnic* and *jogging*. Bring in your own visuals or use *ExpressWays* Picture Cards 154–162 and 173–182.

   a. Point to a visual and ask, "Do you like to _____?" Have students answer, "Yes, I do" or "No, I don't."

   b. Have pairs of students ask each other similar questions and offer appropriate answers.

2. Introduce and practice gerunds and infinitives.

   a. Write on the board:

   > to walk — walking
   > to sit — sitting
   > to drive — driving

   b. Model the following sentences, and have students repeat:

   > I like to walk to school.
   > I like walking to school.

   > We don't like to sit in class.
   > We don't like sitting in class.

   > They like to drive to the beach.
   > They like driving to the beach.

   c. Call on students to practice forming similar sentences. For example:

   Teacher: We like to play tennis.
   Student: We like playing tennis.

   Teacher: Bob likes to go fishing.
   Student: Bob likes going fishing.

   Teacher: Mary likes to play baseball.
   Student: Mary likes playing baseball.

   Teacher: They like singing.
   Student: They like to sing.

   Teacher: We like going bowling.
   Student: We like to go bowling.

   Teacher: Dan doesn't like driving.
   Student: Dan doesn't like to drive.

THE MODEL CONVERSATION

1. **Set the Scene:** "A wife and husband are talking about what to do."

2. **Listen to the Model.**

3. **Class Practice.**

4. **Read.**

5. **Pair Practice.**

6. **Alternative Expressions.**

THE EXERCISES

Examples

---

1. A. What do you want to do today?
   B. I don't know. Do you have any suggestions?
   A. How about going jogging?
   B. Hmm. I don't really feel like going jogging. Any other ideas?
   A. Well, how about driving to the mountains?
   B. Good idea! We haven't driven to the mountains in a long time.

2. A. What do you want to do today?
   B. I don't know. Do you have any suggestions?
   A. What about playing tennis?
   B. Hmm. I'm not really in the mood to play tennis. Any other ideas?
   A. Well, what about playing basketball?
   B. Good suggestion! We haven't played basketball in a long time.

Before doing each exercise, check students' understanding of the vocabulary and introduce any unfamiliar words or phrases. Have students use the footnoted expressions or any of their alternatives as they do the exercises.

Exercise Practice (optional). Have pairs of students simultaneously practice all the exercises.

Exercise Presentations. Call on pairs of students to present the exercises.

Culture Notes

Exercise 5: "Hang out" is an informal expression used by teenagers to mean "spend time."

Exercise 5: "Shopping malls" are large indoor shopping areas with many stores. Most malls have one or more large department stores and an assortment of smaller shops and stores. Malls in the United States are usually surrounded by large parking lots.

ORIGINAL STUDENT CONVERSATIONS

Have pairs of students create and present original conversations based on the model. (You may want students to prepare their original conversations as homework, then practice them the next day with another student and present them to the class.)

EXPANSION

1. Class Poll: What Do You Want to Do?

a. Divide the class into small groups. Give each student a list of recreation activities. For example:

---

go to a ballgame
see a movie
go jogging
drive to the mountains
play tennis
play basketball
go fishing
go swimming
go bowling
have a picnic
take a walk
go to the zoo
go to a museum
go shopping
go to the library

---

b. Tell each student to silently select one activity he or she would enjoy doing. Tell the students that they need to find out what the others in their group would like to do. They can ask questions such as:

   Do you want to (*go to the zoo*)?
   What about (*going shopping*)?
   Do you feel like (*playing tennis*)?
   Would you like to (*take a walk*)?
   How about (*having a picnic*)?

The other students will respond either positively ("Good suggestion!" "Good idea!" "I'd like to _____.") or negatively ("I don't really feel like _____ing." "I'm not really in the mood to _____.").

c. Have students record the name of the person after the activity he or she would enjoy doing.

d. Have the groups report back to the class the activities each student in the group would enjoy.

2. Vocabulary Game

a. Divide the class into teams.

b. Have each team list as many recreational activities as they can think of.

c. After three minutes, the team with the longest list wins.

3. Miming Game

a. Write on separate cards the recreational activities from student text page 134.

b. Have students take turns picking a card from the pile and pantomiming the recreational activity.

c. The class must then guess what the activity is.

Variation: This can be done as a game with two competing teams.

4. Category Game

a. Divide the class into groups of 3–5 students.

b. Write out the following cards, and give a different one to each student in the group.

Outdoor Activities:	Indoor Activities:

go fishing
go swimming
   at the beach
have a picnic
go to the zoo
	go bowling
	hang out at
	   the shopping
	   mall
	see a movie

Activities That Can Be Done Alone:	Activities That Must Be Done with Others:

go jogging
drive to the
   mountains
see a movie
go fishing
go swimming
	play basketball
	play tennis
	take the kids
	   to the zoo
	go bowling

c. Have one student announce his or her category to the group. For example: "Outdoor Activities." That student then gives a clue for the first item. For example:

"It's a very quiet activity."

d. The group members try to guess the item. [*go fishing*]

e. The game continues until all the students in the group have given clues for the items in their categories. The person who guesses the most items wins the game.

5. Research and Presentation Project: *Recreational Activities in Our Community*

a. Brainstorm with students their favorite recreational activities. Write their ideas on the board.

b. Divide the class into teams. Assign each team one recreational activity. Have them find the answers to the following questions:

Where are some of the best locations for doing this activity?
What is the most economical way to enjoy this activity?
How can a person find a team to play with?
Is there an association to join for this activity? What services does the association offer?

c. Have the teams write up a report of their research. Then have each team give a short presentation to the class about what they discovered. Students may wish to publish their findings as a *Recreational Guide to the Community.*

Constructions Ahead!

Have students do the activity individually, in pairs, or as a class. You may want to assign this exercise as homework.

1. go
2. going
3. driving
4. drive
5. see
6. see
7. playing
8. play
9. do
10. doing

CrossTalk

Have students circulate around the room asking for and giving suggestions for weekend activities. Have them share their ideas with the class. Then have the class choose the activity everyone likes best and make plans to do this activity on a future weekend.

FOCUS

TOPIC

Recreation: Recreational and Entertainment Activities

GRAMMAR

1. **Gerunds**

    How about **going** to the town pool?
    How about **seeing** the new Disney film?

2. **Infinitives**

    Where do you want **to go**?
    What would you prefer **to do**?
    I think I'd prefer **to go** to the town pool.

FUNCTIONS

1. **Advice–Suggestions**

    Offering . . .
    How about *going to the town pool*?

    We could always *swim at the lake*.

2. **Want–Desire**

    Inquiring about . . .
    Where do you want to *go*?

3. **Indifference**

    It doesn't make any difference to me.
    It doesn't matter to me.
    I don't care.

4. **Preference**

    Inquiring about . . .
    What would you prefer to do?
    What would you rather do?

    Expressing . . .
    I think I'd prefer to *go to the town pool*.
    I think I'd rather *go to the rink*.

VOCABULARY

Recreation and Entertainment	Community
bike	lake
film	museum
hide and seek	pond
hike	pool
hopscotch	rink
movie	
outdoors	**Sports**
outside	
ride (our) bikes	skating
skate	swimming
swim	

COMMENTARY

People often say, "I don't know" (line 3) when they don't have an opinion or haven't decided about something yet.

THE MODEL CONVERSATION

1. **Set the Scene**: "A husband and wife are talking about what to do."

2. **Listen to the Model.**

3. **Class Practice.**

4. **Read.**

5. **Pair Practice.**

6. **Alternative Expressions.**

THE EXERCISES

Examples

1. A. Let's go skating today.
   B. Good idea. Where do you want to go?
   A. Oh, I don't know. How about going to the rink? Or we could always skate on the pond.
   B. It doesn't make any difference to me. What would you prefer to do?
   A. I think I'd prefer to go to the rink.
   B. Okay. That's fine with me.

2. A. Why don't we do something outdoors today?
   B. Good idea. What do you want to do?
   A. Oh, I don't know. How about going for a hike? Or we could always ride our bikes.

B. It doesn't matter to me. What would you rather do?
A. I think I'd rather go for a hike.
B. Okay. That's fine with me.

Before doing each exercise, check students' understanding of the vocabulary and introduce any unfamiliar words or phrases. Have students use the footnoted expressions or any of their alternatives as they do the exercises.

Exercise Practice (optional). Have pairs of students simultaneously practice all the exercises.

Exercise Presentations. Call on pairs of students to present the exercises.

Culture Notes

Exercise 3: A "Disney film" is a movie produced by Walt Disney Studios, a production company that specializes in entertainment for children.

Exercise 3: A "James Bond movie" is a movie featuring the international spy character James Bond, as created by writer Ian Fleming.

Exercise 5: "Hopscotch" and "hide and seek" are children's games. Hopscotch involves drawing connected squares on the ground, throwing small stones into the squares, and then hopping in the squares on one foot as you stoop to pick up the stones. In "hide and seek," the person who is "it" counts to a number with eyes closed while the other players hide. After announcing "Ready or not, here I come!," the person who is "it" must try to find the others.

ORIGINAL STUDENT CONVERSATIONS

Have pairs of students create and present original conversations based on the model. (You may want students to prepare their original conversations as homework, then practice them the next day with another student and present them to the class.)

EXPANSION

1. Guessing Game: What Do You Want to Do?

a. Divide the class into two teams. Each team decides on a recreational activity (*swimming, going to a museum, having a picnic, playing tennis,* and so on).

b. Tell the students that they need to guess the other team's activity by asking questions.

c. Team A begins to ask questions, each member asking one question. Anyone on Team B can answer. For example:

> Do you play on teams?
> Do you go to a pool?
> Is it for children?
> Do you need a car?
> Can you do this in the summer?
> Do you need a ball?

d. If Team A guesses the activity, they get one point. If everyone on a team has asked a question and they don't guess the activity, Team B gives the answer and they begin questioning the other team.

2. Categorizing: Recreation for Different People

Have students decide what kinds of recreational activities are appropriate for different age groups. If possible, have them explore the areas where these activities take place in their town or neighborhood.

a. Have students tell you various recreational activities for different age groups, and write their ideas on the board. For example:

Children	Teens	Adults
hopscotch	movies	bowling
zoo	shopping	museum
ride bikes	basketball	drive
puppet show	skating	jogging

b. For each of the activities, have students find out where these activities take place (local parks, names of theaters, names of museums, school or neighborhood playgrounds, skating rinks, pools, beaches, and so on).

c. Have students report their findings to the class.

d. You can compile these findings and publish this as a class booklet on recreational activities and places in your area. Students in the class can use it as a reference and share it with family, friends, and other classes in the school.

3. Places and Activities

a. Divide the class into teams.

b. Name a location, such as the following:

> pond
> rink
> mountains
> park
> beach
> zoo
> shopping mall

c. Have each team list as many recreational activities related to that location as they can think of.

d. After three minutes, the team with the longest list wins.

4. Miming Game

a. Write on cards the following recreational activities:

watching a James Bond movie

watching a comedy

ice skating outdoors on a pond

hiking on a high mountain

seeing an art exhibit

seeing a dinosaur exhibit

riding a bike on a city street

riding a bike in the mountains

having a picnic on the beach

swimming in a lake

b. Have students take turns picking a card from the pile and pantomiming the recreational activity.

c. The class must then guess what the activity is and where it is taking place.

Variation: This can be done as a game with two competing teams.

5. Class Survey: Recreational Preferences

a. Brainstorm with students different categories of recreation and entertainment. For example:

> going to movies
> skating
> visiting museums
> swimming
> seeing plays

b. Divide the class into groups.

c. Assign each group a category, and have students create survey questions based on that activity. For example:

> *going to movies*
>
> Do you prefer to go to afternoon or evening performances?
> Do you prefer to sit close to the screen or far from the screen?
> Do you prefer adventure movies or comedies?
> Do you prefer to eat popcorn or candy during the movie?

d. Have students conduct their surveys by circulating around the room asking each other their questions.

e. Then have students tally their findings and share them with the class.

What's the Answer?

Have students do the activity individually, in pairs, or as a class. You may want to assign this exercise as homework.

1. to do
2. seeing
3. go
4. to stay
5. getting
6. to watch
7. get

Fill It In!

Have students do the activity individually, in pairs, or as a class. You may want to assign this exercise as homework.

1. b		5. a	
2. b		6. a	
3. b		7. b	
4. b		8. b	

Survey

Have students ask ten people of different ages about their favorite weekend activities. Have students report their findings to the class and compare the results. Have the class discuss preferences they discovered based on people's ages.

FOCUS

TOPICS

Social Communication: Invitations
Recreation: Recreational and Entertainment
               Activities
Weather: Weather Conditions
          Weather Forecasts

GRAMMAR

1. **Infinitives**

   Would you like **to go** skiing tomorrow?
   Do you want **to go** on a picnic tomorrow?

2. **Gerunds**

   Would you be interested in **going** to the
   beach tomorrow?
   In that case, **going** skiing probably
   wouldn't be a very good idea.

3. **Present Perfect Tense**

   I **haven't gone** skiing in a long time.
   I **haven't taken** a ride in the country in
   a long time.
   I **haven't played** golf in a long time.

4. **Supposed to**

   Isn't it **supposed to** be very warm
   tomorrow?
   I'm pretty sure it's **supposed to** be very
   warm.

FUNCTIONS

1. **Invitations**

   Extending . . .

   Would you like to *go skiing tomorrow*?
   How would you like to *go on a picnic
   tomorrow*?
   Do you want to *go to the beach tomorrow*?
   Would you be interested in *taking a ride in
   the country tomorrow*?

   Accepting . . .

   That sounds great.
   That sounds like fun.
   I'd love to.
   I'd like to.

2. **Asking for and Reporting Information**

   I heard it *on the radio.*
   I read it *in the paper.*
   I saw *the forecast on TV.*
   They said so *on the morning news.*
   The cashier at the drug store told me.

3. **Possibility/Impossibility**

   Inquiring about . . .

   Isn't it supposed to *be very warm
   tomorrow?*

4. **Certainty/Uncertainty**

   Expressing Certainty

   I'm pretty sure *it's supposed to be very
   warm.*

5. **Agreement/Disagreement**

   Expressing Agreement

   I guess you're right.

VOCABULARY

Weather	Sports
cloudy	golf
cold	sailing
foggy	
forecast	
rain	
snow	
warm	
weather forecaster	
windy	

COMMENTARY

1. "But wait a minute!" (line 3). Speaker B is signaling that there is a problem; the weather won't be good for skiing.

2. "Gee" (line 5) is an expression that people use in a variety of ways. In this situation, Speaker A is expressing disappointment. His comment "I hadn't heard that" suggests that he is slightly puzzled — not sure what to think.

3. "Let's . . ." in line 11 is used to introduce a suggestion.

4. "Okay" (line 13) is commonly used to express agreement.

GETTING READY

1. Practice weather vocabulary. Bring in visuals depicting various weather conditions, and have students describe them. Be sure to include examples of the following: *warm, cold, rain, snow, foggy, cloudy, windy.*

2. Practice gerunds.

   a. Model the following conversation:

      A. Do you want to go sightseeing?
      B. Not really. Going sightseeing isn't a very good idea.

   b. Call on pairs of students to continue the practice, using their own activities or visuals that you provide.

THE MODEL CONVERSATION

1. **Set the Scene:** "Someone is inviting a friend to go skiing tomorrow."

2. **Listen to the Model.**

3. **Class Practice.**

4. **Read.**

5. **Pair Practice.**

6. **Alternative Expressions.**

THE EXERCISES

Examples

1. A. Would you like to go on a picnic tomorrow?
   B. That sounds great. I haven't gone on a picnic in a long time. But wait a minute! Isn't it supposed to be cold and windy tomorrow?
   A. Gee. I hadn't heard that.
   B. I'm pretty sure it's supposed to be cold and windy. I read it in the paper.
   A. In that case, going on a picnic probably wouldn't be a very good idea.
   B. Hmm. I guess you're right.
   A. Let's wait and see what the weather is like tomorrow.
   B. Okay. I'll call you in the morning.

2. A. How would you like to go to the beach tomorrow?
   B. That sounds like fun. I haven't gone to the beach in a long time. But wait a minute! Isn't it supposed to be cloudy tomorrow?
   A. Gee. I hadn't heard that.
   B. I'm pretty sure it's supposed to be cloudy. I saw the forecast on TV this morning.
   A. In that case, going to the beach probably wouldn't be a very good idea.
   B. Hmm. I guess you're right.
   A. Let's wait and see what the weather is like tomorrow.
   B. Okay. I'll call you in the morning.

Before doing each exercise, check students' understanding of the vocabulary and introduce any unfamiliar words or phrases. Have students use the footnoted expressions or any of their alternatives as they do the exercises.

Exercise Practice (optional). Have pairs of students simultaneously practice all the exercises.

Exercise Presentations. Call on pairs of students to present the exercises.

ORIGINAL STUDENT CONVERSATIONS

Have pairs of students create and present original conversations based on the model. (You may want students to prepare their original conversations as homework, then practice them the next day with another student and present them to the class.)

EXPANSION

1. Information Gap: It All Depends on the Weather

a. Write the following information on index cards, and make enough copies for the class.

b. Divide the class into pairs. Assign Role A to one member of each pair and Role B to the other.

c. Have students role-play the situations using expressions for inviting and accepting invitations.

1.
> Role A:
>
> Invite a friend to go sailing.

> Role B:
>
> You read in the paper that it's going to be a beautiful day tomorrow.

2.
> Role A:
>
> Invite a friend to go for a drive to the mountains. (You love the snow!)

> Role B:
>
> You heard on TV that tomorrow is going to be a terrible day. It's going to snow more than 10 inches!

3.
> Role A:
>
> Invite a friend to go swimming.

> Role B:
>
> You don't know what the weather is going to be tomorrow.

4.
> Role A:
>
> Invite a friend to go to a museum.

> Role B:
>
> You enjoy doing things outdoors. The weather forecaster on Channel 9 predicted that it's going to be a beautiful day tomorrow.

5.
> Role A:
>
> Invite a friend to have a picnic with you on Saturday and go to the beach with you on Sunday. You read in the paper that the weather for the weekend is going to be partly sunny and warm.

> Role B:
>
> It's going to rain all weekend. Your neighbor told you. But that's okay. You want to stay home and work on your taxes.

2. What's the Weather?

a. Cut out the section of the newspaper that lists the weather and temperatures in cities around the world. Make enough copies for the class.

b. Have students tell about the weather in different cities. (Ask, "What's the weather today in _____?")

3. Suggestion Game

a. Divide the class into several teams.

b. Choose one kind of weather and have the teams come up with possible activities. For example: "It's supposed to rain tomorrow. What can we do?"

c. Have students in each group work together to see how many suggestions they can think of for that kind of weather. For example:

> How about seeing a movie?
> What about going to the Science Museum?

d. The team with the most suggestions wins.

e. Continue with other weather conditions.

4. Class Survey: Where Do We Get Our Information?

a. Write the following categories on the board:

> weather
> sports
> movie recommendations
> book recommendations
> restaurant recommendations
> neighborhood events

b. Assign pairs of students a category. Have them create survey questions about how people get their information for that particular category. For example:

movie recommendations

> Do you read movie reviews in the paper? If so, who is your favorite reviewer?
> Do you watch movie reviews on television? If so, who is your favorite reviewer?
> Do you pay attention to previews and advertisements for movies?
> Do your friends talk about good movies to see?
> What is your best source of information on good movies?

c. Have students conduct their surveys by circulating around the room asking each other their questions. Then have students share their findings with the class.

Fill It In!

Have students do the activity individually, in pairs, or as a class. You may want to assign this exercise as homework.

1. playing
2. taking
3. going
4. driving
5. riding
6. hanging
7. drinking

Listen

Listen and decide which weather forecast is correct.

1. Here's today's weather forecast for the metropolitan area. We're going to have rain this afternoon. Temperatures will be in the low eighties.

2. Here is the weather update for our area. We have a sunny day ahead. The present temperature is forty-five degrees. Tonight's low will be in the thirties.

3. A. And now, let's hear the weather report from Jim Reed.
   B. Thank you, Jane. It looks like we'll have a little snow this morning . . . but nothing to worry about. And put on those heavy jackets! Today's high will be only about twenty-five.

4. It's going to be a hot, muggy evening with temperatures in the mid-eighties. We have a seventy percent chance of thunderstorms throughout the night.

5. Now here's our latest weather update from Rockin' Ninety-Nine Weather Center. The good news is NO MORE RAIN in the forecast. We'll have clearing tonight, but watch out for fog early tomorrow morning while you're driving to work.

6. A. Now it's time to hear from our weather reporter, Mike Martinez. Mike, what does it look like out there today?
   B. Well, Susan, hold on to your hat! We're in for a windy day with gusts up to twenty miles per hour.

Answers

1. b
2. a
3. a
4. a
5. a
6. b

Your Turn

Have students discuss the activity as a class, in pairs, or in small groups. Then have students write their responses at home, share their written work with other students, and discuss in class.

FOCUS

TOPICS

Social Communication: Invitations
Recreation: Recreational and Entertainment
Activities

GRAMMAR

1. **Gerunds**

   Would you by any chance be interested in **going** dancing tomorrow night?
   Going dancing sounds like a lot more fun than **working** overtime.

2. **Infinitives**

   Would you like **to see** a movie this weekend?
   Do you want **to go out** for dinner tonight?

3. **Can**

   I'm afraid I **can't.**

4. **Able to**

   I'm afraid I won't be **able to.**

5. **Have to/Have Got to**

   I **have to** work overtime.
   I**'ve got to** finish a term paper.

6. **Supposed to**

   I'm **supposed to** attend a business meeting.

FUNCTIONS

1. **Invitations**

   Extending . . .

   Would you by any chance be interested in *going dancing tomorrow night*?
   How would you like to *go out for dinner tonight*?
   Do you want to *go to a concert this Saturday evening*?

   Declining . . .

   I'm afraid I can't.
   I'm afraid I won't be able to.

2. **Checking and Indicating Understanding**

   Checking One's Own Understanding

   Tomorrow night?
   This weekend?
   This Saturday afternoon?

3. **Ability/Inability**

   Expressing Inability

   I'm afraid I can't.
   I'm afraid I won't be able to.

4. **Obligation**

   Expressing . . .

   I have to *work overtime.*
   I've got to *finish a term paper.*
   I'm supposed to *attend a business meeting.*

5. **Disappointment**

   That's too bad.

VOCABULARY

Recreation and Entertainment

concert
dancing
dinner
movie
play
roller skating

COMMENTARY

1. In this conversation, Speaker A is inviting Speaker B out on a date. In traditional United States culture, the young man was always the one who would invite the young woman to go out. Nowadays, *who* invites *whom* depends on many factors, such as how well the people know each other and the type of activity that is planned.

2. The expression "Would you by any chance be interested in _____ing?" is very indirect and would allow the person being invited to comfortably decline. Of the related expressions for extending an invitation, "Do you want to _____?" is the most direct.

3. "I'm afraid I can't" (line 3) is a polite expression for refusing an invitation. "I'm afraid" means "I regret that . . . ."

4. The closing "Maybe some other time" is commonly used when an invitation is declined. It is meant to end the interaction positively and encourage the person to extend an invitation again sometime in the future.

GETTING READY

1. Review recreation and work activities. Have students suggest names of things they *like to do* and things they *have to do but don't like doing*. Write their ideas in two lists, one for recreation and the other for work. For example:

Recreation	Work
dancing	doing homework
seeing a movie	cleaning the
going to a	house
concert	baby-sitting
eating out	working overtime

2. Practice comparing activities.

   a. Model the sentences:

   Dancing is more enjoyable than doing homework.
   Doing homework is more boring than seeing a movie.

   b. Have students compare other activities from the two lists by making similar sentences.

THE MODEL CONVERSATION

1. **Set the Scene:** "One friend is inviting another out."

2. **Listen to the Model.**

3. **Class Practice.**

4. **Read.**

5. **Pair Practice.**

6. **Alternative Expressions.**

THE EXERCISES

Examples

1. A. Would you by any chance be interested in seeing a movie this weekend?
   B. This weekend? I'm afraid I can't. I have to finish a term paper.
   A. That's too bad.
   B. It is. Seeing a movie sounds like a lot more fun than finishing a term paper. Maybe some other time.

2. A. How would you like to go out for dinner tonight?
   B. Tonight? I'm afraid I won't be able to. I've got to attend a business meeting.

> A. That's too bad.
> B. It is. Going out for dinner sounds like a lot more fun than attending a business meeting. Maybe some other time.

Before doing each exercise, check students' understanding of the vocabulary and introduce any unfamiliar words or phrases. Have students use the footnoted expressions or any of their alternatives as they do the exercises.

Exercise Practice (optional). Have pairs of students simultaneously practice all the exercises.

Exercise Presentations. Call on pairs of students to present the exercises.

ORIGINAL STUDENT CONVERSATIONS

Have pairs of students create and present original conversations based on the model. (You may want students to prepare their original conversations as homework, then practice them the next day with another student and present them to the class.)

EXPANSION

1. Information Gap: Invitations

a. Make up schedules similar to those below. Put them on index cards, and make enough copies for the class.

b. Divide the class into pairs. Assign Role A to one member of each pair and Role B to the other.

c. Have students role-play the situations. Tell Speaker B to check his or her schedule and either accept or refuse the other person's invitation based on the schedule.

> Role A:
> You enjoy doing things. Invite a friend to join you.
>
> | | |
> |---|---|
> | Friday evening | see a movie |
> | Saturday morning | play tennis |
> | Saturday afternoon | go hiking |
> | Saturday evening | go to a concert |
> | Sunday afternoon | see a play |
> | Sunday evening | go out to eat |

> Role B:
> This is your weekend schedule:
>
> | | |
> |---|---|
> | Friday evening | work overtime/office |
> | Saturday morning | (free) |
> | Saturday afternoon | take/father/doctor |
> | Saturday evening | visit/uncle/hospital |
> | Sunday afternoon | (free) |
> | Sunday evening | work on/taxes |

2. True Regret?

a. Have students reread the model conversation and imagine how it would sound if the woman really *didn't* want to go out with the man and how it would sound if she really *did* want to go out with him but couldn't because of her work.

b. Have students practice the conversation with the two different dynamics of *polite* regret and *true* regret.

c. Have students present their different versions of the conversation to the class. Have the class decide, based on the presentation, whether the woman really wants to or doesn't want to go out with the man.

3. Obligation Game

a. Divide the class into several teams.

b. Tell students to think of all the things they have to do every morning, every weekday, every weekend, and every season.

c. Have students in each group work together to see how many obligations they can think of for each time period. For example:

> *every morning*
>
> I have to get up at 6 o'clock.
> I have to eat breakfast.
> I've got to catch the 8:15 bus.
> I have to be at work by 9 o'clock.

d. The team with the most obligations wins.

4. Cultural Comparisons: Teenage Dating

a. Have students in pairs or in small groups discuss the following questions:

> At what age do young people begin dating in your country?

Do girls invite boys on a date?

Do the girl and boy share expenses on the date?

Are the parents supposed to meet their child's date?

Should teenagers be chaperoned (accompanied by someone)?

Where do most teenagers go on dates?

b. Have the groups share their ideas with the class.

Variation: Have students interview Americans about teenage dating. Then have them share their findings with the class.

Fill It In!

Have students do the activity individually, in pairs, or as a class. You may want to assign this exercise as homework.

1. b   5. c
2. a   6. b
3. a   7. c
4. b   8. c

Listen

Listen and decide whether someone accepted or rejected the other person's invitation.

1. A. Carol, how about going out for dinner tonight?
   B. Tonight? That sounds great.

2. A. Bob, do you want to go bowling tomorrow night?
   B. Tomorrow night? I'm afraid I can't. I've got to baby-sit for my cousin.

3. A. Angela, how would you like to see a ballgame with me this weekend?
   B. I'd love to.

4. A. Lucy, would you by any chance be interested in going to a movie with me this Friday night?
   B. This Friday night? Hmm. Let me think. You know, I think I have to help my parents clean the attic. Maybe some other time, Ronald.

5. A. Howard, what about going to a museum with me tomorrow?
   B. Gee, Irene, I'm afraid I won't be able to.
   A. You won't?

   B. No. I've got to finish an important term paper.
   A. Oh.
   B. Maybe some other time, okay?
   A. Sure, Howard.

6. A. Tim, do you feel like going skating this afternoon?
   B. This afternoon? Sure. That's a great idea. I really should do my homework, but I'd much rather go skating with you.

7. A. Millie, let's get together this weekend.
   B. Great idea. What do you want to do?
   A. Let's take a nice long walk in the park.
   B. Okay. When?
   A. How about Sunday afternoon?
   B. Sunday afternoon? Gee, I won't be able to. I've got to work on my taxes this Sunday. Maybe some other time.

8. A. How would you like to play tennis with me this Tuesday afternoon?
   B. This Tuesday? Gee, I think I'm supposed to attend a meeting this Tuesday. No, wait a minute. The meeting is Thursday. Sure. I'd love to play tennis with you on Tuesday.

Answers

1. a   5. b
2. b   6. a
3. a   7. b
4. b   8. a

CrossTalk

Have students first work in pairs and then share with the class what they talked about.

FOCUS

TOPICS

Social Communication: Making Conversation
Recreation: Recreational and Entertainment Activities

GRAMMAR

1. **Past Tense**

What **did** you **do** over the weekend?
   I **saw** a play.
   I **went** sailing.

2. **Past Perfect Tense**

I **had gone** sailing the weekend before
   THAT, too!
I **had driven** to the mountains the
   weekend before THAT, too!

I **hadn't seen** a play in ages!
I **hadn't worked** in my garden in ages!

3. **Gerunds**

You really enjoy **going** sailing!
You really enjoy **driving** to the mountains!

4. **Infinitives**

I like **to go** sailing whenever I can.
I like **to drive** to the mountains whenever
   I can.

FUNCTIONS

1. **Asking for and Reporting Information**

What did you do *over the weekend*?
   I *saw a play.*

Didn't you *go sailing the weekend before*?
   Yes, I did.

How about you?

2. **Likes–Dislikes**

Inquiring about . . .
Did you enjoy it?

Expressing Likes
You really enjoy *going sailing*!

I like to *go sailing* whenever I can.

VOCABULARY

**Recreation and
Entertainment**

drive to the mountains
fly a kite
go dancing
go sailing
read
see a play
take *my children* to the zoo

Everyday Activities

bake
cook
volunteer
wash the car
work in the garden
write letters

260 EXIT EIGHT

COMMENTARY

1. Asking about weekend activities is a common way to make conversation.

2. "In ages" (line 4) means a very long time.

3. In lines 5–6, Speaker B reciprocates the questions, "What did YOU do over the weekend?" and emphasizes YOU to redirect the conversation to Speaker A.

4. "THAT" in "I had gone sailing the weekend before THAT, too!" (lines 10–11) refers to the weekend before. Speaker A emphasizes "THAT" to clarify that he is talking about the far past.

5. "Boy!" (line 12) is a common exclamation of interest or surprise.

GETTING READY

Introduce the past perfect tense.

a. Write on the board:

Harriet's Vacation Last Week

Sunday:	go sailing
Monday:	go swimming
Tuesday:	ride her bicycle
Wednesday:	write letters
Thursday:	go skating
Friday:	see a movie
Saturday:	go dancing

---

b. Tell the class about Harriet's week:

Harriet was on vacation last week. She **went sailing** on Sunday. She didn't go sailing on Monday because **she had gone sailing** the day before.

She **rode her bicycle** on Tuesday. She didn't ride her bicycle on Wednesday because **she had ridden her bicycle** the day before.

c. Continue telling about the rest of the week.

d. Write on the board:

A. Did she _____ on _____?
B. No, she didn't. She had _____ the day before.

---

e. Model the following:

    A. Did Harriet go sailing on Monday?
    B. No, she didn't. She had gone sailing the day before.

    A. Did she go swimming on Tuesday?
    B. No, she didn't. She had gone swimming the day before.

f. Continue asking students about the other days of the week.

THE MODEL CONVERSATION

1. **Set the Scene:** "Two co-workers are talking about their weekend activities."

2. **Listen to the Model.**

3. **Class Practice.**

4. **Read.**

5. **Pair Practice.**

THE EXERCISES

Examples

---

1. A. What did you do over the weekend?
   B. I worked in my garden.
   A. Did you enjoy it?
   B. Yes. I hadn't worked in my garden in ages! How about you? What did YOU do over the weekend?
   A. I drove to the mountains.
   B. Hmm. Didn't you drive to the mountains the weekend before?
   A. Yes, I did. And I had driven to the mountains the weekend before THAT, too.
   B. Boy, you really enjoy driving to the mountains!
   A. I sure do! I like to drive to the mountains whenever I can.

2. A. What did you do over the weekend?
   B. I took my children to the zoo.
   A. Did you enjoy it?
   B. Yes. I hadn't taken my children to the zoo in ages! How about you? What did YOU do over the weekend?
   A. I wrote letters.
   B. Hmm. Didn't you write letters the weekend before?
   A. Yes, I did. And I had written letters the weekend before THAT, too.
   B. Boy, you really enjoy writing letters!
   A. I sure do! I like to write letters whenever I can.

Before doing each exercise, check students' understanding of the vocabulary and introduce any unfamiliar words or phrases.

Exercise Practice (optional). Have pairs of students simultaneously practice all the exercises.

Exercise Presentations. Call on pairs of students to present the exercises.

Culture Note

Exercise 5: To "volunteer at the nursing home" is to help take care of elderly patients without receiving pay. Volunteering in hospitals, community projects, and schools is very common in the United States.

ORIGINAL STUDENT CONVERSATIONS

Have pairs of students create and present original conversations based on the model. (You may want students to prepare their original conversations as homework, then practice them the next day with another student and present them to the class.)

EXPANSION

1. Find Someone Who . . .

a. Collect some information about what students did last weekend.

b. Put this information in the following form:

```
Find someone who . . .

1. went hiking.              _____

2. took care of her sisters. _____

3. went sailing.             _____

4. flew a kite.              _____

5. saw a movie.             _____
```

c. Have students circulate around the room asking each other questions to identify the above people.

d. The first student to identify all the people wins.

2. Chain Game: What a Busy Day!

a. Begin the game by saying, "After a very busy day, James finally sat down at dinner and told his family what he had done that Saturday. Before he sat down for dinner, he had gone shopping. Before he went shopping, he had gone to the bank."

b. Student 1 adds another item. For example: "Before he went to the bank, he had picked up his check."

c. Continue around the room in this fashion, with each student adding to what the previous one said.

If the class is large, you can divide students into groups to give students more practice with the past perfect.

3. Listen Carefully!

a. Find an interesting newspaper or magazine story, and tell the story to the class.

b. Make several statements in the past tense about the story. Some statements should be true and others false.

c. Students have to listen carefully to the statements and decide if each is true or false. If a statement is false, have students correct it.

Variation: This activity can be done as a game with two competing teams. The teams take turns deciding whether each statement is true or false.

4. Class Discussion

a. Divide the class into small groups.

b. Have students discuss the following questions:

What is a recreational activity you haven't done in a long time?
Why did you stop doing it?
What is a recreational activity you do frequently?
Why do you enjoy doing this activity?

c. Have the groups share their ideas with the class.

Constructions Ahead!

Have students do the activity individually, in pairs, or as a class. You may want to assign this exercise as homework.

1. had gone
2. had played
3. hadn't ridden
4. hadn't seen
5. had written, hadn't
6. hadn't gone

Figure It Out!

Have students write their descriptions individually and then pass them to you. Scramble the papers and redistribute them to the class. Have students circulate around the room interviewing each other about their weekend activities until they can identify the author of the description they have.

FOCUS

TOPICS

Social Communication: Making Conversation
Recreation: Recreational and Entertainment Activities

GRAMMAR

1. **Past Tense**

   How **did** your parents **enjoy** their vacation?

   They **were** really disappointed.
   The weather **was** miserable.

2. **Past Perfect Continuous Tense**

   They **had been looking** forward to their vacation for a long time.
   They **had been talking** about it for weeks!

3. **Possessive Adjectives**

   They had been looking forward to **their** vacation.
   She had been looking forward to **her** dinner.
   He had been looking forward to **his** ski vacation.
   You had been looking forward to **your** flight.

FUNCTIONS

1. **Initiating a Topic**

   Tell me, *how did your parents enjoy their vacation*?

2. **Asking for and Reporting Information**

   How did *your parents enjoy their vacation in Florida*?

3. **Sympathizing**

   That's a shame!
   That's too bad!
   What a shame!
   What a pity!

4. **Agreement/Disagreement**

   Expressing Agreement
   I know.

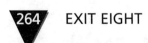

264 EXIT EIGHT

VOCABULARY

Adjectives

bad
boring
bumpy
choppy
cold
crowded
expensive
miserable
old-fashioned
slow
tiny
warm

COMMENTARY

1. "Tell me " is a common way to initiate a topic of conversation.

2. The two speakers are obviously good friends. Speaker A expresses sympathy in line 6 ("That's a shame!") upon hearing about her friend's parents' unpleasant vacation.

GETTING READY

Introduce the past perfect continuous tense.

a. Write on the board:

had been working

Mr. Fay

Mrs. Fay

had been cleaning

had been planting flowers

Michael

Susan

had been vacuuming

had been baking cookies

b. Point to the appropriate cues on the board as you tell the following story:

"I stopped by to visit the Fay family this afternoon, and everybody in the family was exhausted! They had been working hard all day.

Mr. Fay had been cleaning the house.
Mrs. Fay had been planting flowers in the garden.
Their son Michael had been vacuuming.
And their daughter Susan had been baking cookies.

Everybody in the Fay family had been working hard all day. That's why they were all exhausted when I stopped by to visit them this afternoon."

c. Write on the board:

> A. What had _____ been doing?
> B. He/She/They had been _____ing.

d. Ask questions about the Fay family, and have students answer. For example:

A. What had Mr. Fay been doing?
B. He had been cleaning the house.

A. What had Mrs. Fay been doing?
B. She had been planting flowers in the garden.

THE MODEL CONVERSATION

1. **Set the Scene:** "Two friends are talking."
2. **Listen to the Model.**
3. **Class Practice.**
4. **Read.**
5. **Pair Practice.**
6. **Alternative Expressions.**

THE EXERCISES

Examples

---

1. A. Tell me, how did your sister enjoy her dinner at the Ritz?
   B. She was really disappointed. The food was cold, and the service was slow.
   A. That's a shame! She had been looking forward to her dinner at the Ritz for a long time.
   B. I know. She had been talking about it for weeks!

2. A. Tell me, how did your brother enjoy his ski vacation?
   B. He was really disappointed. The weather was warm, and the ski lifts were expensive.
   A. That's too bad! He had been looking forward to his ski vacation for a long time.
   B. I know. He had been talking about it for weeks!

Before doing each exercise, check students' understanding of the vocabulary and introduce any unfamiliar words or phrases. Have students use the footnoted expression or any of its alternatives as they do the exercises.

Exercise Practice (optional). Have pairs of students simultaneously practice all the exercises.

Exercise Presentations. Call on pairs of students to present the exercises.

Culture Note

Exercise 5: The "Senior Prom" is a formal dance for the graduating class in high school.

ORIGINAL STUDENT CONVERSATIONS

Have pairs of students create and present original conversations based on the model. (You may want students to prepare their original conversations as homework, then practice them the next day with another student and present them to the class.)

EXPANSION

1. ***Adjective Expansion Activity***
   a. Divide the class into teams.
   b. Have each team list as many adjectives as they can think of to describe vacation experiences.
   c. After three minutes, the team with the longest list wins.

2. ***Find Someone Who . . .***
   a. Collect some information about students' vacation and travel experiences.
   b. Put this information in the following form:

   Find someone who . . .
   1. went on a ski vacation.   _____
   2. took a cruise.   _____
   3. had a bumpy plane flight.   _____
   4. had dinner at an elegant
      restaurant.   _____
   5. went to the mountains
      for a vacation.   _____

   ---

   c. Have students circulate around the room asking each other questions to identify the above people.
   d. The first student to identify all the people wins.

3. ***Research Project: Places to Go and Things to Do***
   a. Brainstorm with students different vacation possibilities. Write their ideas on the board. For example:

   ---

   taking a cruise
   going skiing
   going camping
   spending the weekend in an exciting city

b. Divide the class into teams. Assign each team one vacation idea. Have them contact a tourist agency to find out the following:

> Where are some of the best locations for doing this?
> What kinds of activities are possible?
> What is the most economical way to take this kind of vacation?
> What should the vacationer beware of?

c. Have the teams write up a report of their research. Then have each team give a short presentation to the class about what they discovered. Students may wish to publish their findings as a *Class Vacation Guide*.

4. Investigation: When Things Go Wrong

a. Divide the class into teams.

b. Have each team take a different aspect of tourism and entertainment, such as: air travel, boat travel, train travel, hotels, cruises, camping, dining, beach vacations, or ski vacations.

c. Have each group brainstorm all the different problems that might arise while enjoying this type of vacation or entertainment. Have them contact tourist agents to find out what to do when such things go wrong. For example:

> *air travel*
>
> Question: What should I do if my luggage doesn't arrive when I do?
> Answer: Contact the airline and give an address where the luggage can be delivered.

d. Have students report their findings to the class.

Constructions Ahead!

Have students do the activity individually, in pairs, or as a class. You may want to assign this exercise as homework.

1. had been planning
2. had been wanting
3. had been telling
4. had been expecting
5. had been hoping
6. had been looking forward
7. had been talking
8. had been leaking

Your Turn

Have students discuss the activity as a class, in pairs, or in small groups. Then have students write their responses at home, share their written work with other students, and discuss in class.

FOCUS

TOPIC

Recreation: Listings and Schedules

FUNCTIONS

1. **Want–Desire**

   Inquiring about . . .

   Would you like to *see a movie tonight*?

   What would you like to *see*?

   Are you interested?

2. **Advice–Suggestions**

   Asking for . . .

   How about *The Missing Jewels*?
   What about *The Missing Jewels*?

3. **Asking for and Reporting Information**

   What's it about?
   Who's in it?
   What time is it *showing*?

   The ad in the paper says . . .

4. **Hesitating**

   Hmm.
   Let me see.

5. **Preference**

   Expressing . . .

   I'd prefer to *go at 7:10*.
   I'd rather *go at 7:10*.

VOCABULARY

Recreation and Entertainment

adventure movie
cartoon
children's film
comedy
documentary
drama
foreign film

mystery
science fiction movie
western

listings
schedule
theater

COMMENTARY

1. "What's it about?" (line 6) is asked when someone wants to know the theme or basic story line of a movie, book, or some other dramatic performance.

2. "Sounds like . . ." (line 9) prefaces a logical conclusion or an *educated guess*.

3. In line 15, the informal response "That sounds fine to me" means "I like that idea."

GETTING READY

Introduce types of movies.

a. Ask students "What kind of movies do you like?" List their answers on the board. Be sure to include: *mystery, adventure, drama, comedy, western, science fiction, documentary, children's, foreign, cartoon.*

b. Have students give the titles of movies they know that fit the different categories.

c. Have students tell names of movie stars they know.

THE MODEL CONVERSATION

1. **Set the Scene:** "A husband and wife are trying to decide what movie to see."

2. **Listen to the Model.**

3. **Class Practice.**

4. **Read.**

5. **Pair Practice.**

6. **Alternative Expressions.**

THE EXERCISES

Examples

---

1. A. Would you like to see a movie tonight?
   B. Sure. What would you like to see?
   A. How about *Dangerous Journey*?
   B. *Dangerous Journey*?
   A. Yes. It's playing at the East Mall Cinema.
   B. What's it about?
   A. I don't know. The ad in the paper says, "It'll keep you on the edge of your seat!"
   B. Hmm. Sounds like an adventure movie. Who's in it?
   A. Samantha Drake and Maxwell Hall. Are you interested?
   B. Sure. What time is it showing?

   A. Let's see. There are shows at 7:30 and 9:45.
   B. I think I'd prefer to go at 7:30. Is that okay?
   A. Sure. That sounds fine to me.

2. A. Would you like to see a movie tonight?
   B. Sure. What would you like to see?
   A. What about *The Final Good-Bye*?
   B. *The Final Good-Bye*?
   A. Yes. It's playing at the Regency Theater.
   B. What's it about?
   A. I don't know. The ad in the paper says, "Bring several handkerchiefs!"
   B. Hmm. Sounds like a drama. Who's in it?
   A. Nancy Haywood and Donald Brewster. Are you interested?
   B. Sure. What time is it showing?
   A. Let me see. There are shows at eight and ten.
   B. I think I'd rather go at ten. Is that okay?
   A. Sure. That sounds fine to me.

Before doing each exercise, check students' understanding of the vocabulary and introduce any unfamiliar words or phrases. Have students use the footnoted expressions or their alternatives as they do the exercises.

Exercise Practice (optional). Have pairs of students simultaneously practice all the exercises.

Exercise Presentations. Call on pairs of students to present the exercises.

Culture Notes

Exercise 1: The advertising statement "It'll keep you on the edge of your seat!" implies that the movie is very exciting and, possibly, very scary.

Exercise 3: The expression "rolling in the aisles" means laughing uncontrollably at a movie or play.

ORIGINAL STUDENT CONVERSATIONS

Have pairs of students create and present original conversations based on the model. (You may want students to prepare their original conversations as homework, then practice them the next day with another student and present them to the class.)

EXPANSION

1. Scanning Exercise: What's Playing?

Practice looking for specific information in the movie listings.

a. Make copies of the movie listings from the newspaper, and distribute them to students in the class.

b. Have students scan the listings for answers to specific questions. For example:

What time does _____ begin?
Where is _____ playing?

I have to work late tonight, and then I want to see a movie. What time does the latest movie start? Where is it playing?

2. Role Play: Let's See a Movie

a. Divide the class into pairs.

b. Make copies of movie listings and movie ads from the newspaper, and distribute to each pair of students.

c. Set the scene: "You want to see a movie tonight. Look at the newspaper and decide which movie you'd like to see."

d. Have the pairs report back to the class and tell which movie they decided on and why.

Variation: Give cue cards to each member of the pair, indicating their taste in movies. For example:

> You don't like comedies or westerns.

> You only like adventure movies.

3. Class Discussion: Favorite Movies

Have students talk about their favorite movies in pairs or in small groups and then report back to the class. Possible questions are:

What was your favorite movie?
Was it a comedy/adventure movie/
   drama . . . ?
Who was in it?
What was it about?

4. Movie Game

a. Divide the class into several teams.

b. Call out any of the following types of movies from page 146 of the student text:

mystery
comedy
drama
documentary
western
adventure movie
cartoon
children's film
foreign film
science fiction movie

c. Have the students in each group work together to see how many titles of movies they can think of that belong to that category.

d. The team with the most titles wins.

5. Make Up Your Own Titles!

a. Divide the class into pairs.

b. Call out movie categories from the activity above.

c. Have the pairs make up titles for each type of movie.

d. Have the class then decide if the titles are appropriate.

6. Adjective Game

a. Divide the class into several teams.

b. Call out a movie category from Activity 4.

c. Have the students in each team work together to see how many adjectives they can associate with that type of movie. For example:

documentary: interesting/informative/
                     slow
adventure movie: exciting/thrilling/fast/fun

d. The team with the most adjectives wins.

Movie Match

Have students do the activity individually, in pairs, or as a class. You may want to assign this exercise as homework.

1. e
2. c
3. f
4. g
5. b
6. d
7. a

Listen

Listen to the movie theater recordings and answer the questions.

The State Theater is proud to present *One Last Kiss*. There are shows this evening at seven-thirty and nine-thirty. Tickets are seven dollars apiece.

Thanks for calling the Town Theater. We're happy to be showing the popular film *The Friendly Giant*. The afternoon show is at one o'clock. Other shows are at three o'clock and five o'clock. Tickets for the one o'clock show are three dollars. All other shows are six dollars each.

Answers

1. b
2. b
3. a
4. b
5. b
6. a

Community Connections

Have students look in the local newspaper to find a listing or an ad for a movie they're interested in seeing. They should call the theater to find out what time the movie starts. Have students go to the movie in pairs or small groups. They should then tell the class about the movie. You can also have students write short reviews of the movie and distribute them to the class.

FOCUS

TOPIC

Recreation: Listings and Schedules

FUNCTIONS

1. **Want–Desire**

   Inquiring about . . .

   What do you want to *watch*?

2. **Asking for and Reporting Information**

   What's on?
   > *Dr. Goodbody* is on Channel 2.

3. **Preference**

   Expressing . . .

   I'd rather not *watch Dr. Goodbody.*

4. **Advice–Suggestions**

   Offering . . .

   How about *Million Dollar Jackpot on Channel 5*?
   How about *watching Pittsburgh Police on Channel 7*?

5. **Checking and Indicating Understanding**

   Checking One's Own Understanding

   Million Dollar Jackpot?
   Pittsburgh Police?

6. **Indifference**

   It doesn't make any difference to me.

   Whatever *you'd like to watch* is fine with me.

VOCABULARY

Recreation and Entertainment

Channel 2
children's show
detective show
drama
game show
miniseries

police show
program
situation comedy
soap opera
TV listings

COMMENTARY

1. "What's on?" in line 2 means "What programs are on TV?"

2. "Oh" at the beginning of line 4 prefaces Speaker B's comment.

3. "Tired of" (line 4) implies that the person has done the activity so much that he or she is now bored with it.

4. Types of TV shows (line 6):

   a. A *situation comedy* is a weekly TV comedy with a continuing cast of characters who are humorously portrayed going through their daily routines. Some situation comedies portray family life in a fictional home. Others portray the lives of a group of people at a particular place of work. Many of these shows have *canned laughter* (recorded sounds of people laughing) inserted at funny moments in the program.

   b. A *game show* is usually a daily show in which contestants compete for prizes. In these shows, people have to answer trivia questions, guess prices of consumer goods, or play word games. Many game shows incorporate some element of chance, such as a roulette wheel or a card drawing for their *grand prize* competition. Winners usually get cash, major home appliances, luxury cars, clothing, or vacations.

   c. A *drama* is a weekly show or special presentation that handles a serious theme.

   d. A *detective show* and a *police show* are shows that feature fast-moving action and occasional violence, often with complicated story lines in which the viewer follows clues to uncover the crime.

   e. A *children's show* is television programming that includes educational shows produced by publicly supported TV stations, such as *Sesame Street* and *Mister Rogers*, as well as cartoon shows produced by the commercial networks. Educational shows generally try to entertain children while at the same time promoting their cognitive and emotional development.

   f. A *soap opera* is a situation drama that usually centers on the personal relationships of a set of characters. These story lines usually involve tragic experiences and petty conflicts. Popular topics for soap operas are the lives of very rich people and the lives of doctors and nurses working in a hospital.

   g. A *miniseries* is a made-for-TV movie often based on a famous novel or historical event. There are several episodes in a miniseries, which is broadcast on consecutive nights.

5. "I'm not really in the mood for" (line 7) is an informal way of expressing a personal preference. It means "I don't really want to."

6. "TV listings" (line 10), the schedule of TV programs for the week, are usually published in local newspapers every Sunday. Special magazines, such as *TV Guide*, also offer these listings in addition to articles about TV stars and their programs.

7. Speaker A says "Let's see" in line 13 as she hesitates while looking through the listings.

8. "That's supposed to be a pretty good show" (lines 13–14) means "It's reported to be a good show." Speaker A has either heard or read somewhere that the show is good.

9. The expression "Maybe we should _____ after all" (lines 15–16) indicates the speaker now agrees with the suggestion he had previously disagreed with.

10. "It doesn't make any difference to me" (line 17) is used when a speaker does not have a preference or wants someone else to choose. The expression "Whatever you'd like to _____ is fine with me" is used to agree with someone else's choice.

GETTING READY

Talk about types of television programs.

   a. Ask students what types of shows are on television. Write their ideas on the board. Be sure to include: *game show, children's show, situation comedy, drama, detective show, police show, soap opera,* and *miniseries.*

   b. Ask students to tell the names of television shows they know and identify what type of program they are.

   c. Model the following conversation:

> A. What's your favorite television show?
> B. *Roommates.* I really like situation comedies.

   d. Call on pairs of students to continue the practice using TV shows of their choice.

THE MODEL CONVERSATION

1. **Set the Scene:** "A wife and husband are trying to decide what to watch on TV."

2. **Listen to the Model.**

3. **Class Practice.**

4. **Read.**

5. **Pair Practice.**

Now have pairs of students create and present original conversations using the model dialog as a guide. Encourage students to be inventive and to use new vocabulary. (You may want to assign this exercise as homework, having students prepare their conversations, practice them the next day with another student, and then present them to the class.) Students should present their conversations without referring to the written text, but they also should not memorize them. Rather, they should feel free to adapt and expand them any way they wish.

EXPANSION

TV Listings

Give all students copies of the complete TV schedule for a particular evening. Divide the class into pairs, and have students play the roles of family members who are deciding what they want to watch.

Reflections

Have students discuss the questions in pairs or small groups, and then share their ideas with the class.

Television Match

Have students do the activity individually, in pairs, or as a class. You may want to assign this exercise as homework.

1. f
2. d
3. b
4. e
5. a
6. c

Reading: *VCRs*

Preview: Have students look at the illustrations and discuss the following questions:

Where are these people?
What are they doing?
Are they enjoying themselves?

Then have students read the passage silently, or have them listen to the passage and take notes as you read it or play the audiotape.

True or False?

Have students do the activity individually, in pairs, or as a class. You may want to assign this exercise as homework.

1. True
2. False
3. True
4. False
5. True

What's the Answer?

Have students do the activity individually, in pairs, or as a class. You may want to assign this exercise as homework.

1. a
2. c
3. b
4. c

CrossTalk

Have students first work in pairs and then share with the class what they talked about.

InterView

Have students circulate around the room to conduct their interviews, or have students interview people outside of class. Students should then report back to the class about their interviews.

Looking Back

Have students look at the list of expressions. Encourage them to ask you any questions about the meaning or pronunciation of any of the words. If students ask for the pronunciation, repeat after the student until the student is satisfied with his or her pronunciation of the word.

Review Activities

To review the language introduced in the unit, do the following activities.

1. Association Game

a. Divide the class into several teams.

b. Call out a topic category from the *Looking Back* section on student text page 152.

c. Have students in each group work together to see how many phrases they can associate with that category. For example:

Making a Suggestion: *go to a movie*

How about going to a movie?
What about going to a movie?
How about a movie?
What about a movie?
Let's go to a movie!
Why don't we go to a movie.

d. The team with the most phrases wins.

2. *Create a Conversation!*

a. Divide the class into pairs of students.

b. Tell each pair they have three minutes to make up a conversation using one item from each category from the *Looking Back* section on page 152 of the student text.

c. Have students share their conversations with the class.

Have students talk about the people and the situations and then present role plays based on the scenes. Students may refer to previous lessons as a resource, but they should not simply reuse specific conversations. (You may want to assign these exercises as written homework, having students prepare their conversations, practice them the next day with another student, and then present them to the class.)

1. **FOCUS: Department Store: Purchasing an Item**

   A customer is talking to a salesperson in a department store. She wants to buy a tape recorder.

2. **FOCUS: Department Store: Purchasing an Item**

   A man wants to buy his mother a gift.

3. **FOCUS: Department Store: Returning an Item**

   A customer is returning a jacket to a department store.

4. **FOCUS: Post Office: Mailing Packages**

   This person wants to mail a package at the post office.

5. **FOCUS: Recreation: Recreational and Entertainment Activities**

   A wife and husband are making plans for the day.

6. **FOCUS: Recreation: Recreational and Entertainment Activities**
   Social Communication: Invitations

   One co-worker is inviting another co-worker to do something.

7. **FOCUS: Recreation: Recreational and Entertainment Activities**
   Social Communication: Making Conversation

   Two co-workers are talking on Monday morning about what they did over the weekend.

8. **FOCUS: Recreation: Recreational and Entertainment Activities**

   Two people are trying to decide what movie to see.

Exit 1

Pages 1-3

A. The Right Choice

1. aren't you
2. am
3. I'm
4. Nice meeting you, too.
5. do you work in
6. What about you

B. Listen

1. Which
2. Who
3. What
4. How
5. Whose
6. Why

C. Wrong Way!

2
1
3
5
4

D. What's the Response?

1. b
2. a
3. b
4. a
5. b
6. b
7. a
8. b
9. b
10. a
11. a
12. b

E. The Right Choice

1. did
2. Am
3. do
4. are
5. Does
6. is
7. Are
8. Do

F. Listen

1. transportation
2. work
3. school
4. health
5. housing
6. work
7. health
8. transportation
9. housing

Page 4

A. More Formal or Less Formal?

More Formal	Less Formal
1. ✓	—
2. —	✓
3. ✓	—
4. —	✓

5. —	✓
6. ✓	—
7. ✓	—
8. —	✓

B. Listen

1. ✓ ___	4. ___ ✓
2. ✓ ___	5. ✓ ___
3. ___ ✓	6. ✓ ___

C. Wrong Way!

1. How are you doing?
2. How are things?
3. I'd like to introduce my wife, Jane.
4. It's nice meeting you.

Pages 5-6

A. Wrong Way!

1.	2.
3	1
5	4
1	5
8	3
4	2
6	
2	
7	

B. Matching Lines

1. e
2. g
3. i
4. h
5. c
6. f
7. a
8. d
9. b

C. Crosswalk (see page 293)

D. Listen

1. Italian
2. Japanese
3. Swedish
4. Spaniard
5. Brazil
6. Korea
7. France
8. Spanish
9. French

Pages 7-8

A. The Right Choice

1. reservation
2. What's
3. spell
4. First
5. correct
6. requested
7. Not really
8. No problem

B. What's the Word?

1. reservation
2. suite
3. staying
4. charging
5. bed
6. alone
7. facing
8. check in

C. Listen

1. a	4. b	7. a
2. a	5. b	8. a
3. b	6. a	

Pages 9-12

B. What's the Question?

1. What's your apartment number?
2. What's your telephone number?
3. What's your zip code?
4. What's your date of birth?

C. What Are They Saying?

1. a	3. b	5. b
2. b	4. a	6. b

D. Analogies

1. This is Tom.
2. university
3. student
4. came
5. difficult
6. Biology
7. Not really.
8. telephone number
9. in a little while
10. work

E. Word Search (see page 293)

F. Matching Lines

1. h	5. j	9. b
2. d	6. i	10. g
3. f	7. c	
4. a	8. e	

Exit 2

Pages 13-15

A. What's the Response?

1. a	5. b	9. b
2. b	6. a	10. a
3. a	7. b	11. a
4. a	8. a	12. b

B. Listen

1. Bad News
2. Good News
3. Bad News
4. Good News
5. Bad News
6. Good News
7. Bad News
8. Bad News
9. Bad News
10. Bad News

C. The Right Choice

1. made
2. left
3. took
4. didn't eat
5. went
6. saw
7. didn't feel
8. got
9. didn't win
10. didn't find
11. got
12. didn't buy
13. wrote
14. had to

E. Greeting Card Match

1. c	4. f	7. d
2. g	5. h	8. b
3. a	6. e	

Pages 16-18

A. The Right Choice

1. ask
2. What
3. Did
4. fire
5. fire
6. did
7. hear
8. heard
9. believe
10. it's

C. Listen

3	7	5	1
6	2	8	4

D. The Right Choice

1. ask
2. wants
3. stop
4. boss
5. strike
6. true
7. people
8. When
9. heard
10. was
11. talking
12. Who
13. overheard
14. quit
15. receive
16. union

E. What's the Line?

1. don't want, want
2. isn't going
3. isn't getting, He's getting
4. doesn't plan, plans
5. aren't going
6. doesn't want, wants
7. weren't, were

F. Yes or No?

	Yes	No
1.		✓
2.	✓	
3.	✓	
4.		✓
5.		✓
6.	✓	

7. ✓ ___
8. ___ ✓
9. ✓ ___

Pages 19-21

A. The Right Choice
1. going   6. are
2. are going   7. going
3. You're   8. have
4. going   9. too
5. How

C. What's the Question?
1. Where   4. How many   7. Why
2. When   5. Where   8. What
3. What   6. Who   9. When

D. Function Check
1. a   4. a   7. a
2. b   5. a   8. a
3. a   6. b

E. Listen
1. _3_ _1_ _2_   2. _2_ _3_ _1_
3. _2_ _1_ _3_   4. _1_ _3_ _2_

F. Crosswalk (see page 293)

Pages 22-24

A. Wrong Way!
1. _2_   2. _5_
   _4_   _3_
   _1_   _6_
   _3_   _4_
   _5_   _7_
                 _2_
                 _1_

B. Listen
1. a   4. b   7. b
2. b   5. a   8. a
3. a   6. a

D. What's the Word?
1. look   9. invite
2. relax   10. visit
3. go   11. sleep
4. see   12. read
5. buying   13. eat
6. do   14. spend
7. rake   15. prepare
8. wash

E. Listen
1. relax   6. zoo
2. brother   7. visit
3. play   8. watch
4. chores   9. rock
5. brunch

F. Matching Lines
1. d   4. f   7. g   10. c
2. h   5. a   8. e
3. i   6. j   9. b

G. Wrong Way!
1. On Friday afternoon he married his girlfriend.
2. On Saturday they won $10,000 in the lottery.

Exit 3

Pages 25-26

A. Wrong Way!
_3_
_8_
_5_
_1_
_7_
_4_
_6_
_2_

B. Fill It In!
1. b   4. b   7. b
2. b   5. a
3. a   6. b

C. Listen
1. ✓   5. ___
   ___   ✓
2. ___   6. ___
   ✓   ✓
3. ✓   7. ✓
   ___   ___
4. ___   8. ✓
   ✓   ___

E. Listen
1. L-A-W-L-E-R   4. P-O-T-S-K-Y
2. Y-I-N-G   5. G-O-M-E-Z
3. M-I-L-L-S   6. J-A-R-V-I-S

Pages 27-28

A. The Right Choice

1. sorry
2. nobody
3. name
4. this
5. isn't
6. apologize
7. dialed

B. Matching Lines

1. e
2. h
3. a
4. g
5. d
6. c
7. f
8. b

C. What Are They Saying?

1. a
2. a
3. b
4. a
5. b
6. a

Pages 29-30

A. The Right Choice

1. doesn't
2. Yes
3. Where
4. gate
5. Thank you
6. Excuse me
7. sorry
8. Oh, no
9. I've got to
10. Let me see
11. I hope so

B. Sense or Nonsense?

	Sense	Nonsense
1.	✓	___
2.	✓	___
3.	___	✓
4.	✓	___
5.	___	✓
6.	___	✓

C. Crosswalk (see page 293)

Pages 31-33

A. The Right Choice

1. Could you tell me
2. get to
3. I didn't get that
4. repeat
5. corner
6. Are you with me
7. understand
8. I've got it

B. The 5th Wheel!

1. *I'm sorry.* (The others indicate understanding.)
2. *Excuse me.* (The others indicate understanding.)
3. *That's right.* (The others are apologies.)
4. *I want to* (The others indicate obligation.)
5. *Okay so far?* (The others indicate that the person doesn't understand.)
6. *Are you there?* (The others are asking for information.)
7. *Do you know?* (The others are asking if the person is certain.)
8. *I didn't follow you.* (The others are ways of indicating understanding.)

C. Listen

1. C
2. I
3. C
4. C
5. I
6. C
7. I
8. C
9. I

D. What's the Line?

[*possible answers*]
1. Can you tell me
   Could you tell me
   Do you know
2. Could you please repeat that?
   Could you please say that again?
3. Uh-húh.
   Sure.
   All right.
4. Are you with me so far?
   Okay so far?
   Are you following me so far?
5. I'm following you.
   I understand.
   I'm with you.

E. What's the Response?

1. b
2. b
3. a
4. a
5. b
6. b
7. a
8. b

Pages 34-36

A. Wrong Way!

3
9
6
1
8
5
11
7
2
12
10
4
13

B. Matching Lines

1.	b	4.	e	7.	c
2.	f	5.	g	8.	h
3.	a	6.	d		

C. What's the Word?

1.	highways	7.	underground
2.	carpools	8.	sites
3.	rush	9.	commuters
4.	midday	10.	intersection
5.	hail	11.	traffic
6.	honk	12.	ancient

D. The 5th Wheel!

1. *artifacts* (The others are adjectives.)
2. *city* (The others are means of transportation.)
3. *carpool* (The others are roadways.)
4. *hail* (The others indicate "building".)
5. *Canada* (The others are cities.)
6. *normal* (The others are related to "old things.")
7. *trains* (The others are people.)
8. *moped* (The others are places related to transportation.)
9. *pier* (The others are means of transportation.)
10. *lunch* (The others are important occasions.)

E. Word Search (see page 293)

F. Listen

1.	b, d	3.	a, d
2.	a, d	4.	a, c

Pages 37-38

Check-Up Test: Exits 1, 2, 3

A. What's the Word?

1.	What	5.	Whose
2.	How	6.	Where
3.	Which/What	7.	When
4.	Who	8.	Why

B. Listen

1.	went	7.	died
2.	wrecked	8.	believe
3.	dial	9.	go
4.	found	10.	rent
5.	overheard	11.	heard
6.	left	12.	gave

C. Matching Lines

1.	d	5.	f
2.	e	6.	a
3.	g	7.	c
4.	b		

D. Same or Different?

1.	different	6.	same
2.	same	7.	same
3.	different	8.	same
4.	same	9.	different
5.	different	10.	same

E. What's the Word?

1.	didn't	4.	don't
2.	doesn't	5.	aren't
3.	wasn't	6.	weren't

F. The 5th Wheel!

1. *wheel* (The others are WH-question words.)
2. *mother* (The others are males.)
3. *Brazil* (The others are people.)
4. *door* (The others are places related to transportation.)
5. *get fired* (The others are happy events.)

Exit 4

Pages 39-40

A. The Right Choice

1.	How	8.	cabinets
2.	apartment	9.	Are
3.	looking for	10.	are
4.	Where	11.	much
5.	neighborhood	12.	Does
6.	safe	13.	electricity
7.	tell		

B. Matching Lines

1.	c	5.	d	9.	l
2.	e	6.	a	10.	k
3.	b	7.	i	11.	h
4.	f	8.	j	12.	g

C. Listen

1.	three-bedroom	7.	dryer
2.	downtown	8.	included
3.	$560	9.	near
4.	electricity	10.	walking
5.	pets	11.	neighborhood
6.	quiet	12.	dues

D. Crosswalk (see page 293)

E. Matching Lines

1.	c	5.	a	9.	k
2.	d	6.	e	10.	l
3.	f	7.	i	11.	j
4.	b	8.	g	12.	h

Pages 41-42

A. Wrong Way!

10
7
4
9
1
11
5
8
2
13
3
6
12
14

B. Listen

1.	b	4.	a	7.	b	10.	b
2.	b	5.	a	8.	b	11.	b
3.	b	6.	a	9.	a	12.	a

C. Fill It In!

1.	b	4.	b	7.	a	10.	b
2.	a	5.	a	8.	b	11.	b
3.	b	6.	b	9.	a	12.	a

Pages 43-44

A. Wrong Way!

4
3
6
1
5
2

B. What's the Line?

1. They're in the Frozen Food Section, Aisle 3.
2. It's in the Dairy Section, Aisle 2.
3. They're in the Imported Foods Section, Aisle 4.
4. It's in the Frozen Food Section, Aisle 3.
5. It's in the Produce Section, Aisle 1.
6. They're in the Paper Products Section, Aisle 5.

7. They're in the Household Supplies Section, Aisle 6.
8. It's in the Dairy Section, Aisle 2.

C. Listen

1.	a	3.	b	5.	b
2.	a	4.	b	6.	a

D. Mystery Products!

1. sponges, Household Supplies
2. tomatoes, Produce
3. skim milk, Dairy
4. napkins, Paper Products
5. frozen peas, Frozen Food
6. taco shells, Imported Foods

E. The 5th Wheel!

1. *rice* (The others are types of bread.)
2. *lemons* (The others are dairy products.)
3. *peanut butter* (The others aren't foods.)
4. *onions* (The others are types of meat.)
5. *coffee* (The others are supermarket services.)
6. *tuna fish* (The others are vegetables.)
7. *mayonnaise* (The others are frozen foods.)
8. *butter* (The others are fruits.)
9. *bug spray* (The others are imported foods.)
10. *toothpaste* (The others are sweet foods.)

Pages 45-46

A. Matching Lines

1.	c	3.	b	5.	d
2.	e	4.	a		

B. Matching Prices

1.	e	4.	g	7.	j	10.	c
2.	k	5.	i	8.	a	11.	f
3.	b	6.	h	9.	d		

C. Believable or Unbelievable?

	Believable	Unbelievable
1.	✓	___
2.	___	✓
3.	___	✓
4.	✓	___
5.	✓	___
6.	✓	___
7.	___	✓
8.	✓	___
9.	___	✓
10.	___	✓

D. Listen

1.	twelve fifty	6.	thirty thirteen
2.	ten fifty-four	7.	one ninety-nine
3.	two forty	8.	ninety cents
4.	six seventy-six	9.	three eighty
5.	twelve twenty-five	10.	one seventeen

Pages 47-48

A. The Right Choice

1.	These are	12.	This is
2.	are they	13.	is it
3.	They're	14.	It's
4.	They're	15.	It's
5.	they're	16.	it's
6.	them	17.	it
7.	little	18.	little
8.	little	19.	little
9.	few	20.	little
10.	little	21.	Is it
11.	Are they		

C. Listen

    3   1   5   4   2

D. What's the Word?

1. them, ground beef
2. it, tomatoes, lettuce
3. it, apples, sugar
4. them, chocolate, eggs

E. What's the Question?

1. What are they?
2. What is it?
3. Are they difficult to make?
4. What's in it?/What's in them?

Pages 49-50

A. What's the Response?

1.	b	4.	a	7.	a
2.	a	5.	b	8.	b
3.	b	6.	b		

B. Sense or Nonsense?

	Sense	Nonsense
1.	___	✓
2.	✓	___
3.	___	✓
4.	___	✓
5.	✓	___
6.	✓	___
7.	✓	___
8.	___	✓
9.	✓	___
10.	✓	___
11.	___	✓
12.	___	✓

C. Fill It In!

1.	a	4.	a	7.	a
2.	b	5.	a	8.	b
3.	b	6.	b		

D. What's the Word?

1.	Cut up	9.	some
2.	some	10.	Add
3.	few	11.	little
4.	some	12.	Put
5.	Put	13.	Bake
6.	little	14.	Serve
7.	Mix	15.	few
8.	little	16.	little

Exit 5

Page 51

A. What's the Word?

1.	saw	5.	Have	9.	done
2.	do	6.	done	10.	sit
3.	We're	7.	have	11.	fill
4.	I'd	8.	I've		

B. Fill It In!

1.	b	3.	a	5.	b
2.	a	4.	b	6.	a

Pages 52-53

A. The Right Choice

1.	Has	10.	Have
2.	gone	11.	eaten
3.	yet	12.	yet
4.	has	13.	have
5.	She's	14.	I've
6.	already	15.	already
7.	gone	16.	eaten
8.	When	17.	When
9.	went	18.	ate

B. What's the Line?

1. She's, given, She gave
2. They've, gotten, They got
3. We've, seen, We saw
4. He's, read, He read
5. I've, met, I met

C. Listen

1. wore
2. write
3. made
4. spoken
5. met
6. eat
7. done
8. seen
9. take

Pages 54-55

A. The Right Choice

1. since
2. for
3. for
4. since
5. for

B. Is or Has?

	is	*has*
1.	___	✓
2.	✓	___
3.	✓	___
4.	___	✓
5.	___	✓
6.	✓	___
7.	___	✓
8.	✓	___
9.	___	✓
10.	___	✓
11.	___	✓
12.	✓	___
13.	✓	___
14.	___	✓
15.	___	✓
16.	___	✓
17.	✓	___
18.	___	✓

C. Word Search (see page 294)

D. Listen

✓	___
___	✓
✓	✓
___	___
✓	✓

Page 56

A. Wrong Way!

3
1
4
2

B. Matching Lines

1. e
2. c
3. a
4. g
5. b
6. d
7. f

C. Analogies

1. met
2. eaten
3. driven
4. did
5. spoken
6. ridden
7. gotten
8. read

D. Listen

1. has
2. have
3. haven't
4. hasn't
5. has
6. have

Page 57

A. The Right Choice

1. repaired
2. haven't
3. going to
4. please
5. repaired
6. I didn't know that

B. What's the Word?

1. given out
2. eaten
3. vacuum
4. getting
5. spoken
6. polished
7. filled out
8. oil
9. typed
10. arrange
11. fed
12. clean
13. set
14. fix
15. make
16. write

Pages 58-59

A. The Right Choice

1. We've been
2. for
3. How long?
4. Since
5. Since you were teenagers?
6. that's right

B. Listen

1. a
2. a
3. b
4. b
5. a
6. b

C. What's the Line?

1. They've been making
2. She's been writing
3. I've been operating
4. We've been repairing
5. He's been fixing
6. I've been cooking and baking

Page 60

A. Wrong Way!

<u>2</u>
<u>4</u>
<u>7</u>
<u>1</u>
<u>6</u>
<u>5</u>
<u>3</u>

B. Listen

1. ✓   3. ✓
    ___   ___
    ✓   ___
2. ✓   4. ✓
    ___   ___
    ✓   ✓

Pages 61-62

A. Good Advice or Bad Advice?

	Good Advice	Bad Advice
1.	✓	___
2.	✓	___
3.	___	✓
4.	✓	___
5.	___	✓
6.	✓	___
7.	___	✓
8.	___	✓
9.	___	✓
10.	✓	___
11.	___	✓
12.	✓	___
13.	___	✓
14.	✓	___

B. Listen

1. b   3. b
2. c   4. c

C. What's the Question?

[*possible answers*]
1. Where have you worked before?
2. How long did you work at the Ajax Corporation?
3. What were your responsibilities?
4. Do you work now?
5. How long have you been a student?
6. What have you been studying?
7. When will you finish school?
8. Do you have any questions about the company?

D. Fill It In!

1. a   3. a   5. a
2. b   4. b   6. b

Exit 6

Page 63

A. Matching Lines

1. d   4. b
2. a   5. c
3. e

B. Listen

1. a   3. a   5. a
2. b   4. b   6. a

Page 64

A. The Right Choice

1. report   6. On
2. Go   7. near
3. overturned   8. say
4. Where   9. right
5. happen   10. be

B. What's the Word?

1. robbed   6. broken out
2. landed   7. crawled
3. fallen down   8. mugged
4. broken into   9. run over
5. overturned   10. fallen through

Page 65

A. What's the Response?

1. b   3. a   5. a
2. a   4. b   6. a

B. Listen

1. a   4. b   7. b
2. b   5. a   8. a
3. a   6. b

Pages 66-67

A. What's the Response?

1.	b	4.	a	7.	a
2.	b	5.	b	8.	a
3.	a	6.	b		

B. What's the Word?

1.	has, for	6.	has
2.	has	7.	has, since
3.	aren't	8.	haven't
4.	isn't	9.	hasn't, for
5.	had		

C. Crosswalk (see page 294)

D. Listen

1.	b	5.	b	9.	a
2.	a	6.	a	10.	b
3.	a	7.	b		
4.	a	8.	b		

Pages 68-69

A. The Right Choice

1.	given	6.	ever
2.	questions	7.	had
3.	Certainly	8.	haven't
4.	have	9.	be
5.	don't		

B. What's the Question?

1. Has your husband ever been hospitalized?
2. Are you allergic to penicillin?
3. Has your dog Rover ever been on a special diet?
4. Does your mother have any objection to herbs or other natural remedies?
5. Do you have any history of heart disease in your family?
6. Has your daughter ever had surgery before?
7. Have you ever had a toothache before?
8. Will you answer one or two more questions?

C. Sense or Nonsense?

	Sense	Nonsense
1.	✓	
2.		✓
3.		✓
4.	✓	
5.		✓
6.		✓

	Sense	Nonsense
7.	✓	
8.	✓	
9.		✓

Page 70

A. The Right Choice

1. a, d
2. b, d
3. b, c

B. Listen

1.	b	3.	b	5.	a
2.	a	4.	a	6.	b

Pages 71-72

A. Wrong Way!

4
6
8
1
5
3
7
2

B. The 5th Wheel!

1. *You could possibly* (The others indicate obligation.)
2. *You need to* (The others indicate possibility.)
3. *You could* (The others indicate strong obligation.)
4. *You have to* (The others are recommendations.)
5. *I urge you to* (The others are suggestions.)
6. *Can you suggest?* (The others are asking about a problem.)
7. *Can you recommend?* (The others are asking for repetition.)

C. Listen

1.	they	4.	their
2.	they've	5.	they'll
3.	they're	6.	they've

D. What's the Ailment?

1.	nose bleed	5.	cold
2.	sore throat	6.	stomachache
3.	stomachache	7.	sore throat
4.	bee sting	8.	nose bleed

Page 73

A. Wrong Way!

<u>5</u>
<u>3</u>
<u>2</u>
<u>1</u>
<u>6</u>
<u>8</u>
<u>4</u>
<u>9</u>
<u>7</u>

B. What's the Problem?

1.	a	4.	b	7.	a
2.	a	5.	a	8.	b
3.	b	6.	a	9.	b

Pages 74-75

Check-Up Test: Exits 4, 5, 6

A. The Right Choice

1.	a few	5.	a
2.	much	6.	a pound
3.	some	7.	many
4.	a few	8.	a head

B. Matching Lines

1.	e	5.	d	9.	a
2.	g	6.	c	10.	h
3.	j	7.	b		
4.	f	8.	i		

C. Fill It In!

1.	a	5.	b	9.	b	13.	b
2.	b	6.	b	10.	a	14.	a
3.	b	7.	a	11.	a	15.	a
4.	a	8.	b	12.	a	16.	b

D. Listen

1.	b	4.	c	7.	c
2.	c	5.	a	8.	b
3.	a	6.	b		

Exit 7

Pages 76-77

A. Wrong Way!

<u>4</u>
<u>2</u>
<u>5</u>
<u>1</u>
<u>3</u>

B. Matching Lines

1.	e	4.	a	7.	d
2.	h	5.	g	8.	c
3.	f	6.	b		

C. Listen

1. ✓   3. ___
   ___   ✓
2. ___   4. ✓
   ✓   ___

D. What Am I?

1.	coat	6.	necktie
2.	videocassette recorder	7.	television
3.	shoes	8.	dishes
4.	pastry	9.	designer dress
5.	stove	10.	headphones

E. Fill It In!

1.	b	5.	a	9.	b
2.	a	6.	b	10.	a
3.	a	7.	b	11.	b
4.	b	8.	a	12.	a

Pages 78-79

A. The Right Choice

1.	May	4.	one
2.	to buy	5.	that's
3.	models		

B. Sense or Nonsense?

	Sense	Nonsense
1.	___	✓
2.	✓	___
3.	___	✓
4.	✓	___
5.	___	✓
6.	✓	___
7.	___	✓
8.	___	✓

C. Listen

1.	gas range	4.	TV
2.	watch	5.	coffeemaker
3.	computer	6.	refrigerator

D. Crosswalk (see page 294)

Pages 80-81

A. The Right Choice

1. Could
2. I'd be
3. do
4. sleeveless
5. daughter
6. What
7. I think
8. would
9. you have
10. one
11. I'll take
12. take
13. card
14. cash

B. Matching Lines

1. e
2. g
3. a
4. c
5. d
6. b
7. f

C. Wrong Way!

1. a red, white, and blue jogging suit
2. a self-cleaning gas range
3. an automatic washing machine
4. light blue designer jeans
5. a dark brown waterproof watch
6. size 7 white sneakers
7. a light blue permanent press shirt
8. a large leather belt
9. an IBM Personal Computer
10. a small yellow plastic purse
11. beige permanent press pants
12. a medium dark green sleeveless blouse

D. Listen

1. a
2. b
3. b
4. b
5. a
6. b
7. a
8. b
9. a
10. b

Pages 82-83

A. The Right Choice

1. I want to
2. receipt
3. Could
4. them
5. They're
6. too
7. exchange
8. them
9. ones
10. I'd
11. refund

B. What's the Word?

1. tight
2. comfortable
3. permanent press
4. in stock
5. low
6. expensive

D. What's the Word?

1. more powerful
2. shorter
3. more lightweight
4. tighter
5. fancier
6. cheaper
7. easier
8. bigger

E. Listen

1. b
2. a
3. b
4. b
5. a
6. b
7. a
8. a

Pages 84-85

A. Fill It In!

1. b
2. a
3. a
4. b
5. a
6. b
7. b
8. a
9. b
10. a

B. Listen

1. b
2. a
3. b
4. a
5. a
6. a
7. b
8. b

C. Matching Lines

1. d
2. g
3. a
4. c
5. e
6. b
7. f

D. More Matching Lines

1. c
2. a
3. b
4. e
5. f
6. d

Page 86

A. What's the Word?

1. finest
2. point out
3. controls
4. reclines
5. passengers
6. trips
7. feature
8. stereo
9. CD
10. particular
11. installment
12. spread out
13. write up
14. shop around
15. decision

Exit 8

Page 87

A. The Right Choice

1. do
2. hanging out
3. hang out
4. playing
5. played

B. Listen

1. ___
   ✓

2. ✓
   ___

3. ___
   ✓

4. ✓
   ___

A. Wrong Way!

5
2
1
4
6
3

B. Matching Lines

1. e   3. f   5. b
2. a   4. c   6. d

D. Listen

1. take a hike   4. play "hide and seek"
2. go bowling   5. visit a museum
3. go to the movies   6. have a picnic

E. What's the Line?

1. driving, ride   4. taking, have
2. do, seeing   5. swimming, going
3. play, play   6. visiting, go

Page 90

A. The Right Choice

1. taking   6. said
2. I'd love to   7. taking
3. haven't taken 8. wouldn't
4. supposed to   9. you're
5. I hadn't heard 10. is

B. Sense or Nonsense?

	Sense	Nonsense
1.	✓	___
2.	✓	___
3.	___	✓
4.	✓	___
5.	___	✓

C. Listen

1. b   3. b   5. a
2. a   4. b   6. b

Pages 91-92

A. What's the Meaning?

1. c   2. a   3. b

B. The Right Choice

	___		___
	✓		
	✓		✓
1.	___	2.	✓
	✓		
	___		✓
	✓		
3.	✓	4.	✓
	✓		
	✓		✓
	___		✓
5.	✓	6.	___

C. Accepted or Rejected?

	Accept	Reject
1.	✓	___
2.	___	✓
3.	___	✓
4.	✓	___
5.	✓	___
6.	___	✓
7.	___	✓
8.	___	✓

Pages 93-94

A. The Right Choice

1. did you do   8. drove
2. flew   9. did
3. Did   10. had driven
4. enjoy   11. driving
5. hadn't flown   12. like
6. did   13. whenever
7. do

B. Fill It In!

1. a   3. a   5. b
2. b   4. a   6. a

C. What's the Response?

1. b   2. b   3. a

D. Listen

1.	watch	9.	hiked
2.	written	10.	wanted
3.	hurt	11.	made
4.	send	12.	skate
5.	said	13.	drove
6.	gone	14.	bought
7.	seen	15.	drawn
8.	flown		

Page 95

A. What Are They Saying?

1. had been predicting
2. had been thinking
3. had been expecting
4. had been wanting
5. had been hoping

B. Listen

1.	a	3.	a	5.	b
2.	b	4.	a	6.	b

Pages 96-97

A. What's the Response?

1.	a	5.	a	9.	a
2.	a	6.	b	10.	a
3.	b	7.	a		
4.	a	8.	b		

B. Matching Lines

1.	d	5.	c
2.	f	6.	g
3.	a	7.	b
4.	e		

D. Listen

1.	a	3.	a	5.	a
2.	b	4.	b	6.	b

E. Crosswalk (see page 294)

Page 98

A. The Right Choice

1.	watch	8.	Are
2.	on	9.	guess
3.	is	10.	watching
4.	not	11.	should
5.	watching	12.	matter
6.	there's	13.	Whatever
7.	mood		

B. Sense or Nonsense?

	Sense	Nonsense
1.	✓	___
2.	___	✓
3.	✓	___
4.	___	✓
5.	✓	___
6.	___	✓
7.	___	✓
8.	___	✓

Pages 99-100

Check-Up Test: Exits 7, 8

A. The Right Choice

1.	larger	4.	lower
2.	lightweight	5.	cheaper
3.	conversative	6.	warmer

B. Matching Lines

1.	d	4.	i	7.	b
2.	g	5.	c	8.	f
3.	a	6.	h	9.	e

C. Wrong Way!

1. a bright green dress
2. a large light blue sweater
3. a size 34 beige belt
4. a white permanent press shirt
5. a light brown plastic purse

D. Listen

1.	a	5.	b	9.	a
2.	b	6.	a	10.	b
3.	b	7.	b		
4.	a	8.	a		

E. What's the Line?

1.	hadn't gone	4.	hadn't gone
2.	hadn't played	5.	hadn't worn
3.	hadn't seen		

F. What's the Line?

1. had been planning
2. had been telling
3. had been looking forward
4. had been hoping
5. had been talking
6. had been leaking

Page 6

C. Crosswalk

Page 11

E. Word Search

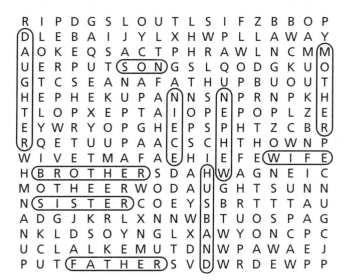

Page 21

F. Crosswalk

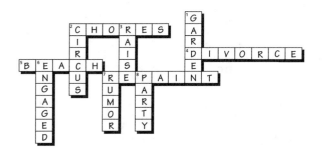

Page 30

C. Crosswalk

Page 36

E. Word Search

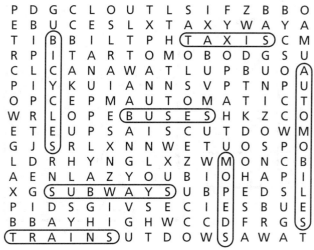

Page 40

D. Crosswalk

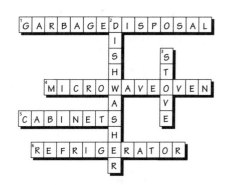

Page 55

C. Word Search

Page 79

D. Crosswalk

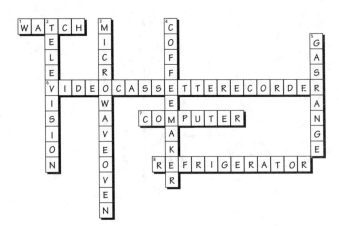

Page 67

C. Crosswalk

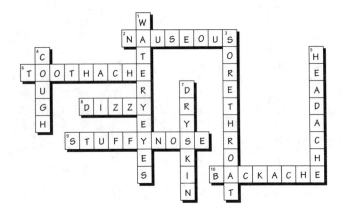

Page 97

E. Crosswalk

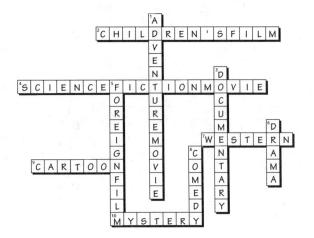

#1	supermarket	#52	lamp	#105	blouse	#156	have a picnic
#2	bank	#53	bed	#106	shoes	#157	go to a museum
#3	library	#54	rug	#107	hat	#158	go swimming
#4	post office	#55	picture	#108	sweater	#159	watch TV
#5	laundromat	#56	crib	#109	jacket	#160	go out for dinner
#6	clinic	#57	TV	#110	suit	#161	relax
#7	park	#58	plant	#111	vest	#162	play golf
#8	school	#59	cookie	#112	jersey	#163	plant flowers
#9	museum	#60	tomato	#113	bathrobe	#164	wash (my) car
#10	mall / shopping mall	#61	apple	#114	raincoat	#165	clean (my) house
		#62	banana	#115	sweatshirt	#166	paint
#11	movies / movie theater	#63	egg	#116	evening gown	#167	go sailing
		#64	orange	#117	pajamas	#168	listen to CDs
#12	airport	#65	milk	#118	sneakers	#169	fix (my) roof
#13	zoo	#66	bread	#119	boots	#170	rest
#14	fix (my) car	#67	cheese	#120	rubbers	#171	read
#15	study	#68	lettuce	#121	belt	#172	bake
#16	clean	#69	ice cream	#122	socks	#173	drive to the beach
#17	do (my) homework	#70	coffee	#123	skirt	#174	play tennis
#18	make breakfast	#71	carrots	#124	gloves	#175	go jogging
#19	dance	#72	butter	#125	watch	#176	play basketball
#20	eat	#73	potatoes	#126	earrings	#177	go to the beach
#21	look for	#74	sugar	#127	necklace	#178	take a walk
#22	wash the dishes	#75	rice	#128	boots	#179	go to the zoo
#23	walk the dog	#76	peaches	#129	camera	#180	drive to the mountains
#24	comb (my) hair	#77	yogurt	#130	stockings		
#25	brush (my) teeth	#78	teacher	#131	typewriter	#181	go skating
#26	do (my) exercises	#79	repairperson	#132	fan	#182	do yoga
#27	take a shower	#80	writer	#133	jeans	#183	kitchen sink
#28	feed the baby	#81	salesperson	#134	purse	#184	light fixture
#29	bus station	#82	assembler	#135	stamps	#185	front door
#30	drug store	#83	architect	#136	package	#186	stove
#31	hotel	#84	chef	#137	money order	#187	radiator
#32	parking lot	#85	secretary	#138	registered letter	#188	toilet
#33	grocery store	#86	baker	#139	aerogramme	#189	orange juice
#34	gas station	#87	mechanic	#140	change of address form	#190	mayonnaise
#35	police station	#88	delivery person			#191	tuna fish
#36	hospital	#89	security guard	#141	see a play	#192	ketchup
#37	fire station	#90	musician	#142	go dancing	#193	potato chips
#38	bus	#91	headache	#143	go to a concert	#194	apple juice
#39	train	#92	earache	#144	visit	#195	grapes
#40	plane	#93	stomachache	#145	go for a bike ride	#196	peanut butter
#41	ship / boat	#94	toothache	#146	write letters	#197	chocolate milk
#42	bedroom	#95	sore throat	#147	take (my children) to the zoo	#198	refrigerator
#43	living room	#96	backache			#199	air conditioner
#44	kitchen	#97	cold	#148	rain	#200	stereo system
#45	bathroom	#98	cough	#149	snow	#201	computer
#46	dining room	#99	shirt	#150	sunny	#202	mattress
#47	patio	#100	tie	#151	cloudy	#203	armchair
#48	balcony	#101	dress	#152	hot	#204	bookcase
#49	sofa	#102	pants	#153	cold	#205	cassette player
#50	chair	#103	coat	#154	see a movie	#206	coins
#51	table	#104	umbrella	#155	go skiing		

CORRELATION KEY

ExpressWays 3 Student Text & Workbook	Navigator 3 Companion Book	Word by Word Picture Dictionary
Exit 1	Chapter 1	pp. 1-7
Exit 2		pp. 8-9, 34-37
Exit 3	Chapter 2	pp. 4-5, 34-37, 94-97
Exit 4	Chapters 3, 4	pp. 13-29, 46-53, 66
Exit 5	Chapter 5	pp. 80-91
Exit 6	Chapter 6	pp. 70-74, 94
Exit 7	Chapter 7	pp. 40-41, 56-65, 75, 92-93
Exit 8	Chapter 8	pp. 98-119

Navigator is a five-level course in a unique magazine format. It is designed to serve as a supplement to the *ExpressWays* series, as a stand-alone classroom text, or as a take-home text for students' independent learning and enjoyment.

The *Word by Word Picture Dictionary* presents over 3000 words through full-color illustrations. Its interactive methodology gives students conversational practice with every word on every page. It serves as a vocabulary enrichment companion to the *ExpressWays* series.